Shadow Living...

Paintings of Grief

By

Deborah Slappey Pitts

Author of bestseller *I Feel Okay*

you and always
Deborah Slappy Pitt

www.deborahslappeypitts.com
Email the author: slappeyterrymax@aol.com

ISBN: 9780978789701
Library of Congress Control Number: 2007923227

Cover and Interior Designs: Michele DeFilippo, 1106 Design

Editors: D.L. Carpenter, Creative Ink
Cheryl Dunlop, Christian Writers Institute
William Phenn, Readerviews

The information in this book is for information purposes only.

The actual names of physicians, psychologists, and hospitals have been changed in this book because of delicate issues and privacy. However, the accounts are true to the best of my ability and memory.

Scriptures are quoted from the King James Version of the Bible.

Printed in the United States of America

Shadow Living...

Paintings of Grief

HarobedHouse™
Edifying the World Thru Words
Post Office Box 9105
Columbus, Georgia 31908

Also by Deborah Slappey Pitts

I Feel Okay

*If I have touched one person's life after reading this book,
I will have succeeded in my quest to help my neighbor.*

Table of Contents

Dedication

I would like to dedicate *Shadow Living…Paintings of Grief* to the millions of people around the world who grieve daily for their loved ones. I pray that you'll find solace in *Shadow Living…Paintings of Grief* as you read my story of loss, grief, and my earnest struggle to live again and reach beyond the shadows of my pain. I know Clyde would have wanted me to live again. With God's strength, I will, and so will you.

Lovingly,

Deborah Slappey Pitts

Acknowledgments

I would like to thank everyone who embraced my family and me as we struggled throughout the years to cope with the tremendous devastation of losing Clyde to death, and to communicate to a world audience about the devastating effects of primary amyloidosis. The disease is now exposed to the world, and to this end, I'm grateful and indebted to you.

Because of your continued kindness and support, many people are learning about primary amyloidosis and are actively engaged in conversations with their physicians. This is in itself a tremendous milestone.

My humbled thanks to you for purchasing the series—*I Feel Okay* and *Shadow Living…Paintings of Grief*. You are a blessing to my family and me, and we will always think kindly of your generosity and for spreading the word about primary amyloidosis. I couldn't have done it without your support.

I am also grateful to my editors for their unwavering support. I couldn't have produced this second book without their input.

I'm grateful to my husband, Marshall Pitts, for his unwavering support and sacrifice, and for giving me his love and understanding and the opportunity to write *I Feel Okay* and *Shadow Living…Paintings of Grief*. I couldn't have succeeded without his unconditional devotion.

Now my work is done and I can pen other topics that are near and dear to my heart. Thank you and God bless always.

Thanks for your continued support,
Deborah Slappey Pitts

Prologue

My best friend, my Innisfree, Clyde Slappey,
died on April 19, 1995, and on that day I died as well. The only
thing that remained of me was fragmented pieces of putty. But
God extended His loving hand toward me and gave me the
strength to rise up and walk once again through the crystal
shores of time.

Through God's unmerited favor, He molded those fragmented pieces of me with His unending love and allowed me to
stand in the sunshine of the day, no longer pummeling through
the shadows; no longer being afraid of the dark. Though I was
shaken and pulverized both in body and spirit, I've recaptured
the sunshine on my face and I am able to walk in the rain again.
When I was a young girl I adopted the name *Innisfree* as the person who would be my all and all forever and ever. He would be
the man of my dreams and we would be one. And for 21 years,
Clyde and I were one in total mind and spirit.

In 2003, through God's uncompromising wisdom and grace
I was able to write Clyde's personal story of faith, perseverance,
and courage. I described his battle with the silent killer, primary
amyloidosis, in *I Feel Okay*, my first work. In it, I described
our family's tragedy in losing Clyde to this disease. This is the
sequel, *Shadow Living…Paintings of Grief*.

I was urged to tell the whole story, that is, my story of pain, despair, and the anguish we faced as a family. I was urged to tell how we suffered through the very dark months, even years in coping with Clyde's death. To this day we're still coping.

It was a very difficult fight when Clyde and I became separated by death. I couldn't touch him anymore. I couldn't stroke his mustache or brush his hair in that downward stroke which he had always adored. And as I prayed to God that Clyde's story in *I Feel Okay* would be an inspiration and encouragement to others, I pray also that *Shadow Living…Paintings of Grief* will be helpful and uplifting to the world as well.

In *I Feel Okay*, I had something to say about this killer disease, primary amyloidosis that destroyed our happy family. Primary amyloidosis is a disease of the immune system caused by the abnormal accumulation of protein fibrils in body organs and tissues. The proteins are small fragments of antibody molecules, which are normally present in the blood and give protection against infectious agents and bacteria in the body. However, in primary amyloidosis, a defect occurs in the immune system where excessive amounts of antibody molecules are produced and deposited in the body's organs and tissues. These tissues enlarge and damage normal tissues practically in every organ of the body. As the tissues continue to enlarge they interfere with normal body functions, causing kidney failure, loss of sensation, heart failure, and even death.

Now, I have something to say about grief and living with grief. I'm here to tell you that there is no such thing as closure. How can there ever be closure when you lose someone to death? It just doesn't happen. As the months transformed into years, I learned that you simply cope with the person being absent from your life. You begin to acknowledge that his physical presence is no more, and that's about it. At least that's what I've tried to do. Sometimes I'm not successful with my coping skills, but I keep on trying, looking to God for my strength and courage to make it through the day.

I think of grief as a fragile scab encrusted over an unhealed sore. As long as you don't touch it, bump it or knock it around, the scab remains intact and in its place. Silent. But once agitated in any way, it hurts and it bleeds, and bleeds much. I've learned to live one day at a time without seeing Clyde. And each day after I open my eyes and listen to the birds sing the pain retreats. But it never goes away. It has a face and it's called grief.

Over the 12 years since Clyde's death, I've learned the best that I can do is to walk with God and take life one day at a time. It's the safest route. I've reckoned with the reality that Clyde's physical presence is no more, but his spirit remains within his family. But make no mistake about it, I miss Clyde every day and in every way imaginable. I miss him terribly and I always will.

We, like so many families, are living with grief. We are surrounded by thousands, perhaps even millions of people around the globe who live in the shadows of grief daily. It's time to talk about those shadows. I've learned to go on with my life as much as I can. And through my story I hope to reach those who suffer daily with the heartache of living with death. You aren't alone.

In *Shadow Living...Paintings of Grief,* I describe grief as a superficial entity that takes a life of its own through suffering and pain. I have learned that you have to fight back with all of your being to break away from the shackles of grief in order to live again. If you don't, grief will consume you until the only thing left is pieces of you, not a whole person anymore.

Your journey won't be easy. It's never easy and you can't do it alone. You'll need help. You'll need divine intervention from God to guide you spiritually, physically, and psychologically. God, along with His dedicated health care professionals, family and friends will guide you to the light of day once again. God will guide you through your journey of grief. If you allow Him to do so, He will bear your tremendous burden of pain and suffering. Most assuredly, He will.

I became a widow at 40, and frankly I didn't know what I was going to do without Clyde. We'd done everything together. But God saved me from myself. And now I stand here as much as I can be, whole, thankful to my Lord and Savior Jesus Christ for taking care of my family and me. It's never easy living with the loss of a loved one, but believe me when I say God will help you, He will guide you through the burning sands of pain and agony. He'll walk with you every step of the way. I know what I'm talking about. I know from the inside out.

Jesus Christ will do the walking for you when you can't walk, and He'll carry you through the dark, shadowy dungeons of grief to the other side where you are welcomed with serenity, laughter, and yes, life in the light of day once again. But you'll have to work through your grief to reach the other side. Don't be afraid because you can do it. You can do it because I did. I'm here for you in words to guide you all the way. Just don't give up. You can do it! Our Lord and Savior Jesus Christ will help you find your way out of the dark days of grief and He will give you purpose and determination and the desire to live again.

In *Shadow Living...Paintings of Grief,* I share my very personal walk with you through the world of grief onto the other side where joy and heavenly peace awaits. I put a face to grief. Though my story's not a pretty one, I felt it needed to be told. This is my story, and it begins on a brisk spring day on April 24, 1995...the day we buried Clyde and the day my shadow living began.

Part One...
Leaving Clyde Behind

Chapter One

Leaving Clyde Behind

I was oblivious to the days of anguish ahead as I watched my dear husband being laid to rest. I could barely hold on. I didn't know it at the time, but I was in shock, the first of many stages in the grieving process.

I STARED AT THE AMERICAN FLAG that draped the golden, caramel-colored casket in front of me, trying desperately to make sense of the muted reality that Clyde was gone. He wasn't with us anymore. Even though he was laid before my eyes, I couldn't believe my husband was in a coffin. Everything had happened very quickly, right in front of me, and I hadn't had time to recover.

During the viewing of Clyde's body on that late April morning, my mind kept trying to grapple with the reality that it was my husband lying in that casket, so still and motionless. And even though my eyes saw him, my mind was incapable of comprehending that Clyde was gone. He had died, slipping away from me into the dungeon of death, and I couldn't do anything about it.

"Oh Lord! Oh Lord!" I screamed inside as I looked at Clyde's casket that chilly Monday noonday, April 24, 1995. "What do I do now? Where do I go? What's gonna happen to me? Our children? How will they cope without their father? Is this real? Is this really real, Lord? I see the casket, but is this really real?"

I was frozen in time. I had touched Clyde's face the previous day at the funeral home. I had felt his hand and rubbed it against mine. But nothing happened. He didn't respond to me. So I stroked his cheeks. Still. Nothing—absolutely nothing. Everything was simply beyond my comprehension as I stared down at the Star-Spangled Banner that draped Clyde's casket so handsomely.

Standing in front of Clyde's coffin was our elder, Brother Eddie Clayton of the Church of Christ; standing near him was the undertaker who waited patiently for Brother Clayton to finish the prayer. As I approached the canopy, I stared at the small chairs aligned along the left side of the tent.

At any other time this would have been a beautiful, tranquil setting of family and friends, who traveled from around the country to give their last respects to a loving husband, father, brother, and friend. Yes, there were many people standing around the canopy braving the brutal, unforgiving wind and the cheerless noonday sun at the Andersonville Cemetery in Americus, Georgia. I sat down in one of the tiny chairs and felt the cold wind quietly beat against my cheeks, making me shudder as the chill penetrated my body.

I felt an unimaginable loneliness as my eyes panned the crowd. I missed my husband and I wanted to be with him. I felt abandoned as I stared at Clyde's casket. I was frozen in time. I had ceased living. I was empty inside. My best friend had left me here alone to pick up the pieces and go on, but where to? I didn't have a clue. I didn't know what to do with the pieces; let alone how to go on without him.

The pain that lay ahead was just beginning to sink into my brain as I stared at the coffin. But I knew for sure that none of the people under the canopy would ever be the same. My eyes remained fixed on Clyde. Even the wind couldn't disturb my gaze at that moment.

"I hope he's okay," I said silently. "I hope he's not in pain, Lord. Please don't let him be in any more pain. Please…" My thoughts continued to race.

"Lord, I can't leave him here," I said under my breath. "I just can't." But no one heard my words. Only the Lord.

The ending didn't seem fair. Clyde and I had traveled as far as the Mayo Clinic in Rochester, Minnesota, trying to find someone to help him before it was too late. We had seen many doctors and graced the halls of many hospitals around the country. Surely it wouldn't end this way. Surely it wouldn't.

"Oh God!" I screamed inside. "Are You going to let it end this way?…Please don't let it end this way!" My heart sank.

I stammered vehemently within myself. "Don't let it end this way. Don't let them put him in the cold, dark ground. I need to take my husband home," I screamed silently as the tears rolled relentlessly down my cheeks.

"Don't hurt him, don't let them hurt him…I have to take care of him…I must take care of him, Lord!"

I sobbed in agony and despair. I shook my head from side to side, closing my eyes in naked pain, hoping against all hope that when I opened them, the casket and the rest of this horrible nightmare would be only a figment of my imagination—even better, a dream. But it wasn't my imagination and it wasn't a dream. It was real. It was all real.

"Lord, we were so close. We were very close."

I closed my eyes tightly as I tried in vain to fight back the tears. But the tears were insistent and came rushing out as if they had a mind of their own.

"This just can't be," I said under my breath. "It can't be. Clyde isn't in that casket! He just can't be!"

At that moment I turned to look at Clyde Daryl and Alex Keith, our two sons. They were sitting next to me with their eyes fixed on Clyde's casket.

"Oh, Lord!" I said silently as I looked at them. "Please bring their father back to them...please. There's nothing in me. I don't have the strength to even comfort my sons. Please help us get through this, please. If only Clyde could get out of that casket. If only he could, Lord. If only he could rise like Lazarus...I would take care of him!"

I turned my head to the next row of seats and stared at Clyde's eight brothers and sisters: Lewis, Mattie, Annie Bee, Bessie Mae, Mozelle, Marvin, Clarence, and Jeannette. And standing close by were Clyde's sisters-in-law, Gertrude, Val, and Geneva. They were all staring straight ahead in shock and disbelief.

"Lord, I want my family back," I said. "I want Clyde back with me. I want you to wake me up from this nightmare. I'm desperate inside. I'm ripped inside! I don't understand this. Please bring him back to us! Please Lord! We want to be a family again—Clyde, Debbie, Clyde Daryl, and Alex Keith—the way we used to be! That's all. I just want my family back!" I screamed silently as my frail body ached with anguish.

A flicker of memory flashed across my mind as I continued to stare at the casket. We would be together once again and all would be well, I assured myself. Clyde would get up early on Saturday morning and would prepare breakfast. The boys and I would awake to the mouth-watering smell of country-cured bacon, scrambled eggs, cheese-buttered grits, and some lightly browned toast with just a hint of strawberry jam that would tickle our nostrils. It would be wonderful to see his face and listen to his outrageous tales of adventure, rescue, and bravery.

From the bedroom, I would hear Clyde loud and clear while he talked and laughed like a crazy man in the kitchen, reliving one of his tall tales to Alex Keith and Clyde Daryl. His tales were so vivacious. I could hear him say clearly as if he was standing next to me, "Well Charlie Man, you see I was on the coast of Africa in the South of Wales and before I knew it, I was caught up, wrestling with a big blue whale and I knocked it out, and taking one breath I…"

My mind snapped back to reality.

I wouldn't hear Clyde tell any of his wonderful stories of adventure anymore. All of his stories were now permanently bound in the casket in front of me.

If only Clyde could get out of the casket and come back to us, then we would be together again and everything would be alright. We would be one happy family again.

"We are gathered here…" Brother Clayton's deep, grinding voice ripped through the wind-chilled curtain of silence and interrupted my thoughts. All eyes turned toward him.

We had decided to have Clyde's funeral at 10:00 a.m., so Clyde Daryl, our eldest son, could get back to college. Clyde wanted it this way and I wanted to make sure we followed his wishes. Yet I had my reservations about that decision. I prayed it was the right choice for Clyde Daryl and Alex Keith, and even for me. But Clyde's will was stronger than mine, and I wanted to follow his.

My attention soon turned to a whistling sound coming from the other side of the canopy. Next, my ears tuned to a marching sound that was approaching not too far in the distance. The sound whistled through the trees near the canopy where we were sitting. All heads turned in the direction the sound was coming from. I turned my head toward the left side of Clyde's casket and, as I peeped through the tiny opening of the canopy, I saw three uniformed soldiers marching forward; embellished with green Army suiting.

The three soldiers marched in unison—right, left, right, left—as the sound became more intense. Then one of the soldiers stopped abruptly and broke rank from the other two. He marched directly in front of the canopy, to the right side of Clyde's coffin. The third soldier, as if on cue, walked quickly in front of the casket, and together the other two soldiers lifted their left hands in an arch to give Clyde the soldier's farewell salute. They moved with purpose as if they had received instructions from some divine presence.

I watched the undertaker remove the family flower arrangement from the top of Clyde's coffin and lay it gently on the ragged green carpet. The flower arrangement was an intricate grouping of roses, carnations, orchids, and green sprouts of peace lilies, accented with baby's breath.

With white, satin-gloved hands, the two soldiers grabbed both ends of the flag from Clyde's casket, stretched the four ends and folded the flag in a triangular fashion, one fold after the other until they met in the middle. The third soldier walked forward and gently tucked the remaining end pieces of the flag into the fold and handed it to the second soldier. With the folded flag in hand, the second soldier did an about-face turn and walked toward me very carefully, holding the flag respectfully in front of him.

"Mrs. Slappey," he said in a quiet voice, bending toward me.

Unable to respond to him in words, I acknowledged his presence by looking up and nodding to him as he gently laid Clyde's flag in my arms, touching me slightly on the hands with a loving gesture of gratitude and respect for my family. After a few seconds, the soldier stepped back, saluted me out of respect for my husband, and turned to rejoin his fellow soldiers. They marched away from the canopy.

My eyes remained glued on the soldiers as I pulled Clyde's flag close to my chest, touching the edge of the flag against my face. I breathed in the scent of the flag, feeling very honored to be Clyde's widow and to bear his flag. I knew I would hold onto it forever. Clyde had weathered the storms of war in Vietnam, but he wasn't able to overcome the devastating effects of primary amyloidosis.

I looked at Brother Clayton and felt the pain in his eyes. I looked around at the faces of those in attendance who came to pay their last respects to Clyde. Their eyes told the true story. Their eyes were filled with sorrow and pain. I was very grateful to them for coming with me to bury Clyde. We were all gathered together in that one place, some 60 miles from home to bury my dear husband. Our journey had ended.

Without warning, gunshots pierced through the silence. One…then two…then three. The shots echoed through the cemetery, vibrating through every barrier and open space. And then the deafening silence returned. No breathing, only stillness in the wind.

My breathing became shallow and I felt as if I was about to pass out. I saw dark spectacles of light as I began to feel sick to my stomach. I felt paralyzed. I gazed at the soldiers as they marched away from Clyde's burial place. I didn't want them to leave; I wanted them to stay with us. Although I couldn't speak, I thanked the soldiers very much in my heart and appreciated them being there to send my husband home with military honors.

The undertaker thanked everyone for coming, breaking the silence. He informed everyone that the family would receive friends and visitors at the church building.

After Brother Clayton gave the ending prayer, people began to embrace us tenderly. But I didn't want to leave Clyde in Andersonville. I didn't want to leave my chair. My breathing returned to normal as many people surrounded me with hugs, kisses, and embraces. I desperately needed to feel those hugs and warmth from the crowd. I felt so alone, abandoned with no place to go.

"I just can't, Lord. I just can't leave him here," I said. "He will get cold and he needs me. He really needs me."

The tears blinded me from seeing the sympathizers' faces as I continued to stare at the golden casket. The undertaker walked toward me and I knew what he was going to say. It was time to go, but I didn't want to leave.

With Alex Keith on one side and Clyde Daryl on the other, I reluctantly stood up from my chair and walked toward my husband's casket. I touched his casket at the top where I had envisioned his head was resting and raised my left hand to stroke the area where his head would be. Clyde had always enjoyed me rubbing and stroking his head; it was very soothing and relaxing to him after a long day at work. I knew he liked it and I wanted to do it one last time.

Touching his beautiful flowers, I pulled four roses from his arrangement. I wanted to keep them close to my heart because they represented us—the Slappey family. One loving, happy family.

With the four roses in hand, I turned and walked away with Clyde Daryl and Alex Keith, one on each side. Together, we walked away from Clyde and the canopy and started the long walk to the limousine to travel back to Columbus.

As we walked to the car, I looked up at an oak tree that was rather old with few branches. I could tell that the tree was dying. As I watched the branches dance in the wind and saw the leaves dangle with the whistling wind, I knew then that it was finished. I didn't know what I was going to do, but I knew that it was finished. Clyde's journey had ended. Our journey had ended, too.

My strength was fading and my legs were beginning to buckle. I could barely lift my feet as we walked to the limousine. I had no strength in my being. Not one drop. I didn't want Clyde to be in pain anymore. I wanted to take him home with me. But sadly as I turned to look at Clyde one last time, I knew I had to leave him there. I couldn't take him home anymore. I walked back to the limousine, one foot and then the other, as if I needed someone to guide me. The tears inter-rupted my vision. I couldn't see much in front or to the side of me. I remembered where I was, what we were doing, and what had happened as I softly turned my face to the green canopy where Clyde's coffin lay buried in handsome flowers of every kind.

Clyde would be lowered into the ground as I had seen done with many others, but no matter how many times I'd seen it, the pain never eased, especially not now. The undertaker took my hand and I knew it was time to leave. I climbed into the limousine and immediately turned to look at Clyde's grave. I closed my eyes in pain and kept them shut for a few seconds. I shook my head and didn't say a word. I just didn't know what I was going to do.

"Lord, I just don't know," I said to Him as I looked at the cascade of flowers towering over Clyde's resting place. "I don't know what I'm going to do now."

From my seat in the limo, I turned my head again to see Clyde's casket before they lowered him into the ground. I said my final goodbye. Beneath the roses, orchids, peace lilies, and carnations, lay my husband of 21 years.

As I stared at his casket, my mind drifted to when we first met on a hot, clear summer evening in 1972. We were so young and full of energy and adventure. We had loved each other all the way and our love was very special. The birth of our children flashed before my eyes. Clyde Daryl, our firstborn, came into the world on January 16, 1976, and all was well. And then Alex Keith came into the world, rather rambunctiously, on April 2, 1981. He definitely was the image of his father.

Our happy family moments flashed before me at lightning speed. The tears began to race down my short-sleeve, front-button black dress. I had done all that I could for Clyde and I knew that God was taking care of him now, but I still wanted to stay close to him. We were one, always and forever. What was

I going to do without him in my life? I didn't have the answer and I shuddered to think of what tomorrow might bring for my family and me.

We had loved one another through the best and worst of times, and I wasn't quite ready to give him up to God, at least not yet. The love of my life had gone ahead of me and left me on this earth—alone. And I knew that the pain and anguish was just beginning for me, Clyde Daryl, Alex Keith and the rest of the Slappey family. Without a doubt, I knew I would never, ever be the same again after that day. Not ever.

CHAPTER TWO

The Long Ride Home

I felt numb; pretty much empty. Nothing seemed real anymore. I was wandering in a dark, shadowy world of despair. I was alone with my grief as joy had abandoned my soul. I was stuck between endless clouds of sadness coupled with misery after losing my best friend.

ANDERSONVILLE NATIONAL CEMETERY is very rich in history. It's a place where thousands of soldiers died and were buried during the Civil War. The cemetery is nestled among hefty pine, oak, and dogwood trees off Georgia Highway 49 and is respectfully maintained by the federal government.

As we drove out of the cemetery, I peeked out of the passenger's side of the limousine at the trees. As the years passed I became passionately close to every tree and statue that graced the roads at Andersonville. During the first two years, I visited Clyde quite often, many times every week. And 12 years later, little has changed except for thousands of new graves.

Beautiful oak trees outline the entrance to Andersonville National Cemetery; their branches add a subtle distinction. An old but well-renovated white and crimson brick building welcomed mourners and visitors near the front gate. Within 200 feet of the entrance stood the first sign of the burial grounds where thousands of heroes lay; many dying agonizing deaths from hunger, thirst, and lack of medicines. The graves were close together, about two feet apart. I learned that during the Civil War soldiers were buried vertically to save space for the thousands of soldiers who died in prison and during the war.

White headstones, no more than 12 x 25 inches tall aligned each end of the cemetery. A horde of indigenous trees including magnolias, oaks, pines, and cedars overshadowed the gravestones. I learned later that more soldiers from New York were buried at Andersonville than from any other state.[1]

Statues from across the United States, representing Pennsylvania, Massachusetts, New York, Maine, Ohio, Iowa, Idaho, and more were strewn amid the graves as a reminder of the rich history within Andersonville's hallowed walls.

I was proud that my husband would be resting among heroes who fought in the Civil War, World Wars I and II, and the Korean and Vietnam Wars. Knowing that Clyde would be resting alongside war heroes brought some comfort to me. Clyde was a Vietnam veteran so it was fitting that he would rest with them.

They were all lying in rest, waiting for that special day when the Lord would come back and put all things in order. As we waited for the rest of the family to get into the cars, the undertaker turned toward me and patted me on the hand.

"Mrs. Slappey, are you okay?" he asked. I lifted my head and turned toward him, slowly turning away from Clyde. I wanted to keep a detailed memory of where Clyde was located so I would be able to find my way back to his grave when I returned to visit him.

"I am okay," I said in a lamenting voice. "Thank you for asking, but I'm okay."

Once everyone was seated, we began to move slowly as all four limousines followed behind one another heading back to the Church of Christ for the repast. I knew it was going to be a long ride back home.

I watched cars pulled to the curbside out of respect for the procession. Even though the drivers didn't know who had passed, they saw the hearse and string of limousines. Since childhood, I had watched many funeral processions, and when it was safe to do so, I would pull to the side of the road. I now knew what those families felt while in the procession. And on that Monday in April, I mentally thanked each driver who took the time to stop and show respect for my husband. Now, whenever I see a procession, I make sure I pull over out of the same respect those drivers had for us.

As the limousine careened through the tiny city, I stared out of the window, looking aimlessly at the trees bending in the wind. I saw people look at the procession wondering who had died. The dogwood trees were so brightly arrayed with white buds, a significant indication that we were in the middle of spring.

What will you do now, Debbie? What will you do now? The question replayed in my thoughts over and over again. I didn't have an answer. *I just don't know. I don't know what I'm going to do now, without Clyde, Lord. We did everything together. Everything—and now I had to leave him in this sad place...I just don't know.* I shook my head to shut out the pain and kept peeping out of the window. My mind began to race.

Lord, if only I could have gotten Clyde to the Mayo Clinic earlier. They might have been able to help him. I agonized about it over again in my mind. Our lives would be so different. I would be reading to Clyde in the bed. I knew he was weak, but still we would be together. I would be close to his side. And that was all that mattered. And I would lay my head next to his and pucker up my lips toward him and plant a big kiss on his forehead. I smiled and I shook my head as I meandered in my pleasant thoughts.

Yes, I thought, *I would plant a big kiss on his forehead with all of my brick red lipstick.* I would plant it right in the middle of his forehead—where he disliked it the most.

The limousine continued to travel on Highway 26 to Columbus. I looked around at Clyde Daryl and saw the look on his face. He looked pensive and I knew he was thinking about his dad. I didn't dare ask him his thoughts. He needed time. He'd just buried his father and wouldn't be able to talk to his "Pop" again. He wouldn't be able to talk to him, not even man-to-man. I closed my eyes in pain at the thought. I wanted to bury those thoughts; cover them up in hot ashes of amnesia. And if I could have, I would have buried our reality deep into amnesia.

I turned to look at Alex Keith and trembled inside as I gazed into his eyes trying to unearth his thoughts. I shuddered to think how he would go on without his dad. They were the best of friends; so very close, respectful and crazy about each other. Alex Keith was 12 years old and his dad was very special to him. He would do anything for his daddy. Now, he had to face the reality that his father was gone. I just didn't know what he would do. But as I stared at him, I knew that only God could help him now. I knew he had buried his best friend and father today, and I didn't know what would lie ahead for him. I knew that I couldn't help him. We were all involved in our own thoughts that early afternoon, wondering where we would go from here.

"Is he really gone?" I asked myself. "Yes, I saw him in the casket." I saw the undertaker place the laced, white handkerchief across his face, but I still couldn't accept him as dead.

What does dead mean, Lord? Does it mean that I can't talk to him anymore? Does it mean that I can't laugh with him and squeeze his hands during the evening?

I have been with Clyde my entire adult life. I met him when I was 18 and now I'm 40, and you want me to keep going without him? How do I handle that Clyde's not with me anymore? Oh Lord, please help me now.

"Mrs. Slappey." The undertaker touched me lightly on my shoulder. "We're back at the church."

We had returned to the Church of Christ around 2:00 p.m. and I was very tired. The four limousine drivers got out of the cars and opened the doors for the family. As I approached the door, I noticed a frail, limp-looking tree near the flower bed next to the gate. I felt sad as I gazed at the little tree. All it needed was some tender loving care. As ridiculous as it sounded, I saw Clyde in that little tree. Looking at the tree reminded me of his weakened body finally giving way. But the little tree was still alive, at least for the moment. A little water would probably do wonders for it. I inhaled the cool air as I turned to look at the four limousines all parked, one behind the other.

One by one the Slappey family walked into the fellowship hall at the church—Annie Bee, Jeannette, Mozelle, Bessie Mae, Louis, Marvin, and Clarence. Once inside we embraced and held each other close. I knew that we had to keep going as a family, which was what he wanted me to do. I vowed to do everything that I could do to ensure that I abided by his last words.

Lord, how do I handle this? I thought. *What do I do with this pain? You said You would walk with us in the darkness as well as the light, but You took him from us. You took him from me. Just where do I go without him, Lord? What do I do now? You made us one and now you've left me here without him. For what?* I thought angrily.

The anger fueled inside of me as I walked to one of the tables. The day's pain had left me drained. All I wanted to do was to fall on my bed and drift into a coma-like sleep.

"I don't know, Lord what I'm going to do without Clyde," I said out loud. "I just don't know what I'm going to do now."

CHAPTER THREE

When Darkness Falls

I was lingering in the first stage of grief, shock. I couldn't believe that Clyde was gone. It was unreal. God protected me from the cold reality that Clyde was dead by wrapping His loving arms around me.

I WATCHED MOM-MOM, my grandmother, gulp down the remaining piece of pound cake in her hand, and knew I had to stop her. I didn't want her to hurt herself. Mom-Mom was growing senile, it seemed more and more each day. She had done well until age 85, but then she slowly started to decline. We all had noticed how she had started to repeat the same thoughts. These subtle changes made us more aware of her declining condition. She was becoming more forgetful each day. Mom-Mom reared my sisters, brother, and me and we loved her dearly.

I looked around at everyone in the fellowship hall. I was very happy that most of the family came back to the church for the repast so we could all be together. We desperately needed to be with one another. I yearned to be close to everyone who was close to Clyde.

I turned my attention back to Mom-Mom and smiled at her. She smiled back, eating another piece of pound cake. I didn't want her to choke, so I walked toward her, took her hand in mine and led her back to the table where we were sitting so she could sit next to me comfortably.

"Mom-Mom," I said. "You can sit next to me, okay," motioning her to come sit next to me. "Just sit right here," I said to her, pointing to the chair for her to sit.

She smiled obligingly and touched the corner of the chair to steady her legs as she sat down.

"Okay, sweetheart...Are you doing okay?" she asked, holding the chair to steady herself some more. "Where is Clyde? Where is he?"

"I'm okay, Mom-Mom. I just want you to be okay," I replied, intentionally not answering her second question. Mom-Mom scooted into her seat as I placed my hands midway on the chair to gently push her closer to the table. At 93 years old, Mom-Mom was still moving around fairly well.

Mom-Mom just loved Clyde. She would talk to Clyde and me for hours on end. She adored him. Clyde helped her around the house—we both did. But I wasn't sure if she understood that Clyde was gone.

I remember one time when Clyde and I didn't have a dime to our names. It was around Christmas. Clyde and I had slaved for hours earlier that week picking pecans to pay our furniture bill. After picking them all day, we finally had enough pails of pecans to make an installment on our furniture. Even though we didn't have anything left for Clyde Daryl's Christmas, we had paid our bills.

Mom-Mom walked in the kitchen where we were sitting and handed six dollars to Clyde. At first, Clyde didn't know what she was placing in his hands, but when he saw it, he refused to take it. But Mom-Mom was relentless in her determination to give him the money. She told Clyde that he needed to put some money in his pocket, and so he did. Clyde and I never forgot the six dollars that Mom-Mom gave us that Christmas morning, and we pledged then and there to help her when she needed our support. She helped us get back on our feet again.

Mom-Mom was just that way. She always helped others, sometimes giving her last. Mom-Mom died three years after Clyde on August 11, 1998. I miss her terribly.

I was deeply saddened when she passed, but she had lived a very good life.

I looked at the next table, where most of Clyde's sisters and brothers were sitting. Their sad faces spoke volumes in pain. Clyde was the baby brother of the family and they loved him dearly. I watched them as they tried to comfort each other, holding on to each other solemnly, wanting to speak some word to ease the pain, but finding none. I then turned another direction and fixed my eyes on my mother, Mae. She loved Clyde and had always spoken highly of him because he treated her with genuine respect and admiration. My mother and L.C., my stepfather, came to our house many, many times to take care of Alex Keith while Clyde and I traveled. Because of my parents and many others, we were able to travel at a moment's notice when we received word about a doctor or hospital that had information on primary amyloidosis.

The pain was so vivid in Mae's eyes. I knew that she was upset by Clyde's death and was hurting even more for me. I strolled over to the end of our table and walked up to Mae and hugged her lovingly.

"Debbie, it's going to be okay," she said. "Clyde is all right now. He's out of his pain. He wants you to take care of yourself now," Mae said as she put her arms around me and hugged me warmly.

I closed my eyes, cherishing the warm hug from her for an extra moment or so as I choked back my tears.

"I know that he's okay, Mae. I know that he's all right now." I hesitated for a moment. "We were just so close… but I know that God's taking care of him now. And as much as I want to take care of him, I know that I can't anymore," I replied as I pulled out some tissue from my purse to wipe away the tears that were running down my face.

The fellowship hall was located in the basement of the church. Next to the hall was a tiny area designated as the kitchen. I was able to manage a smile as I thought over the numerous times Clyde and I would be in the kitchen together cooking for church homecomings, the after-school tutoring program, graduation, and just about everything else in between. Clyde was a deacon in the Church of Christ so we were always at the church working, doing something for the Lord.

"Mrs. Slappey, are you ready to go now?" the undertaker asked, tapping me on my shoulder. I sighed momentarily as I looked around the sanctuary. Many people had left.

"It's finished, Clyde," I said reluctantly. "It's finished now, Sweetheart." I turned to the undertaker. "Yes, I guess we are ready to leave," I replied. "Thank you so much."

I dreaded going home because Clyde wouldn't be there. And I hated to face this fact. I wasn't ready. I didn't think I ever would be.

"I think we better go," I said to everyone. I motioned to Clyde Daryl and Alex Keith and the rest of the family as we gathered to walk out of the building. Brother and Sister Clayton came over and hugged us. I will always appreciate their love and care while Clyde was sick and even more so after his death. They were so sweet and will always be my second parents.

I walked toward the car and sat in the backseat. The ride home was uneventful. I kept looking out the window, perhaps hoping that everything had been a dream. Would I stay in Columbus or would I return to Albany, Georgia where we had lived for ten years before relocating to Columbus. I really didn't know at this point what I was going to do. I only knew that I had to keep the family together. It didn't really matter where we lived as long as we were together.

I was glad that the Slappeys came to the house. I felt a tremendous sense of longing to be near Clyde's brothers and sisters. I felt a spiritual connection to his siblings. Being near them felt as if I was still with Clyde. I would always cling to them.

I didn't say much to Clyde Daryl and Alex Keith during the drive home. I had tried my best to comfort them earlier, but the thought of having to walk into our home after burying Clyde was far more painful than I had expected. I didn't have the power within me at the time to comfort them. I was emotionally drained. I didn't think I could lift one foot in front of the other and walk into the den without Clyde. It just didn't seem real.

I've always known that God was in the midst of trouble and pain and that He would direct me into His glorious love and comfort. I needed His words that I had memorized long ago to hold me together as the driver neared our home. I began to pray like I'd done so many times in my life.

"God, I pray, please give me the strength and courage to walk into our home, one step at a time. Clyde's not there and I'm having a hard time with it. I need your strength now. I need it now, Lord, I humbly pray to You."

I kept praying silently as I acknowledged I needed God to help me.

"I need Your help, Lord. I don't have much strength within me. I just buried my husband, and I don't have the strength to even walk into our home. I know that he wouldn't want me to feel this way. I know that he would want me to be strong, but I'm…not strong right now, Lord. I need Your help. Please help me…I'm broken now, Lord. I'm broken in tiny pieces!"

I closed my eyes, hoping to stop the tears as I continued to pray silently. "Mom, are you okay? Are you all right?" Clyde Daryl asked with concern.

"I heard you mumbling something. Mom, Dad's okay," he said to me softly as he lightly placed his arm around my shoulders. "Dad's okay now."

"Oh, I'm all right, son. I'll be all right. I'll be okay." I told him I was okay, but I wasn't, and I knew he knew that I wasn't okay.

"I know Mom, I know. Dad wanted us to all be well. He told me to take care of you and Alex Keith if anything happened to him…and I am going to do what he asked me to do…to take care of the family," he said sadly as he dropped his head. He looked away in the distance and continued, "You know I really miss him, too."

The undertaker pulled into our driveway while Clyde Daryl and I continued to talk. I turned toward the undertaker and thanked him and his crew.

"I appreciate you and everyone today," I said to him. "Everything went according to plan as my husband would have wanted it. And for this I'm very thankful to all of you."

"You are quite welcome Mrs. Slappey," he said while handing me his card. "Whatever you need, please don't hesitate to call us. We will be happy to help you and your family in any way that we can. God bless you in His care."

We emerged from the limousines and walked into the house. I listened as the four limousines back out of the driveway onto Dearborn Avenue. By this time, I was completely exhausted and all I wanted to do was fall headfirst onto my bed and sleep forever. Clyde's funeral had lasted only one hour, but the repast was more like two hours after returning from the cemetery. This had been his wish.

As we walked into the house, Clyde Daryl and Alex Keith hugged my neck and kissed me softly. The wind seemed to take on a life of its own as the cool breeze whisked against my cheeks in the sun's glow. Clyde Daryl took Alex Keith's hand in ours and we joined in unison with Lewis, Marvin, and Clarence—Clyde's brothers, and walked into the house to pray together.

Once in the house, we prayed as a family. I had dreaded walking into my home, but I knew that I had to do it sooner or later. I don't remember much else after I walked back to my bedroom to change clothes. I wanted desperately to get out of that black dress and slip into something a bit more comfortable. I knew that folks would be arriving to sit with the family and I wanted to be ready for them. Even though I was extremely tired I wanted to greet everyone and let them know how much I appreciated their prayers and support.

Later that evening, around 5:00, we drove Clyde Daryl to the airport. I knew that he wanted to stay around the family a little while longer, but I didn't want him to miss out on his second semester of college.

Clyde wanted to make sure that Clyde Daryl didn't miss out on any schooling. In their last conversation together he told him to stay in school no matter what happened to him. I knew the best thing that any of us could do was to get back into our routine. But it wasn't going to be easy for any of us. Clarence, Clyde's brother, drove Clyde Daryl to the airport so he could get back to Winston-Salem, North Carolina, before dark. Winston-Salem was around 400 miles from Columbus and it took about an hour to get there by plane.

By 8:00 p.m., I didn't have any strength left in my bones. I was beyond tired. I didn't want to leave my company, but I could barely keep my eyes open as I sat in a chair in the den. I thanked everyone for coming and told them that I was going to lie down for a little while. I walked back to my bedroom and lay across my bed, hoping to rest for a few minutes so I could go back and sit with family and friends.

I opened my eyes and the clock read 10:00 p.m. I had slept for almost two hours. Clyde Daryl had made it back to Wake Forest University. By now, our company had gone home and Mae, L.C., and Alex Keith were asleep. I stared at Clyde's dresser until finally I pulled myself out of the bed and walked toward it. I touched his cologne bottles, and as my fingers danced around the bottles, my mind began to wander.

"Lord," I said, "I just hope and pray that I did the right thing with Clyde Daryl today. I know he wanted to stay with us, but I know he was better off being back at school. Please Lord, I pray, let him be okay at school alone."

I lamented at the thought that he would have to deal with his father's death alone. My prayer was that he would remember his father's words even though physically he was no longer here.

I kept looking at Clyde's cologne bottles and picked up his favorite, Old Spice. I sprayed some into my hands and inhaled the fragrance, rubbing the scent on my face, cheeks, and arms. I closed my eyes and screamed inwardly as I beat my fist against my chest. Crying franticly, I started to shout toward the ceiling, "Lord, please, Lord, please, help me now." Before I knew it, the cologne bottle had slipped from my hands and fallen to the floor. I became frantic and stooped down to grab the bottle from the floor. Shaking profusely, I was barely able to hold the bottle with my hands. I didn't want to break it. It was horrifying to think that I had almost broken Clyde's favorite cologne. I wanted to keep it forever. I held it close to my chest, holding onto that cologne bottle with my life.

"Oh, Lord, don't let me break it! Don't let me break it. It's all that I have of him. I should have been more careful. I'm so sorry, Lord. I'm so sorry, Clyde. Please don't let it break. I need to smell him. I need to be close to him. Lord, help me now. I don't know what to do without him. I need to hold him tight. He's in the ground! He's alone! I can't take care of him there! He needs me, Lord. I need him so much right now!" I cried.

"Please help me right now. I only have him in his clothes and his cologne. I have his toothbrush, I have his shaving items, but I don't have him! Lord, please help me now."

I wobbled back to the bed and lay on the left side, Clyde's side, so I could be near him. I tasted the salt from my tears and tugged Clyde's pillow tightly under my head. All I could do was close my eyes and see him in my thoughts, which made me feel close to him.

Darkness Is Painful

I didn't like the darkness. Darkness just wasn't a good thing for me because when it came, I felt more pain. "Lord, please, I pray. Let the light come back," I said. "Let your light shine again." I squeezed Clyde's pillow tightly and turned over to my side. I was hurting inside. I felt as if someone was ripping through my flesh with a jagged-edge knife; the pain was horrid. I picked up the remote from the bed and clicked the television on, turning to the Weather Channel.

I couldn't go back to sleep, not without Clyde next to me. This was my first night after Clyde's burial and I didn't want this reality. I hated it and trembled to think what tomorrow would bring. How was I going to face the reality that Clyde wouldn't be coming back home to me and our children? He wouldn't be back even the day after tomorrow. I buried my face in Clyde's pillow and sobbed helplessly, wanting with everything that was within me to see his smiling face again. I longed to hear him tell a joke…to see his smiling face again.

"Lord, what will I do without him?" I asked with a deep sigh. "What will I do, Lord? Where will I go from here? I don't even know who I am, Lord. I don't know anymore. Lord, please help me. I need You so much. Why us, Lord? Why did You break up our happy family? This is too big. This is too big for me. I can't handle this. I need my husband, Lord. I need him so much now!"

The tears wouldn't stop. I buried my head in my pillow. I didn't want Mae, L.C. or Alex Keith to hear me crying. My head began to pound, and without realizing it, I drifted off to sleep clutching my pillow tightly.

This would be the beginning of many lonely, bleak nights without Clyde. He was my partner for life. Our lives were joined together to make one. That's why I called him my Innisfree. Now, I had to learn to live without him. I didn't know what I was going to do, but I knew I needed to keep my family together no matter what. The family was the most important thing and I knew that only God could see us through this terrible situation.

Chapter Four

Feeling Out of Place

I yearned to see Clyde's smiling face again. As loneliness got the best of me, I began to deny that he had died and left me here alone. It's difficult to imagine, I know, but the mind can create a world, even a faux reality to survive. Though I didn't go to this extreme, I did grapple between living in the shadows of the past and my new reality of living without Clyde. I knew one day I would have to face the fact that he was gone, but it wouldn't be today.

THE SUN'S GLOW PIERCED through my bedroom window and imprinted its own signature of warmth on my forehead. I had managed to fall in and out of sleep most of the night. I looked out the window and saw daylight. I was very glad. I guessed it was somewhere around 7:00 a.m. and all was quiet in the house.

Today was Tuesday morning and I had survived the first night after the funeral.

"I made it, Lord!" I said with thanksgiving. "I've survived the first night and I thank You, Lord, so very much."

I looked around the room and for just a second or two gazed at our modest furnishings. Clyde and I had always bought things together. We went to church together, we took fun vacations together and we even bathed together. As I lay in the middle of the bed, my mind drifted to our first home—an apartment in Plains, Georgia. It was a very small apartment; even though we bumped heads because of its small size, we loved it because it was our first home as husband and wife.

Clyde and I got married in 1973. In the early years, it was just Clyde and me. Clyde was just a big old country boy. He liked vegetables, lots of vegetables. So, I knew that I had to learn to cook them for him. Of course, I knew how to cook, but I had become accustomed to someone else cooking for me while in college. I was used to going to the dining area at Clark College in Atlanta, Georgia, to sit down to eat. Since we had married, I had to make a quick adjustment to cooking for my husband. It took me a while initially to adjust, but with time, I was cooking every day and eventually pulling back to every other day.

I smiled as I reflected on a day I cooked fried pork chops and fresh fried corn. I knew that Clyde loved fresh corn so I decided I would prepare it for him. I had seen Mom-Mom cook it, so I called for her recipe. She told me that I needed to add a "touch bit of flour." But of course, she didn't tell me how much a "touch bit of flour" was, so I added several tablespoons to the mixture. I shucked the corn, grated it off the cob, and poured the mixture in a frying pan on the stove top. I added vegetable oil and several tablespoons of flour and it was ready to go...or so I thought.

I waited about 30 minutes and added a little more flour since I didn't see too much going on in the fryer. To make a long story short, by the time Clyde came home for dinner, the corn was pretty much saturated with flour. As a matter of fact, there was more flour on his plate than corn. Clyde kindly thanked me for fixing the corn and never said anything unkind about that fresh corn in our 21 years of marriage. He knew I had made it with love, even though it didn't turn out the way I'd expected.

Clyde just smiled and said, "It's good, Debbie. Thank you for the meal. I appreciate it very much."

I won't ever forget what he said because I knew it hadn't turned out so well. The corn was drowned in flour, but still Clyde appreciated my efforts.

"Thank You, Lord, for my life with Clyde," I said. "I appreciate him more than ever now. Please give me the strength and the courage to keep going—for my kids and for me. I know they need me and we all need You desperately more than ever. Please, just keep me going. I don't know how I will do it, but I know that You'll help me — You'll help all of us. I know that You will. I know what Clyde would want. He would want us to go on. It's just very hard to do right now, Lord. Please, help us Lord."

I kept remembering our times together as a couple and as a family. We had a beautiful family and a beautiful life together. I thought the best thing that I could do for myself was to stay focused on our memories.

Clyde and I didn't have much when we first married. I was a sophomore at Georgia Southwestern College in Americus, Georgia, and Clyde was attending South Georgia Technical School (name at the time) in Americus, Georgia, majoring in electrical technology. There were times we didn't have much gas to put into our 1970 Dodge Reliant. We really struggled in the early days.

Our Reliant wasn't much to look at, but it took us from Plains, Georgia, to Americus, Georgia, and back home. We did the best we could and we learned early in life to appreciate the little things.

I won't ever forget one time when our electricity was turned off because we didn't have the money to pay the bill. We had no electricity and I was hungry. I had prepared chicken to bake in the oven, but after the lights had been turned off, I couldn't cook it. Something told me to go ahead and place the already seasoned chicken into the oven, and that's exactly what I did. Those chicken pieces baked slowly for about an hour since the oven was still warm. By the grace of God, Clyde and I were able to eat some savory baked chicken breasts an hour and a half later in the dark.

I didn't ask any questions. I was thankful to God for His blessings in allowing us to eat a warm meal, even with the electricity turned off. I smiled at that beautiful memory we shared even before our children had arrived on the scene. And then I cried.

"Lord, he's gone!" I said. "He's gone! He's left me here alone. Oh, Lord, I want to be with him. I can't stand to be without him. I'm nothing without him."

The tears flowed from my eyes into my mouth, and the taste was very salty. I buried my face into the gold-colored blanket and looked once more at the clock that read 7:30 a.m. I was very tired. All I wanted was for God to bring Clyde back to me and my family. The idea of having to go on without him was just too excruciating to bear.

I continued to pray: "God, when You wake me up from this nightmare, please let Clyde be here with me. Please let him come to our bedroom the way he used to with my coffee and a big smile. Lord, just let me see him again. I want to close my eyes and see him near me. We both would be smiling and acting crazy together. Lord, I just want to hear him say, 'Debbie, what are you doing?' and then I will know that all is well with me. Please Lord, please, bring him back to me. I can't keep going without him. I just can't...."

My mind raced as I continued to pray to God for strength. I knew God wouldn't bring Clyde back, but for some reason I kept asking Him to do so. I would have done anything to see his face, even to see his spirit.

Worn and tired, I pulled the blanket over my face and turned to face the window. I closed my eyes and sighed in much anguish and pain and slowly drifted back into sleep. Sleep was providing some relief from the pain, even if it was for a short while. In sleep, I didn't cry. I dreaded waking up to the same reality.

The Birds' Songs

I woke up to the sound of birds fussing right outside my window. I guess they were fixing up their nest. The sounds of the birds were so soothing to my soul that morning. I wanted to stay immersed in their song, listening to every chirping sound they made together. I wanted to forget about my own life.

And then my sad reality invaded my thoughts once again and I began to cry. I had buried Clyde and had made it through my first night of being without him. I shrugged my shoulders and turned toward the left side of the bed, Clyde's side. I glided my hand along his pillow back and forth, ever so gently. I laid my head down and closed my eyes as I took in Clyde's scent from his pillow. For a moment in time, at least, in my mind, Clyde was next to me.

"I can stay here forever," I said as I continued to caress Clyde's pillow.

I closed my eyes and pretended that he was near me. It felt so good, warm and nice to see him again. I didn't want to open my eyes ever again, no, not ever. Then suddenly a knock on the door interrupted my perfect moment.

"Mom, are you okay?" Alex Keith asked as he peeked into the room.

Startled, I looked away toward the window, hoping he wouldn't see my tears. I managed to choke back the tears and responded to Alex Keith quickly.

"Good morning, son…How did you sleep last night?" I asked him kindly, hoping he didn't detect the sound of my cracked voice.

"I'm okay, Mom. I want you to be okay," he said as he walked toward the bed and hugged my neck. "Grandma is cooking some bacon and eggs for breakfast. I'm gonna bring you some, okay," Alex Keith said excitedly.

Alex Keith was really trying to be the little man of the house; being very brave. I knew that he was missing Clyde very much, but I didn't want him to hold in his pain because of me.

"I'll get up. I need to since it's almost 8:00 a.m.," I said to him. "I'll come to the table and eat. Just tell Mae that I'll be right there, okay. Just give me a few minutes and I'll eat in the kitchen."

I couldn't believe that I had slept so long. I was tired and worn out, I probably could have slept for hours more.

"Oh, Lord," I said as I lifted myself from the bed and walked into the bathroom. I gazed straight in the bathroom mirror at swollen, bloodshot eyes from crying last night. I pulled my washcloth from the bathtub curtain and dropped it into the sink. It didn't take long for the warm water to saturate the washcloth. I squeezed out the excess water and held the cloth over my face. And then, I broke down into tears again. I was missing my best friend and didn't know what I was going to do.

"Lord, I need you so much. I can't do this without you. I miss my friend. I miss him so much," I cried out.

I placed the warm cloth against my swollen eyes, hoping that the heat would soothe some of the swelling. I went on to brush my teeth and pulled my hair toward the back of my head. I hadn't bothered to roll my hair last night. What was the point? Before walking back into the bedroom, I reached behind the bathroom door and grabbed Clyde's burgundy and cream-colored robe and wrapped it around my body. Walking to the dresser, I picked up my Bible. I turned to Proverbs 3:5-6 and read it aloud.

Trust in the Lord with all thine heart; and lean not unto thine own understanding. In all thy ways acknowledge Him and He shall direct thy path.

This Scripture had saved me from myself many times. I longed for God's word to penetrate my mind that morning. I was in much anguish and could feel that I was very weak — physically, mentally, and emotionally. I reached for the covers to make up the bed before walking into the kitchen. I kept praying intently for a few minutes and then walked into the kitchen and sat down with Mae. Alex Keith had already finished eating.

"Thanks Mae for the breakfast," I said. "I appreciate it very much. I didn't feel like getting up, but I have so much to do. But I'm going to take it easy today."

"That's good Debbie. You need to rest yourself. You've gone through so much," Mae replied. "So just sit down and eat you a little something. You need your strength."

"Where is L.C.?" asking for my stepfather.

"He just stepped outside. I believe he's in the backyard. He ate already," Mae replied.

"Thanks so much for the breakfast. I really appreciate it, Mae. I'm just tired, but I'll be okay. The Lord is with us. He'll take care of us. I just know that with all my heart. It's just a little hard right now," I said.

"It will get easier. You know Clyde would want you to go on. He would," she said, touching my shoulder. "Just remember the things that he said to you and God will do the rest," Mae added.

"I know. I know He will."

"Has Alex Keith said anything about Clyde—about yesterday?" I asked Mae.

"No, he hasn't. He just keeps playing as though nothing has happened. But I'm sure that he will come around. Children behave differently than adults about death. Just give him some time."

Mae and I finished eating and ended up talking for another 30 minutes at the kitchen table. I walked out of the kitchen into the den to stretch out on the sofa. I was still very tired. Mae joined

L.C. and Alex Keith outside as I relaxed on the sofa, staring at the television in front of me.

After about 10 minutes or so, I stood up from the blue and rose sofa and began wandering through the house. It had been a long time since I had the time to walk from one side of the house to the other. I walked into the kitchen and spotted the chrome faucet that Clyde had installed some years ago. After 10, maybe even 15 years, the Delta faucet remained securely intact, with no leaks! Clyde had installed the faucet when we first moved into our house in 1989. He was a master craftsman.

"You know," I said, "Clyde, you're good. It's one of the best installed faucets that I've seen." Clyde also had an extraordinary gift as an electrician. I told him many times over our 21 years together that he needed to start his own business. Clyde always smiled when I complimented him and said that when he retired from Georgia Power he would do just that, start his own business.

With my left hand, I touched the mouth of the faucet with the tip of my finger and smiled. "You were very good, dear," I said. As I walked into the dining room, I panned the room and spotted the huge mirror that was nestled between the ornate cherry buffet table and the kingly shaped golden sconces decorating the wall on each side of the full, single window. I remembered when Clyde and I installed that heavy mirror on a beautiful Saturday afternoon. We had such fun doing it. I looked around at the pictures on the wall, nodding my head in confirmation, and I knew that Clyde would always be special. He had installed almost everything on the wall in the room. Of course, we'd done it together.

The wall decorations had been strategically placed. Clyde was not the kind of guy who would just stick a nail in a wall and slap a picture or mirror here or there. Not Clyde. He would go to his toolbox, take out his measuring tape and work magic on just about anything he touched.

"Man," I said out loud, "I miss you so much. I really miss you." I danced my fingers along the edge of the mirror's ornate design.

Lord, I miss him so much." I slumped down on the living room sofa as I folded my hands together on my face.

"God, I know that You are here with me. But it's not enough. Please give me the strength to get off this sofa so I can take care of Alex Keith. I know that he needs me now. Clyde Daryl needs me now, too, but I just don't have the strength to pick myself up and move. Just help me," I said to God as I fought within myself to rise from the sofa.

God had always taken care of my family and me. As a family, we had many close calls with Clyde being sick, but through it all, He protected us from the storms. But this was a different storm. We were no longer a family of four. Clyde was gone. He was really gone and no amount of tears was going to bring him back.

I couldn't think past a few hours at a time, sometimes not even one hour, because the pain was much too powerful. "I have to get up," I kept saying to myself. "I have to get up." I heard a voice deep within me saying, *Debbie, get off the sofa. Get up off the sofa,* so I did.

I swung my legs close to the floor in obedience and lifted my upper body from the sofa.

"Thank You Lord, thank You," I said. "I need to get up and try to do something around this house."

Mae was talking to the postal lady when I walked into the den. I walked toward them and greeted her with a simple smile. She expressed her condolences and I thanked her for her concern and for delivering the mail that day.

I was able to beat back the pain. I walked back into the den and sat on the sofa for a little while. Mentally drained, I walked back into the living room again and lay on the sofa. It had taken all the energy that I could muster to tear myself from the sofa to greet the postal lady.

My mind was bulging with memories of our lives together. I didn't want to go anywhere. I really didn't want to face the day, nor did I want to walk outside. I felt strange, out of place, even in my own home; I felt detached, numb. If I could have stayed in our memories together as a family, I would have. Even though I knew that God was with me, it still was painful and even horrifying during the first six months living in the house without him. But I knew I had to keep trying no matter what.

I lifted myself from the living room sofa and walked over and touched the beautiful English rose-colored drapes that cascaded on each side of the full-length double window. I remembered so well when Clyde and I worked most of a Saturday afternoon in early spring 1989 to hang those drapes. It was some kind of ordeal, but once we'd finished, the drapes hung majestically.

I wanted to make a huge statement in the living room, and everything had to be color-coordinated. By the time Clyde and I had hung the drapes, I knew that the room spoke volumes when it came to style and finesse. I touched the whisper-soft panels detailed with woven prints of roses that nestled serenely between the silk chiffon drapes. Everything was pristine and comfy in the room. My eyes then rolled toward the cream-colored background of the walls where Clyde and I had decided to hang floral paintings on each side. Just about every color of the rainbow could be seen in the pictures — handsome pastels of peridot, citrine, blue topaz, smoky quartz, and even little dazzles of white topaz. These colors were magnified with green tourmaline, English rose quartz, golden citrine, and blue sapphire florals throughout the sofa's color scheme.

It was an absolute showplace of comfort and enjoyment for many guests during the first six years in our home. I picked up one of the matching sofa pillows as I walked closer and breathed deeply, hoping to detect Clyde's scent. I hugged the pillow very close to my chest and breathed deeply again to relive the scent of times past.

The Basketball Game

I walked out of the living room with the pillow clutched under my arms, dragging my feet over the thick gold carpet. I opened the back French door and walked out to join Alex Keith, Mae, and L.C. sitting in the backyard. Mae and L.C. were comfortably sitting in the lounge chairs located next to the garage while they watched Alex Keith compete against himself in a basketball game. Each time he threw the ball up toward the goal, he would quickly dart under the ball and swoop it up again before it fell to the ground. Of course, Alex Keith was beating himself.

"Mom, come on and play!" He shouted to me. "I am winning! Come on, Mom, and play some hoops with me, just for a little while," Alex Keith pleaded.

Playing basketball was the last thing I wanted to do that afternoon, but I knew that I had to make sure that Alex Keith wouldn't see me moping around. So I lifted my shoulders in defiance of my own dazed disposition and replied, "Okay, I'll play one round, just for a few minutes, okay. You know, it's been a while. You, Clyde, and Clyde Daryl are pretty good with this stuff, but I'm not."

A few minutes turned into an evening of playing basketball as Alex Keith and I played one-on-one. I jumped, I screamed—well, we both screamed, and we had fun together. I was glad to see Alex Keith smile, even through his pain. For a moment in time, even if it was for a brief moment, the stress froze and I was happy. As Mae and L.C. cheered us on, I knew that they were happy to see the smile on Alex Keith's and my face. I was drenched in sweat after playing with Alex Keith, but it was all worth it after seeing Alex Keith's face beam with joy.

"Lord, please let Alex Keith be okay," I prayed. "Please let him be okay." I watched him dart from one end of the court to the other with his big smile.

"I know that he misses his father so much. Lord, I know it." I spoke a silent prayer for Alex Keith and Clyde Daryl. I knew that only God could help them both now. God was the only one who could help me now, too. No one else could bear this pain but God.

It would be my second night without Clyde. I hoped it wasn't too cold for him. At night, the temperature would drop to the 50-degree mark, even in late April. I prayed Clyde was okay. And as the sun's face began to hide under the clouds and trees, I dreaded another night of being without him.

Later that evening, I checked Alex Keith's homework and decided to take an early bubble bath to relax my mind and muscles. I was a little sore from running and jumping with the basketball. Of course, I knew better. I was acting just like a teenager and I was far from it.

"Girl, you are crazy," I said to myself. "You know better than to run and jump like you did today with Alex Keith. You know you can't keep up with him." I smiled at myself and ducked my shoulders under the warm water to soothe the soreness some. I was very tired. I only wanted to sleep. Just sleep.

I kept praying to God quietly. "Help me sleep tonight."

I felt I needed to keep talking to him. My soul was literally intertwined with anguish and desperation. I wanted only to close my eyes and pretend that Clyde was still with me physically. I wanted to pretend even if it was for a little while.

I finished my bath and walked into the den to say good night to Alex Keith, Mae, and L.C. By that time it was around 9:00 p.m., Alex Keith was getting ready for bed so I knew that it wouldn't be long before he would be fast asleep and snoring. After getting a glass of water from the kitchen, I walked back to my bedroom.

I felt very awkward and alone. I stared at the television, but there wasn't much to watch. Nothing really held my interest. Eventually, I found the Weather Channel and watched the forecast for the next day over again. I stretched vertically on the bed and began to feel sleepy. There was really nothing to do.

Slowly as I began to drift off in sleep, I felt a sense of calmness and peace slowly creeping over me. The feeling started at my legs, my shoulders, and then my eyes. I was going to sleep and I thanked God for letting me have peace in sleep. Even though it was for a short while, I appreciated it.

I woke up and lifted my head to look around the room. I gazed at the blinds and could tell that it was still dark outside. The clock read 2:30 a.m. It was early morning, and my eyes had suddenly opened. Had I been dreaming? Had I dreamed about Clyde? I hoped I had. And I so wanted to go back to my dream. But I knew that I couldn't; so I began to pray.

"Thank you Lord for letting me get some sleep tonight. Thank you, thank you," I said over and over again through mumbled whispers.

It was very quiet. I only heard the humming sound coming from the television, which had been on all night. I wasn't ready for silence. I still wanted to hear noise, even laughter. I turned over to Clyde's side of the bed and gently pressed my lips against his pillow.

As I held his pillow close to my face, I whispered in the still of the morning, "I want to see you, that's all. I want to see you, Clyde, and I know that I'll be okay. Lord, please, let me see him. I just want to see his face, his big smile. He has such a handsome, jolly smile. I just want to make sure that he's okay. That's all."

I stopped talking and closed my eyes with Clyde's pillow snuggled against my lips, kissing it softly.

"Clyde, I hope that you're okay," I said. "I hope you're not cold. I don't want you to be cold. It's cool outside. Please don't be cold. I miss you so much."

I held his pillow tightly against my chest as I inched closer to Clyde's side of the bed. I laid my head on his second pillow and stared at the ceiling. With tears flowing down my cheeks, I lay in the bed and cried myself back to sleep.

My 41st Birthday

On April 30, 1995, I turned 41 years old. We buried Clyde on April 24, 1995, on a Monday. My 41st birthday was very solemn for me as it was only one week after Clyde's burial. I really didn't feel like celebrating anything, much less my birthday. But I kept going and smiling because I knew that my family was trying to cheer me up.

I was glad when April 30 finally passed. It would be the first time in 22 years that I had celebrated my birthday without Clyde. We always made a big "to do" about each other's birthdays. Losing him to death and not having him with me on my birthday heightened my anxiety. Nevertheless, I kept going and pushing forward. I knew that there was no turning back. I had to rear Alex Keith alone and I knew I had to keep going. Even if I didn't want to do it myself, I had to keep going for Alex Keith and Clyde Daryl. They needed me and I needed them as well.

"Happy birthday, Mom," Alex Keith said excitedly as he presented me with a brownie cake. It was quite an interesting cake to say the least. The brownie was round and decorated with the cutest little eyebrows, a spongy-looking nose and a big smile planted in the middle of the brownie, accented with delectable cool whip. The brownie was good!

Clyde Daryl and Alex Keith wanted me to know that they were thinking of me. Many of my family and friends sent me cards and called me on my birthday. Clyde Daryl had made arrangements and coordinated everything with Alex Keith.

I appreciated it very much, even though I was in no great mood to celebrate. I knew that from that day forward my birthday wouldn't ever be the same. It would be a constant reminder that Clyde had died within two weeks of my birthday. The month of April would always signify sadness and pain for me.

Spring Festival at Waddell School

Morning came quickly for the household. Alex Keith had his upcoming Spring Festival at Waddell Elementary School and I wanted to make sure that I was there on time. Alex Keith had already dressed for school and was eating his breakfast. I sat and watched him as he finished eating his oatmeal and toast.

Alex Keith seemed to be sleeping well and I was thankful. He finished drinking his milk before picking up his rather heavy satchel and ran to the back door.

"Mom, I'll see you later. Have a good day!" Alex Keith shouted as he dashed out the back door.

Before I could get out the words, "You, too, Alex Keith. Have a good day," he had already darted out the door. I waved at him at the bus stop. He seemed to be doing well.

Maybe too well, I thought.

For Alex Keith's sake, I knew that eventually I would have to talk to someone about our tragedy. I didn't want Alex Keith to push things down so far that he didn't acknowledge what had happened to his father. It wouldn't be a good thing.

As I waited for the bus to come, my mind wandered to Clyde Daryl. I was worried about him as well. I knew he didn't have much time to grieve with the family because he had to concentrate on his studies; I knew that it was best for him to keep busy. I said a silent prayer for him, for both of our boys, as I waited for Alex Keith's bus to arrive.

"Lord, please take care of Clyde Daryl, being so far away. I know he's struggling, but I also know that it's probably the best thing for him. We're all hurting, but with your help, I know we'll be okay. I pray and I plead for his peace, Lord."

The bus came around the corner and Alex Keith and the other kids began to line up. As I watched Alex Keith get on the bus, I thought about Clyde Daryl's excellent semester at Wake Forest and I was so proud of his progress. He was doing well in school—exceptionally well under the circumstances. To tell you the truth, both of our kids were doing very well in school. I was proud of them and knew that Clyde would be very proud of them.

I lifted my left hand and waved at the bus driver. He was a very nice man and kept the kids in check. My eyes followed the bus as it disappeared around the corner on Dearborn Avenue.

L.C. and Mae needed to get their lives back to normal, as they had been at our house over the last five months, taking care of Alex Keith off and on. I knew that it was time for them to put their lives back together again. But I was terrified at the thought of being alone in the house without Clyde.

I thought about the many times Clyde went on business trips and how the two of us talked for hours on end on the telephone. We both knew full well that he would only be gone a few days at a time. But we were just like that. We did everything together. You didn't see Clyde without me, nor did you see me without Clyde. We would talk to each other late at night and say how much we missed and loved each other. We couldn't wait to see each other again.

The crazy thing was that Clyde was never too far away. He either was in Atlanta or somewhere close to Atlanta—no more than a few hours away.

Clyde and I were one with each other. We took it to heart when God talked about becoming one. I guess that's why it was very painful to be without him now, because I knew that he wouldn't be coming back to me ever again. No matter how much I cried and screamed and cried again, Clyde wouldn't be coming back to me.

I hadn't begun to fathom the reality that Clyde was no longer on this earth. My mind couldn't go to that reality, not yet. The only thing I knew was that he was in a freshly dug grave just about an hour's drive from our home.

Closing the door in the den, I turned toward the east and watched the sun rise. It was very peaceful and wondrous to behold. I rejoiced to know that it was daytime again. I didn't like the darkness because it made me very sad. I wasn't afraid of the dark, but I didn't like the pain and sadness that worsened when evening arrived.

I walked back into the house and looked at our family picture above the fireplace. It was one of the best things we could have done as a family, I thought. We took our last picture in December 1994. I saw the laceration on Clyde's face and knew that he didn't feel well. He still went ahead and took the family portrait, and I would always treasure it. I smiled for a few seconds as I remembered our time at the portrait studio on that rainy Saturday afternoon in December.

I tip-toed past Mae and L.C.'s bedroom door and slowly closed my door to cry in private. As it was only 8:00 a.m., I sat back on my bed and decided to lie down again. I would have plenty of time to rest a bit before leaving for Alex Keith's school. The annual spring event wouldn't begin until 1:00 p.m., so I laid my head on my pillow and before long I was fast asleep. I found it much easier to sleep in the daytime than at night.

I arrived at Waddell School for the annual spring races. I walked through the hall corridors and felt out of place. Without Clyde, I felt incomplete, lonely, miserable, and pretty much depleted of any energy. I longed to be near my husband. I wanted to turn and walk back to the door and jump into my car and drive to Andersonville to be near him. It was all I wanted to do.

But I knew I had to keep walking toward the back of the school where the festival was being held. I knew I had to go and cheer Alex Keith on during the competition. After all, Clyde would have wanted me to do so; I knew he would have. I prayed for strength and the ability to smile for Alex Keith as I walked through the corridor. He needed to see me smile. And by the time I reached my hand to open the door to walk outside where the kids were having fun, God gave me the strength I needed. I began to smile.

I looked around for Alex Keith and found him having a great time and enjoying the competition. I was very glad to see him laughing. He ran up to me and dangled the several blue ribbons he had already won in front of my face.

"Mom, I won first place in the 100-yard dash!" Alex Keith said with much excitement. "They couldn't catch me. I just passed them by like a bullet!"

"That's great Alex Keith," I replied, grabbing one of his ribbons to look at closely. "Wow! That's pretty neat. I'm so proud of you, son!" I hugged him closely. He was dripping with sweat.

"Mom, I have to go to the blind scarf competition. Come see Mom," Alex Keith said excitedly as he ran to catch up with his buddies for the next competition.

I was so glad to see him smile and have fun. It had been a long time since he was able to smile and relax. We were always on guard just in case we received a telephone call from the Mayo Clinic about Clyde. I was deeply moved by his genuine joyfulness that day. I wished that I could keep smiling as he was that day. But there were no prolonged smiles for me. I pretended to smile just for a little while until he wasn't looking anymore. I felt as if I had been dumped in a bottomless hole and there was no leverage or foundation on which to anchor. It was one big void without Clyde in my life. I was going through the motions of living, but I wasn't living. It was more like shadow living—existing in the shadows.

"Hi, Mrs. Slappey," a lady said while walking up to me and extending her hand. "I'm Alex Keith's teacher."

I was so deep in thought that I hadn't noticed her walk toward me.

"I'm doing okay." I managed to paint a smile on my face. She wasn't one of Alex Keith's regular teachers; I knew them all.

"How did you know my name and that I was Alex Keith's mom?" I asked her.

"I saw the expression on your face and I knew it was you. I lost my husband sometime ago, and I know that look," she said. "I know what you are going through, Mrs. Slappey. But in time, you will get better. I had such a rough time when my husband died, and many times it wasn't easy, but God will see you through it. He will."

She placed her hand over mine with a gentle touch to assure me that it would be okay. "Believe me," she continued. "In time, you will learn to go on with your life." I appreciated her for taking the time to talk to me.

"Thank you so very much," I said, extending my hand to her. "I appreciate your words very much. I'm just trying to keep going. Alex Keith needs me and I need him as well. I just want him to be okay. Right now, it's not about me, it's about him."

"You also have to take care of yourself, Mrs. Slappey. I didn't know your husband, but I can tell you—you all have raised a fine young man there," she said, looking at Alex Keith as he lined up for the competition.

"Yes we did." I nodded in agreement. "I'm so proud of him. He's just like his daddy. Just infinite in energy.

"It means a lot to me for you to share what you've said," I continued, "I will always appreciate your words. I'll see you another time, okay. I have to get to Alex Keith. Thank you so very much. " I hugged her to show my gratitude.

I still remember the conversation I had with the teacher even though I don't remember her name. There were so many mothers with their children that day and she knew exactly who I was and that I had lost my husband.

Even though I felt out of place and out of touch that day, God gave me the strength to keep placing one foot in front of the other. Alex Keith placed first and second places in several events. I survived that afternoon with Alex Keith and he had a wonderful time as I cheered for him during the competition.

CHAPTER FIVE

Lord, Where Do I Go from Here?

As the days turned into weeks, my shock and numbness gave way to anger. I was angry with God, I was angry with Clyde, and I was angry with myself. I didn't want to go on without Clyde. I just didn't know how.

I TOSSED AND TURNED IN MY BED over the next few nights as I attempted to sleep. I wanted to travel to the cemetery to be near Clyde. I yearned for his presence.

"If only I could be near him and even touch his grave, I would be okay," I said. I knew the cemetery was closed, but it didn't matter. "I want to be near him, Lord…that's all. I just want to be close to him," I said as I pressed Clyde's pillow close to my face and hugged it tightly. I breathed deeply into his pillow.

"Just let me see him again, Lord. I want to touch him—just to let him know that I still love him and always will love him. You said that we were one and now we are separate. You told us to love each other and to be one. Now, you've taken him away from me, Lord. You want people to become one in marriage and then you separate them. It's not fair. It's not right. Lord, where do I go from here? I can't get to him. I can't touch him. I can't see him. I can't do anything now but cry. What do you want me to do, Lord?" I asked sadly.

There seemed to be nothing but tears. The only thing I could do was cry. But no matter how much I cried, Clyde still didn't walk in the door. Angrily, I wiped the tears and shouted into the pillow at the top of my voice, "What's the point! I can't see him anymore. I won't see him ever again...not in this life."

I ranted on as I shook my head in disbelief. In my anguish I began to pound my fists into the pillow with tears streaming effortlessly on the bed. I cupped Clyde's pillow and pulled it close to my heart and closed my eyes. I was thankful to God that early morning, when I cried myself to sleep, because I was no longer in pain. And this was a good thing.

⁓

"Thank you Lord for letting me sleep. I'm sorry about what I said last night. I really don't mean those words. They just come. I'm tired and worn. I'm tired of the pain. I'm tired." My eyes opened partially and then closed again to sleep.

Two days had passed. I didn't know it at the time but I was learning to take each day — each hour, even each minute — moment by moment. It was the only way I could survive the day. I kept going, kept trying to push reality out of my mind. But the pain always came back as horrible and unending as I saw the life drift out of my husband's body.

I heard no answers, only silence and more silence. I knew the Lord heard me. I knew He did, but He didn't answer me, or so I thought. The days began to pass and each day appeared to be the same. I would stare at the TV and cry until I fell asleep. Mae and L.C. would be leaving soon. I didn't want them to worry about me. I knew that with God's help I would be fine.

I couldn't keep up with the days, let alone the month. I only knew that a week had passed by. For me, time pretty much stood still. I wanted to stay in time where Clyde was. I wanted to stay with him. To me, moving on was acknowledging that Clyde had gone away and I couldn't bear that thought. Not yet.

My mind couldn't imagine that Clyde was really dead, even though I had seen him motionless in the casket. I felt many times over that I was in a nightmare. I was walking around, talking, but I was still in a dream world. Nothing appeared to be real. I learned later, after I began to read about grief, that many grieving people experience similar shadow living episodes.

I became a widow at age 40 and I remember thinking about how my new reality was similar to a *Lifetime* television drama, but instead of fiction, mine was quite real. I was living a double life, living and walking and breathing reality, but at the same time, living and breathing in the shadows of the past. My husband, the father of my children and a brother of many, had died of a terrible disease that few people would encounter in their lifetime.

Mae and L.C. Return Home

As weeks passed, I knew that Mae and L.C. needed to take care of their business, so I told them that Alex Keith and I would be okay. And I knew that we would, eventually. Of course, I shuddered inside at the thought of being without them. I knew that Alex Keith was in the house, but it wasn't the same because he was 12 years old. He was still a child, and this would be the first time I would be alone without Clyde.

I didn't know how I would survive the first night without Mae and L.C., but I knew I would. Phyllis Wright, my youngest sister, came to drive them home to Americus. Phyllis is a beautiful, caring sister. She was always close to Clyde and me. She knew I was hurting and she'd had a special bond with Clyde. They would talk for hours and Phyllis appreciated his straightforwardness.

"How are you doing, Debbie," Phyllis asked me after walking into the den. "I'm so sorry about Clyde," she said as she hugged me tightly. I saw the tears swell in her eyes.

"I'm doing okay...Clyde would want me to be okay," I replied as I helped Mae and L.C. gather their belongings. "We'll just have to keep going. I'm trying to keep moving and doing things. I think that's the best thing I can do right now. I don't know what else to do," I responded as I looked at Clyde's picture above the mantle in the den.

Phyllis grabbed my hands and hugged me gently around the neck.

"I know you miss him and I know Clyde wants us to keep going," I continued. "We fought with everything we had against the disease. And I got him to the Mayo Clinic, but he wasn't strong enough to last for the transplant. I ache inside and wish I'd learned about Mayo Clinic earlier. I believe he would have had a heart by now and wouldn't have had to wait so long. He would be here with us today," I said sadly as I hugged her tightly.

"Debbie, you did all you could. Y'all traveled everywhere looking for someone to help Clyde. Don't beat yourself up, girl. You did all that you could. And I know that Clyde appreciated it," she reassured me.

"I know, Phyllis. I know. But it's just so hard to realize in my mind that he's gone. I only wish that I knew then what I know today. He probably would be alive. I just have to live with that. But God knows I tried to get him help. I just have to deal with it in my mind.

"Clyde and I had something special and I've always known that. I thanked God for our beautiful relationship and for our family. We had something special…Phyllis, I just want it to come back. That's all. I just want it back."

We hugged each other for a moment and cried. Phyllis loved Clyde. He had always been there for her in trying times. He was very easy to talk with.

"Phyllis!" Mae rang out, "come help me put this bag in the car, please ma'am." She raised her voice to get our attention.

"Okay," Phyllis returned, "I'm coming." She wiped the tears with her blouse.

I walked behind Phyllis and placed Mae and L.C.'s luggage in the car. L.C. was blind, so I guided him out the door and through the tight opening in the garage between my car and the house. L.C. placed his left hand on my right shoulder and together we walked toward Phyllis's car.

"May the Lord bless you, Debbie and Alex Keith," L.C. said as he hugged Alex Keith and me. "Just ask God for strength and he will give it to you. God will always be with you. Clyde taught me some beautiful things in life and I won't ever forget 'em. I love y'all," he ended.

We hugged each other tightly and said our goodbyes. Mae finally walked out the door, loaded with bags and boxes in her arms. "I'm ready now, Phyllis," Mae said, breathing rather deeply.

"Now, Debbie, we can stay for a little while longer, you know," Mae said, turning to hug me. "We don't have to go yet. We can stay a little while longer." She emptied one of the brown bags into my hands.

"No, Mae. We're okay. Alex Keith and I have to learn to be here, alone. It's okay. Really," I said hugging her tightly.

I rested my right hand over hers and reassured her that Alex Keith and I would be fine.

Phyllis and I hugged one last time before she climbed into the car and backed out of the driveway. We waved at them until the car disappeared from our sight. When I saw Phyllis's car disappear, I knew I was alone, but I also knew that I had to learn to live alone, without Clyde.

"Lord," I said under my breath. "What do I do now, Lord?" Without even thinking, I spoke the words as Alex Keith walked next to me into the house.

"Mom, what did you say?" he asked me intently.

"Oh Alex Keith, I was just praying out loud to God, asking Him to strengthen you and me to take it one day at a time. That's all.

"How do you feel, Alex Keith?" I asked. "I know it's tough for you."

"I'm fine, Mom. I really am," Alex Keith replied. "I didn't want to see Dad that way. I'm glad he's not suffering anymore. I didn't want him to suffer. He was suffering and I will always remember him lying in that bed. No one should suffer that way, especially my dad," he said solemnly as he gazed into the distance and then downward to the pebbled pavement of the driveway.

"Yeah, son, I know. I understand what you're saying. God will take care of us. He always has and I know he always will."

We held each other close and walked back into the house. As we approached the back door, I looked around at our home. The lawn was neatly tailored, thanks to our neighbors who had come by to cut our lawn again. The yard tools were neatly arranged near the storage house.

The azaleas had burst open in full bloom and they were beautiful to see. Nature had come into spring and everything was very beautiful, yet sad at the same time. The dogwood trees paraded with elegance with their lustrous white petals. The rose bush was postured high above the ground shadowing its pink, silken rose petals. Everything stood exquisitely in the midst of the warm, spring morning.

I was thankful that I was blessed to see God's magnificent grandeur of a springtime painting. I hadn't paid much attention to my surroundings lately. But now as I wrestled with my pain, I embraced the beauty of that spring day in May as Alex Keith and I talked softly and walked back into the house.

After a few moments, Alex Keith went into his room and I walked back to mine to lie down for a little while. After 30 minutes or so, I pulled myself off the bed and walked over to my dresser to pick up my King James Bible. I flipped through passage after passage, but ended up pretty much at the same place, Proverbs 3. This chapter of Proverbs had always been a favorite of mine, and I began to read these words:

Trust in the Lord with all thine heart; and lean not unto thine own understanding. In all thy ways acknowledge Him, and He shall direct thy path.

As I finished reading, I prayed: "Lord, please help me now. I know I have to go on. I know I have to, but right now I just don't feel like it. I feel out of place! I feel empty inside. I feel inadequate," I repeated.

"I don't feel like eating. I don't even feel like reading Your word....please help me now. Help me to be here for Clyde Daryl and Alex Keith. Please give me the strength to keep trying, to keep moving on. I want to, but I just don't have the physical or spiritual strength in me to do so. Please Lord help me."

I was extremely tired and wanted to lie back on my pillow and close my eyes. A little voice within me kept repeating that Clyde was dead, but I wouldn't acknowledge the voice. I just couldn't.

I knew that Alex Keith didn't hear me. He was busy watching one of his favorite TV shows. Somehow Alex Keith was able to zone out his pain, and at that moment I would have given just about anything to zone out mine. But I couldn't stop crying. My head continued to pound in agony as I stretched across the bed. One minute I would be smiling as I watched a show on the television; the next moment I would be crying, praying that Clyde would come back home to me and the kids.

I only wanted to close my eyes and pretend that everything was okay. I didn't want to think about anything. I just wanted a peaceful, serene moment of time. Sleeping during the day had become routine for me. I wasn't sleeping well at night, but I did okay during the light of day.

It was early afternoon and I felt extremely tired and worn, and decided to get into my bed and go to sleep. As I stared at the television, the next thing I remember was listening to the meteorologist describe the weather in the Rocky Mountains. I fell asleep under the bright sunlight of the early afternoon and thanked God for letting me sleep.

Clyde's Will in Probate

I was determined to make sure I took care of everything. Brother Clayton accompanied me, along with my attorney, to place Clyde's will in probate on Monday. It was a very cold process that showed me that it's important for everyone to have a will because when it comes to death and taxes, everything is black and white in terms of the legal process. There are no grey areas. Thank God Clyde and I always were realistic about the "what ifs" of life. We planned and created our wills together. I handed over Clyde's death certificate to the clerk. She looked at it and entered certain information on the computer. Clyde was just another number. Just as he had a number at birth, he now had a number recorded at death.

We made sure that the kids would have the funds to continue their education in the event one or both of us died. I also learned that it's important not to make quick or important decisions during the first year of grief. It's okay to delay some decisions until later. At the time, I didn't know if I would remain in Columbus or relocate. Most of our close relatives and friends lived either in

Americus, Plains, or Albany, Georgia; West Palm Beach, Florida; New Haven, Connecticut; and Tulsa, Oklahoma. I did contemplate moving back to Albany, but I decided to postpone my decision until later. I'm very glad I did because I decided later not to relocate at all. I was fine with living in Columbus, Georgia.

When I submitted Clyde's will into probate, the process forced me to acknowledge again that he was gone. I stared at the papers they gave me at the Probate Court: "Letters of Testamentary issued to Deborah Maxine Slappey as Executrix of the Last Will and Testament of Clyde Slappey, deceased."

I read the chief clerk of Probate Court's remarks and it seemed too surreal at that moment. "Lord, that judge shouldn't be saying that about Clyde. Clyde is just sleeping. He's not dead. He can't be dead. I can't make it without him. That judge must be out of her mind to type 'deceased' by Clyde's name. He's not dead," my thoughts continued to race. "He's just sleeping. Any moment now he'll open that door and walk in and say, 'Hey Debbie. How're you doing? Did you have a good day today, Baby?' I'm so angry with her for typing that on that form. Clyde's not dead. She is so cold to say something like that. So cruel, so cold."

I knew that Clyde had passed, but now it had also appeared on paper from the judge. That made it final. Clyde might not come back to me and this made me sad.

I began to pray as I stared down at the Letters of Testamentary...Executrix of the Last Will and Testament of Clyde Slappey, deceased.

I didn't know what to do at that point. I was angry at the judge and at the whole world. I stared out the car window as Brother Clayton drove me back home. I kept seeing "last will and testament of Clyde Slappey, deceased" on the document. I wanted to scream and keep screaming until my reality was only a dream. Brother Clayton didn't say much as he drove me back home. He knew that I wasn't myself and he probably knew that the ordeal of entering Clyde's will into probate was a mind-blowing experience for me.

"Thank you so much, Brother Clayton, for taking me to the judge," I said as I broke the silence in the car after riding for about 20 minutes. "I appreciate you helping me see this through. I had no idea about the paperwork you have to go through when someone...passes," I stuttered.

"I'm just here for you, daughter," Brother Clayton replied.

I don't remember all of what Brother Clayton said, but I always remember him calling me "daughter." It was nice. He was very affectionate and concerned about me and the children. I won't ever forget his acts of kindness that day. Brother Clayton stayed with me just about the entire afternoon at the Probate Court with my attorney. He was a one-of-a-kind Christian man and I will always appreciate his love and devotion for me and my family during our darkest days.

I was determined not to use the word *dead* or *deceased*, not even in my home. We arrived home somewhere around 4:00 p.m. Most of that day was pretty blurred, but I managed to capture some details of my first months without Clyde through my journal.

Brother Clayton spoke with Alex Keith before leaving. I was glad that Alex Keith had Brother Clayton and Brother McCray. They had become Alex Keith's grandpas, and this was a good thing.

It had been a very tiring day. I was still very angry with the probate judge. "She should be more sensitive with folks, instead of being so cold with her words," I thought out loud. Her words penetrated deeply within me and rocked my being.

"Hi, Alex Keith!" I said as I walked toward him after getting out of Brother Clayton's Mercedes.

"Did you have a pretty good day at school?" I asked him, pushing the paperwork behind me so he wouldn't ask what I had in my hands.

"It was fine, Mom. Just fine. We only have about one more month in school and I will be in the seventh grade, going to Fort Middle School! Yeah!" he said proudly.

I could see that Alex Keith was very excited about going to middle school. I guess I would be too; that was a really big thing for kids his age.

"How is Ms. Banks doing?" I asked.

"Ms. Banks is doing okay. She always checks on me to make sure that I'm doing okay."

"Well, I'm glad she is checking on you. You know, it's good to have someone to check on you. She's taken care of you while your dad was sick and now she's taking care of you while he's…"

Alex Keith looked at me rather intently, waiting for me to finish my sentence.

"Well, taking care of you while your dad was sick," I said quickly.

"Have you eaten since you've been home?" I asked him, hoping to change the subject.

"I had some of the chicken and rice and green beans that you cooked. Mom, the chicken and rice is delicious! I ate a lot of it," he said, pointing to his stomach. "Look at my stomach. It's so big!" he said with a big smile.

I was glad he could smile and even laugh at himself. Surely, we needed some smiles in the house.

"Mom, you better get some of that chicken and rice before it's gone. I'll probably eat it all up, if you don't eat some quickly," he said energetically.

"I'm glad to see you eating so well, son. I probably will eat some later on. I really don't have an appetite right now. I'm just going to lie down. I am a little bit worn from moving around today. You just enjoy yourself. I'm going to lie down a bit now."

"Sure, Mom. I have a lot of homework, so I'll be working on it."

I opened my bedroom door and heard Alex Keith ask, "Mom, you are going to check it, aren't you?"

"Of course I will. Don't I always check your homework?" I asked him.

"Yes, you and Dad always checked my work. I miss Dad, Mom. I really miss him."

His words pierced my heart. "I know you miss your dad, Alex Keith. I miss him, too.

"Try to get some sleep okay," I said as I comforted him with a big hug.

Barely able to get into my bedroom door, I closed it hurriedly and grabbed my pillow to muffle the sound of my tears. I buried my head in the pillow and sobbed like a lonely child lost in a snowstorm. I didn't want Alex Keith to hear me crying. I didn't want him to worry about me, and I knew he didn't need to see me sobbing like a baby. I crawled into the middle of my bed, one knee behind the other and lay down. I felt with my hand in the bed for the remote and flipped the television to what had become my favorite channel—the Weather Channel. In a frail, weakened voice I asked aloud, "Lord, where do I go from here?"

I pulled the blanket over my head and cried myself to sleep in the quiet calmness of that lonely evening.

CHAPTER SIX

Retreat into the Shadows

I was overwhelmingly lonely and I missed Clyde so much. I missed holding hands with him and sitting down on the sofa discussing current events. I missed sitting with him at the kitchen table, laughing and having fun together. I would see couples walking and holding hands together. I wanted to walk with my husband again, too. It reminded me of my loss as I had to relive the day Clyde died a thousand times.

WEEKS HAD PASSED SINCE we buried Clyde and I still couldn't sleep well at night. I tried my best to fall asleep around 11:00 p.m., sometimes 11:30 p.m., but my body wouldn't have it. My eyes would routinely pop open early in the morning, sometimes 3:00 a.m. and on a bad night even 2:00 a.m. I would stay awake the rest of the early morning.

I wanted to be strong. I tried so very hard, but the pain was relentless, razor sharp as if someone was deliberately pulling back my skin, slicing my insides without mercy; exposing the delicate layers of my anatomy. The weight of the despair throughout my body was dreadful, especially at night. I began to despise nighttime. I dreaded seeing the sunshine leave the sky. I wanted daylight to last forever. If I could manipulate the night into day, I would have.

What do you do at 2:00 a.m., other than stare at a man pointing at a map of the United States with potbellied grey clouds, seemingly pregnant, waiting for the birth of rain. It was all too unreal as I watched the man wave his hand from one side of the U.S. map—from east to west, from north to south, and back to east and west again. The meteorologist kept reiterating the same thing as my body starved for sleep. But my mind couldn't rest; it was constantly moving from one thought to the next.

I pulled the composition book from my bedside table and began to write these words...

I feel so alone, nothing is the same. I don't have much to give. I try hard, but I don't have much left in me. I am trying to keep my health intact. But it's not working. As the days pass by, the reality seems to set in more and more...

"If only I could have gotten Clyde to the Mayo Clinic one month earlier," I said, "he would be alive today, Lord. I would nestle close to him and we would be all right together. I would take care of him. I would make sure he took his medicines. Oh Lord, I would take care of him forever. I would. If only I'd known about the Mayo Clinic earlier in December. Everything would be different. Clyde would be here. He wouldn't be lying in a cemetery. He would be smiling and laughing because he knew he had escaped the jaws of death. Lord, how can anyone make it through this?" I asked. "How can I make it through this agony? How will my family make it through this?"

During the first few weeks, I would cry myself to sleep in hope that for just a few hours I would escape the reality of death. But as always, I kept praying. I couldn't read because I couldn't concentrate. But I could pray, and I did. God always comforted me in my tears and He took care of me in my sorrow.

The next morning, I decided to go in and check on Alex Keith, hoping he would be sound asleep. To my relief, he was asleep. I was simply amazed at the way he had pushed Clyde's death far from him so he wouldn't have to deal with it. I knew it wasn't good. He appeared to be acting as though nothing had happened. Clyde was more than a daddy to Alex Keith. Clyde was Alex Keith's hero. I gently stroked his forehead back and forth and whispered softly to God:

"Lord, please protect him. Please watch over him. I know he's in a lot of pain, losing his father at such a young age. I know he's hurting, but please comfort him in his sorrow. Please help him deal with it. Help Clyde Daryl to deal with Clyde not being here, and please help me. We don't have anywhere else to go. We only have you. Please help us now Lord. Help us. We miss Clyde terribly."

I shut my eyes tightly and stood motionless for a few seconds. I couldn't pray. I couldn't speak and I couldn't move as I stood in Alex Keith's room. Finally, I mustered the strength to place one foot in front of the other and walked out of his room into mine. I slumped my body on the bed, closed my eyes, and wept silently in the darkness of the night. I felt so bad for Alex Keith, Clyde Daryl, and myself. I didn't know how we would ever make it through without Clyde or even if we could. Sleep was a welcome relief. There were rare moments when I felt we would be okay. Clyde would want us to keep going, I would say, even though he wasn't with us physically. I knew that fact with all of my heart, but most of the time, it wasn't enough. All I knew was that God was with me and my family. I knew this fact without a shadow of a doubt, but still the pain was unbearable.

Mourning my better half was worse pain than having a baby. It was worse than having a toothache or any physical abnormality or condition on this earth. Grieving someone in death takes on a life of its own. It takes over physically, mentally, and even spiritually. It's a mind-absorbing pain that penetrates the essence of one's mental abilities to discern reality from dreamland. I was a walking zombie—living in the shadows of death while fighting desperately to remain with the living. For the first few years of living as a widow, I walked through the motions of living day by day, but deep within I wasn't doing much living at all. I was existing—simply existing in the wind. I felt part of me had been cut off; my best half had been torn, ripped from the rest of my body.

That's the kind of pain I experienced throughout the days, the weeks, even the years. There was no one prescription to ease the pain. My mind dripped with sorrow. I tried to read, but I couldn't decipher the words. But I could listen. Anything would trigger my pain. I would experience fond family memories. Sometimes I would be watching TV, listening to the radio, or just cooking in the kitchen. I remember on one occasion when I was watching a movie and someone died. Had I known the person was going to die, I wouldn't have watched the show. The experience of seeing someone die on television was devastating to me. I would be "out of things" for days—crying, hoping the sorrow would leave me. Many times I thought I was losing my mind. As years passed, I learned more about grief and the stages of grief and began to protect myself from situations that would trigger episodes of anguish and pain. I learned that grief is a journey to the other side. It takes hard work to work through the stages of grief, because you naturally don't want to work through your pain and sorrow.

Three weeks had passed since Clyde's burial. I didn't plan to go back to work so soon, but Mattie, Clyde's oldest sister, talked with me and told me that I needed to keep busy. I did appreciate her wisdom.

"Debbie," she said, "you need to go back to work. It's not good for you to be in the house alone. It's just not good. You need to go back and keep yourself busy."

I heeded her advice and went back to work three weeks after the funeral. Even though I hadn't been able to sleep much most nights, I knew I needed to go back anyway. *Maybe work*, I thought to myself, *will help me sleep better at night.*

I had already spoken to my manager earlier in the day to let her know that I would be returning to work on the following Monday. I knew Clyde wanted me to take care of everything—the children, the house, and I knew that he wanted me to keep things together. I wanted to respect his wishes. I wanted to do all the things he would have wanted me to do.

I was trying to rely on God, but the pain still remained. I didn't understand it. There were so many questions and thoughts, and I had very few answers. The pain was insistent and at times I felt there was nothing I could do. I felt helpless, but not hopeless.

The grief was feverishly painful as if it was determined to drive me out of my mind. Sleep, when it welcomed me, was a sigh of relief for my soul, and a quiet moment was an escape from my dismal reality of living without my better half. And Clyde was the better half of me. The pain would be unbearable and there was nothing that I could do about it.

No matter how much I screamed at the top of my voice or threw furniture from one wall to the other, the reality was Clyde had gone away and left me to suffer a miserable existence. So, I began to feel sorry for myself. I didn't know at the time that I was progressing into another phase of grief—leaving the shock of seeing Clyde die before my eyes and now facing true reality that Clyde would no longer walk into the door saying, "Hi honey, I'm home."

I couldn't bear this thought. Not yet. I just wasn't able. How would I ever survive the next stage—anger? The first stage of grief, shock, had nearly killed me.

Darkness overwhelmed the daylight once again as I found myself surrounded with sadness, watching the darkness engulf the daylight whole. I felt choked with pain and agony as I tossed and turned each night. I tried desperately to go to sleep. I would have given anything to simply close my eyes and drift into a deep sleep, but I couldn't.

"Oh Lord," I spoke very loudly this time. "Help me," I said as I stared at the ceiling, hoping that God would answer me quickly as he'd done numerous times.

"Clyde, where are you, sweetheart? You need to be here with me; with Alex Keith and Clyde Daryl, with the whole family, sweetheart. It's lonely without you being close to us. It's so lonely. Please come to me. Please let me see your face. I need to be with you. I need to touch your handsome face."

I kept looking at the ceiling and rubbing my forehead. I became very aggravated, even agitated.

"It's lonely without you, sweetheart. I'm so lonely. I need for you to come home to me. Please come home now. Please!"

I clenched my fist and began to beat against my face furiously and yelled at the ceiling.

"Clyde, why did you leave me here? I can't do this without you. I can't keep going without you. Please come back. Don't leave me here alone. It's just too painful. Why didn't you stay with me?"

Tears streamed down from my eyes as I lay against the blanket that night to remember our beautiful family.

"I miss you being here. I miss you Clyde," I said as I wrapped myself into one of his crisp white cotton shirts. "I've cried for you, but God won't bring you back to me. He won't."

I buried my face into my hands and pulled Clyde's pillow close to my face. Finally around 12:30 that night, I drifted into sleep. Sadly, I would have many nights of pain-wrenching hours of agony and despair of trying to come to grips with the reality that Clyde was gone and wasn't coming back. I couldn't feel his presence against his pillow anymore. His scent was fading and even though I desperately wanted to hold on to his scent, it was fading away.

The Telephone Call to the Mayo Clinic

For some reason, I was drawn to call the Mayo Clinic just to see how everyone was doing. I felt a connection to the hospital and staff and I still do to this day. I knew they had done everything possible to save Clyde, and I would always appreciate their service, their generosity, and their very special compassion for our family. I decided to call the transplant unit. The nurse told me that every patient had received a heart transplant, and was doing well. She asked me how I was doing and I told her we were taking it one day at a time. I also told her to tell everyone that I was very happy for all of them. Now everyone would be able to go on with their lives with new hearts.

After a few minutes, I hung up the telephone and closed my eyes in devastating pain. My face displayed the sheer horror and anguish as I replayed her words in my mind: *Everyone received a heart transplant. Everyone...Everyone...Everyone... Everyone except Clyde got a heart! He was the only one who didn't.*

I was totally devastated by the news. I was very happy for the patients who had waited for months on end to receive heart transplants, but I was stricken in throbbing horror that Clyde was the only one who didn't get a chance to receive a life-saving heart. Instead Clyde, the youngest of all of them, had died a few weeks earlier.

"If only, Lord, he could have lasted a few more weeks! Clyde would be smiling with everyone else in the transplant unit. If only, Lord, you could have allowed him to receive his heart. He would be here with us. He would be here. Lord, he was only 43 years old."

I cried and cried, and before I knew what was happening, I lifted the lamp from the nightstand and threw it violently against the wall.

"It's not fair! It's not fair!" I said screaming. "Why Lord, why did you let him die? What are we going to do?"

I was alone and Alex Keith was at school. Thank God he didn't see me this way. I was devastated. My beautiful love story, my Innisfree for life, had left me here.

"Tell everyone I'm happy for all of them," I said as I said my goodbyes to her.

After that day I didn't speak to them again until nine years later.

I was never the same after that day. Older patients had waited for a heart and received it. Clyde was the youngest patient in the transplant unit, and he didn't get a new heart. His body was riddled with the amyloid tissue. I was deeply disturbed that my husband wasn't one of them. It just wasn't God's will that Clyde would have another heart. It wasn't God's will for Clyde to live. As the afternoon turned into evening, darkness covered my heart in despair.

I became angry with Clyde because I felt he should have been able to hold on, even by a thread, so he could be with his family. He was a strong man. I remember him being so strong…so why didn't he hang on? My anger dissipated because I knew deep down that Clyde held on as long as he could. And if it was God's will for Clyde to recover from the debilitating effects of amyloidosis, he would have done so. I believed that without a shadow of a doubt.

But still my anguish kept returning, and it hovered over me as a dark, rain-soaked cloud. I began to retreat into the shadows of my pain. "Oh Lord, I failed him! I failed Clyde and it's my fault. All my fault! Clyde, please forgive me!" I yelled out in pain.

I paused for a moment and longed to hear Clyde's voice in my ears. I yanked myself from the bed and walked over to the other side of the bed to reach the telephone answering machine. Clyde's voice was still on the answering machine, so I pressed the recording to hear his voice:

"Hello, this is the Slappey residence. We're not at home right now. Please leave a message and we'll get back with you. Have a nice day."

His voice was very comforting. I pressed the answering machine again and again that afternoon:

"Hello, this is the Slappey residence. We're not at home right now. Please leave a message and we'll get back with you. Have a nice day."

Calm descended upon my face as I listened to his voice. I began to feel a sense of peace as I felt his presence near. His voice calmed my soul. I felt at ease and began to smile. I started to remember our good times together. Clyde always had a tremble in his voice. I played the recording over and over, and after awhile I laid down across my bed, sensing his warmness close to me. I turned over, lay on my back, and drifted quietly off to sleep.

Part Two...
Living Within the Shadows

CHAPTER SEVEN

Returning to Work

It took more energy than I expected to return to work. I felt out of place and kept reliving that sad Wednesday morning when I was told that Clyde had passed out. As I approached the South Center, I hoped with all my being that I had dreamed everything, and Clyde hadn't passed out, but was still alive.

GOD IS WORKING ON YOU when you don't even know it. As I prepared for work I looked through my closet, hoping to find something suitable to wear on my first day back. I could tell I had lost weight as my slacks slid off my waist and hips.

I began to pray. "Lord, please help me get back into the work routine. I can't seem to focus right now. My mind keeps wandering from one thought to the other. Please help me to keep my focus…I need you to stay with me. I feel lost right now, like I don't belong here anymore. I don't understand my feelings. I know it has a lot to do with Clyde, but I need your help to figure it out. Please, let me go back to work and be okay, I pray."

I felt much better after I had prayed. As I looked around the room, I knew that I should get some sleep. The clock struck 11:30 p.m. and I prayed that I would be able to sleep that night.

Thankfully, I fell into a deep, well-needed sleep. I woke up to the sound of music blasting from the radio. I looked at the clock and the bright red digital read 6:30 a.m. I rubbed my hands over my cheeks and remembered suddenly as if I had been shocked by electricity, "I slept for seven hours!" I was elated to realize that I had slept a full night.

"Thank you Lord for letting me sleep."

I lay down for about 10 more minutes and then said my prayers. But still, I glanced over to Clyde's side; hoping he would be lying down. Of course I knew where he was, but for a split second, I turned to say good morning to him.

"I want to see him, Lord. I want to touch his face and hold it and caress my face next to his — next to his warm, loving face," I said painfully. I touched his pillow once again and attempted to climb out of bed. It seemed I had been away from work for light years, not just a few weeks. But I didn't want to start crying again. So I kept praying.

"Lord, I'm thankful. Just thankful to you so much. Help me to get out of this bed and get started this morning. I need you to help me put one foot in front of the other and go in the bathroom and wash my face. Please Lord! Help me!"

And God did. I arose slowly and walked into the bathroom to run my bath water.

"Another day without Clyde, Lord," I repeated. "I'm living another day without his smile."

The tears didn't let up. I kept crying as I ran my bath water. I didn't have any control anymore. I walked out of my bedroom toward Alex Keith's room. Alex Keith was one deep sleeper. If ten Mack trucks came barreling into our house, he wouldn't hear them. He slept even harder than Clyde.

"Alex Keith! Alex Keith!" I called out his name. "It's time to get up, son," I said as I shook him to awaken him.

Alex Keith slowly turned over with one eye just barely opened. "I'm getting up Mom," he replied. "Just give me a few more minutes."

"Nope, son," I said. "You need to get up now. I don't want to come back in here and wake you up again, okay. Now, get up and get ready for school," I said smiling, popping him lightly on his head.

I walked slowly into the kitchen and opened the cabinet to get one of the small steel pans to cook some oatmeal. I opened the pantry door, picked up the Quaker Oatmeal box and looked inside. Thank goodness there was still enough oatmeal for one more breakfast. I poured the remaining oatmeal into the pan and turned on the stove.

I fumbled my way through the cabinet, feeling my way to the decaffeinated coffee. After about five minutes, I walked to my bedroom, but stopped short at Alex Keith's room to make sure he was out of bed and getting ready for school. To no great surprise, I found him still lying down.

"Alex Keith!" I yelled, "Get out of the bed, now!" He immediately jumped out of bed, stretching both hands above his head and finally dropping to his knees to say his morning prayer.

We found ourselves moving on a fast track out of the house. Alex Keith had to get to school by 7:45 and I had to be at work by 8:30. I wasn't looking forward to going back to work. I was very nervous, but I knew it probably was the best thing for me. I knew I had to get back into the world again. I knew I had to try.

My First Day at Work

The buses at Waddell Elementary School were lined up one after the other dropping off children.

"I'll see you later, Alex Keith," I said. "Have a good day at school, okay," I hugged him tightly as he threw his book bag over his shoulder.

"You too, Mom. Have a good day. I'll see you later," he said, looking me dead in the eyes. He knew that it was my first day back to work and he was concerned about his mom.

"I sure will, Alex Keith. I sure will," I replied as he closed the door and raced toward the front entrance of the school. I stared at him for just a moment, watching him walk into the entrance.

"Lord," I said, "I hope he'll be all right. I pray with all my heart and soul that he'll be okay. He needs time to adjust. I hope he'll be okay. Let Alex Keith be okay."

I moved my right hand to turn on the radio as I drove away from the school.

Maybe a little music will help, I thought.

I felt nervous about going back to work. I wasn't the same person anymore. I knew I needed to get back to life again, whatever that meant. Clyde would have wanted me to keep going. And I wanted him to be proud of me.

I smiled. "I can hear Clyde saying, 'Debbie, I want you to go on, go on without me, take care of everything. I'll be okay."

I knew exactly what he would say. He wanted me and the children to go on with our lives. But it was easier said than done. I didn't know what was playing on the radio, but it didn't matter because I wasn't listening anyway. I was preoccupied with the thought of placing one foot in front of the other, stepping off the third floor elevator and walking to my desk. That was my concern.

I coasted to the stop sign, looked both ways, and turned right onto Miller Road. There was steady traffic as people were hurrying to work. I passed through the traffic light and careened down the road onto Manchester Expressway. My heart began to race as I drove close to the intersection of Manchester and Veterans Parkway. I tried to calm myself, but it didn't work.

I began to pray, closing one eye on occasion for concentration, but with one eye open on the traffic. I continued to pray as the traffic light changed to green, prompting me to turn left onto Veterans Parkway. As He's done many times in my life, God took care of me that morning. As I pulled into the parking lot at work, God calmed my anxious spirit. I knew He was with me. I knew that He would always be with me, even on my darkest days.

I walked onto the third floor and to my cubicle. Everything felt strange and out of place. Maybe I was the one who was out of place. I turned the corner to my cube and stared in horror as I replayed that awful morning in my mind.

"Lord," I said silently, "how do you expect me to do this? It's too much." I buried my face in my hand and cried silently. "I just don't have the strength. I can't do this! Please take me back home. Please!"

My eyes found my chair, and I sat down in slow motion. I didn't want to move one muscle as I stared at Clyde's picture at my workstation. I knew that nothing would ever be the same in my life. Anguish poured from my heart.

It's too soon, Lord. It's just too soon for me! I should go back home! Let me go back home, Lord! Please let me go back home. There aren't many people here yet. No one will notice. Please let me go back home! My thoughts raced.

Reliving the Sad Day

I stared at the telephone and the memories of that Wednesday morning, April 12, replayed the voice of the Mayo Clinic nurse in my mind. I knew that I would spend the rest of my days remembering her words...

"Mrs. Slappey, are you alone," she asked. I remembered the matter-of-fact tone in her voice. "Yes, I am," I replied to her.

"Mr. Slappey has passed out." As I'd done many times before, I told her to pull his feet up toward his chest so the blood would reach his heart quickly.

And she said, "Mrs. Slappey, we've done that, and he's still out."

"How long has he been out?" I asked.

She replied, "Forty-five minutes."

"Forty-five minutes. He's been out for 45 minutes!" I screamed through the telephone.

My whole world crumbled into a billion pieces. I lost it after I heard her confirm that Clyde had been out for 45 minutes. I dropped the phone and couldn't utter another word.

I placed my hand on my face in despair. It had seemed a lifetime since I'd heard those words from the nurse at Mayo. Clyde had been out for 45 minutes and I knew that the brain could function for about five minutes without damage, but not 45 minutes. As I replayed those moments, I stirred the heap of documents that were neatly stacked on my desk. Everything was untouched from where I'd left it a few weeks ago. It all seemed surreal.

Within 30 minutes or so, several people came into my cube. They all hugged and squeezed me tightly. It felt good to be comforted and I was very glad to see everyone and knew that they genuinely were concerned about me. I was grateful to them for welcoming me back. After talking to everyone, I sat down in my chair and kept staring at the telephone, replaying that telephone call in my thoughts.

"Clyde was so close, Lord," I said very quietly. "He was so close. Why did it have to happen to him? He had come to terms with having the transplant and everything was coming together. Everything. Why now, Lord?"

I knew there were no answers, but I continued to ask the same question anyway.

I sat at my desk and thumbed through the pile of mail. My mind wasn't in gear, but I knew I would keep trying. As I flipped through the mail, my mind wandered to one of the times when Clyde and I were in Rochester. I laid against his shoulders as he talked about the heart transplant and what it would mean to the family. He told me that he wanted to go back to the Church of Christ, and help build our new sanctuary. He was very excited that the Church was moving closer to finalizing plans for constructing the new church.

I didn't do much that morning other than relive April 12 in my mind. Before I knew it, it was noon, time for lunch. Thank God I'd survived my first morning at work. I was very thankful I'd made it through a half-day so far.

I'm sure my boss knew that I wasn't mentally at work that day. I appreciated her understanding and won't forget her unwavering support. My manager stood by me in my worst time. She was with me all the way, and for this, I'll always be grateful to her and TSYS.

I can't remember much of the afternoon from my first day. I do remember pushing papers around on my desk, and that's about all. But time passed and I was very thankful. Everyone hugged me, but they all understood. They all knew that I needed time to myself, so they kept their distance out of respect for me.

I looked at my clock and it read 4:16 p.m. I didn't feel like staying until 5:30 so I decided to leave about an hour early. I turned off my computer, picked up my handbag from underneath the desk, and walked to the third floor elevator. I waved good evening to the secretary before stepping onto the elevator.

I don't know why, but I quickly pressed the elevator button so the door would close instantly. At that moment I felt an overwhelming urge for the door to close quickly so I could hide from the rest of the world in the sanctuary of the elevator. It didn't make sense to me then, nor does it make sense to me now. It was just how I felt at that moment. My mind raced insatiably from one thought to the next. I was a walking basket case and I didn't want anyone to know. So I hid it. I rushed into the elevator because I didn't want anyone to see me burst into tears.

When the elevator reached the first floor, I pressed the release button to open the door and I ran out of the building. I did everything that I could think of to contain my emotions and keep from bursting into tears. I walked exceptionally fast to reach my car parked in the main parking lot. I hoped no one was watching my erratic behavior. I didn't want anyone to see me the way I was, shattered and in pieces.

"Oh Lord!" I screamed silently. "Please help me with this. I don't know what's happening to me. I did okay all day. And then at the very end, I want to run away and hide...I don't understand me. I don't know what's happening to me. I just want to leave here quickly."

I fumbled for my keys in my handbag and was relieved to pull them out of the bottom of my purse. I fidgeted at the door key to open it. I finally swung open the door to my 1993 dark grey Oldsmobile, placed the key in the ignition, and raced out of the South Center parking lot. And as quickly as I closed the door to the world, I was calm.

I sped down Fourth Avenue onto Veterans Parkway. As I sat waiting for the traffic light at Veterans, I heard a siren and froze in throbbing fear as I relived a sound from the past. The sound became louder and louder and my nervousness soon elevated to a frightening panic again.

"Is Clyde all right? Is Clyde okay?" I spoke out loud unknowingly. "I have to get to him. I have to get home to Clyde!"

And then reality punched me in the face. "Clyde isn't home. He's not there! I can't take care of him! He's gone! He's in Andersonville! I can't take care of him anymore. I can't talk to him anymore!" I yelled hysterically. "He's not home anymore, Lord!"

Melancholy filled my face as I realized again that Clyde was gone. My thoughts raced as I confirmed again that Clyde had left me and I didn't know what I was going to do without him. The panic attacks heightened.

"How do I go on, Lord?" I asked God. "How?"

I buried my face in my hands, and within a few minutes, the sirens faded into the distance. I moaned in desperation. I had nowhere to go, nowhere to hide from my anguish and pain. I stared at my hands on the steering wheel. Both hands appeared melted into the leathery steering wheel. It took a few seconds for my hands to loosen from their death grip. I had been petrified after hearing the sirens.

It took me a while to regain my composure before resuming my drive home. I literally felt sick inside from clutching the life out of the steering wheel. It didn't seem real, but I knew that it was. The sirens had startled me and had flashed episodes of memories when I had to call the ambulance to take Clyde to the hospital during one of his blackouts. I was torn asunder from hearing the siren.

And then I heard a car horn. Someone in the car behind me was blowing the horn relentlessly to alert me to move on since the ambulance had passed by. I don't know how much time had passed, maybe a few seconds, but the drivers seemed very impatient. I waited a few more seconds just to be sure all was clear and then placed my foot on the gas pedal and slowly drove down Manchester Expressway. Still shaken from the episode, I drove home to my place of refuge.

I had to call the ambulance numerous times when Clyde passed out. I would watch the siren flicker its amber lights as I trailed behind it en route to the hospital. The lights had reminded me of the painful times I had watched Clyde leave the house in the ambulance in a semi-conscious state. I had remembered the flickering lights as the ambulance had darted by earlier and the sad memories of seeing Clyde stretched out unconscious came rushing back to me. Several times I had to revive him by stretching him out, then lifting his feet upward so that his blood could easily travel back to his heart again. And by the time I revived him, the ambulance would arrive to take Clyde to the hospital. As I followed the ambulance in my car,

I would watch the red light spin until we finally arrived at the hospital. It happened at least four times.

I eased slowly into the flow of traffic again. Within 20 minutes from leaving downtown, I had arrived home. Finally, I was able to sit down on the sofa and bury my face into my hands. I sobbed like a baby.

"This is just too hard for me. I can't bear this pain," I said. "I can't even drive down the road without getting emotionally sick. What am I going to do?"

Alex Keith was at baseball practice and I was happy he didn't see me broken. I would be leaving to pick him up in about an hour. I felt very unnerved that afternoon. I pondered how I would ever survive another day without Clyde. I'd fallen to pieces after being back at work one day, even if it was at the end of the day.

I wanted to hear sound, so I picked up the remote from the coffee table and flicked on the TV to watch the news. I decided a warm bath would probably make me feel better, so I walked back into my bedroom to run some bath water for a soothing hot soak. It had been a very long day and I wanted to relax my mind before leaving for the baseball park to pick up Alex Keith. I wanted to be alone. I was thankful to be at home away from sirens and people. I didn't want anyone to see me in my current state. It wasn't pretty. I would have given just about every cent that I had to be totally quiet and free from any thought or pain. I grabbed one of Clyde's watches from his dresser and held it tightly in my hands. I felt Clyde's presence close to me, even if it was for a moment.

"God," I said as I arose from the bed to step into the bath water, "please take care of me and my sons. There is so much pain in this world, so much. Please ease our pain."

After my warm bath, it was time to leave and pick up Alex Keith from the baseball park. But I didn't want to leave home. Home had become my sanctuary. I didn't want to go back outside my house, but I knew I had to. I was glad that Alex Keith was beginning to do some of the things he had done before Clyde became sick. Fifteen minutes later, I was out the door on my way to pick up Alex Keith.

We arrived home about an hour later. Alex Keith had had a good practice and was exhausted, so he took a bath and got ready for bed. The siren ordeal drained me, and before I knew it I had fallen asleep around 11:00 p.m. I didn't wake up until around 3:45 a.m. In the quietness of the morning, I pulled my journal from underneath the mattress and began to write...

I love you Clyde. I miss you very much. You had been sick for a long time. I remember when you complained so much. You went to many doctors. You knew something was wrong with you. But no one listened. Why didn't anyone listen to you? I wish they had. I'm so sorry that you aren't here with us. I'm truly sorry...

Before I knew what was happening, I drifted off to sleep with the pen in my hand. I was grateful.

My Second Day at Work

I was grateful that I had survived one day at the office. Everyone was happy to see me. I awoke that Tuesday morning, pretty much accustomed to what was now my regular routine. I hurried Alex Keith off to school and prepared for work. I took a bite of my bagel and a sip of coffee before racing out the door. I looked around at everyone as they hurried off to their jobs. I wondered if there were other people who had lost a loved one.

Easing up to the parking lot at the South Center, I was able to park on the side of the building. As I closed the car door, I turned around to look at the Recorder's Court and the police station across the street. There were no people around the building yet. Mondays were always busy with court appearances, but the rest of the week was relatively quiet, except for visitors at the jail.

As I approached the entrance, I pulled out my badge and swiped it against the reader. The door made a jolting sound, which indicated that the door had opened, accepting my badge swipe. I walked toward the elevator, and as soon as the doors shut, I began to feel very anxious with sweat beading off my hands. I didn't know why I was feeling this way. It all seemed ridiculous, yet this was how I felt.

I stared at the colors of the elevator's interior to redirect my attention. I'd been inside the elevator numerous times, and even though I had seen the décor many times, it never made any difference to me. I had no opinion about it one way or the other. It was just there. But this time as the elevator ascended, I concentrated on the wall design. The diamond-shaped fabric was encased against the steel walls with a lighter side of brownstone and a hint of cinnamon. It wasn't attractive, nor was it ugly. It was just a wall with brown-colored designs.

"Bling! Bling!" The sound from the elevator interrupted my thoughts. I was glad that God helped me focus my thoughts away from the anxiety attack that was building within me. For a moment, even for a minute or so, I was unable to feel the pain or the anxiety. And for this I was grateful.

I placed my brown and tan leather shoulder bag on the desk. I was grateful for the job I had. I was a technical writer and most of my work was sitting in front of a computer writing technical manuals about software enhancements.

It was pretty much the best job that I could hope for in light of my current situation. Even though I couldn't think coherently at the time, I thanked God for giving me the opportunity to have a job at TSYS. I sat in my dark green plaid armchair and scooted comfortably under the desk to start my work and the day. I was glad I had something to do. I wanted to keep my mind busy. Idle time was the worst thing for me.

I stared at the pictures surrounding my cube, touching the rim of our family picture with my index finger. It was Clyde, Clyde Daryl, Alex Keith, and me. We were very happy and our smiles radiated sunshine from that picture.

"I miss my family, Lord. I miss having Clyde close to me," I said in a whispered voice. "We were a beautiful family. Why did it have to end?"

I knew I needed to concentrate on doing something before giving in to my pain, so I picked up an information bulletin I had been working on before leaving for Rochester.

I tried to read the bulletin, but couldn't seem to concentrate. The words didn't penetrate my mind. I squinted at the small 10-point font on the paper and couldn't make out the words on the document. I panicked for a moment. I couldn't read words anymore. Everything appeared very blurry. The words seemed to roll into one on the paper. But when I glanced at the document again, my vision appeared normal again, thank goodness. I didn't know what had happened to my sight, but for a moment, I couldn't see. Before Clyde passed away I read a book of some kind practically every week. But since his death I hadn't had a desire to read or study.

I closed my eyes and prayed. As the early morning drifted into late morning, I finally was able to read through some of the documents and mail stacked on my desk. Many of my teammates, including Virginia and Tanya, came by to check on me. And they would continue to check on me as I struggled throughout the years. They are real friends and I appreciate them very much. I always will.

The Drive to Andersonville

Around 2:00 p.m. I was able to eat a little lunch by forcing the food down. As I was finishing my sandwich, Clyde's picture caught my peripheral vision. It was the last picture we took as a family in December 1994.

I looked at the picture with a prolonged stare, with my left middle finger touching the scar above his right eyebrow. That cut had really bothered Clyde. He hated to think that he fell trying desperately to run out of the hotel room to avoid another blackout episode. But he still passed out again. I replayed his facial expression in my mind as he dashed out of the bathroom, hoping to reach the cool, damp night air. But Clyde fell chest first onto the floor and the left side of his head struck the bed rail, resulting in a deep gash above his right eyebrow. I was very thankful that Clyde didn't puncture his eye. He came very close to doing that.

"If only I can touch him, Lord," I said as I stared down at our family picture. "If only I could feel his presence right now."

I was overcome with an overwhelming urge to go to the cemetery and be near Clyde. Without thinking, I grabbed my handbag and walked hurriedly to the elevator door. I didn't look back and I didn't tell anyone where I was going. I simply walked out of the building because I didn't want another minute to go by. And off to Andersonville National Cemetery I drove.

I felt desperate to see Clyde, to be close to him. And I knew that the closest I could get to him was near his grave. I missed him very much and needed to see him at that moment. I felt the air in my lungs was being sucked out of me. I knew I needed to get to the cemetery quickly or I would lose my mind. I didn't get the chance to tell my manager I was leaving before rushing out the door.

"Lord, I hope she understands," I said. "I need to go now."

There were times when I felt I was losing myself; I felt helpless to do anything about it. I backed out of the parking lot and turned left on Fourth Avenue. As I waited for the traffic light to turn green, I looked down at my hands and they were shaking uncontrollably. I tried to squeeze them together to stop the shaking, but it didn't work. It felt as though a million ants were crawling under my skin. I knew I was on the edge.

It took all I could muster to keep my hands glued to the steering wheel. I couldn't wait to be near Clyde. The anxiety worsened as I pictured Clyde in Andersonville—lying in a grave, away from his family. I would be driving some 60 miles to be near him. I desperately needed to be near him. Trying to calm myself, I clasped my hands tightly together and prayed for the anxiety to calm.

"It's not right, Lord," I said as I drove down Victory Drive. "Why did Clyde have to die and leave me here, Lord? It's just so hard to be here without him. I don't have the strength to keep going without him. I feel out of place, empty."

My attention soon shifted to the horde of traffic lights that scanned the landscape on Victory Drive. I began to reminiscence about a moment in our life when we went down to the Civic Center in Columbus for a carnival. The center was overflowing with people so we had to park in the old cemetery and take the shuttle to the center. It gave me a very eerie feeling having to park in the cemetery. Now as I passed it, I recalled that moment once again.

What I was doing didn't make sense. Here I was at 3:00 in the afternoon speeding down the road to the cemetery, hoping I would arrive before it closed at 5:00 to see my husband. I had walked out of the South Center and I hadn't told anyone. I know my actions didn't make much sense, but I didn't make much sense to myself either.

I kept driving, headed for my destination. I was calm now as I listened to the voices on the radio. I wasn't a fast driver. I took my time and most of the time maintained the speed limit. I guess the cars behind me soon discovered this fact as they changed lanes and sped on by. It was okay, though. I would soon be near my husband and that was all that mattered to me.

"Now I should be in Andersonville in about 45 minutes," I said confidently. I reached forward and pressed the radio buttons to change the station. I smiled in pleasure. The caliber of music was much better than the previous station. It was a very nice scenic route and because I normally wouldn't travel on Victory Drive, I was enjoying the view.

I finally reached the outer parameters of the city of Columbus and saw the sign to the Fort Benning Infantry entrance. I approached the final traffic light on Victory Drive and was thankful to be moving to the outskirts of the city. Though the scenery was colorful, Victory Drive was long and full of short stops. I felt a sense of calm in my being as I drove closer to Clyde. I knew I would have only one hour to sit with Clyde, but it was fine.

My thoughts turned to Alex Keith and Clyde Daryl. They had experienced one of the worst things that could happen to them—to lose a parent. I shook my head in disbelief at the chain of events that paralyzed my mind over the past months. I had brought Clyde home to be buried with his fellow soldiers. I had watched their father suffer and breathe his last breath. And driving some 60 miles to sit with him, even if it was just for a little while, was necessary for me.

The school year would be over in a few weeks for Alex Keith and he would be going to Fort Middle School. It would be another life-changing event in his life and I wanted him to have some stability in his life by living in the same home. His life didn't need any more changes, so I decided to stay in Columbus.

It was comforting for me to be near Clyde. He and I had a connection that was beyond the grave. And I learned how special it was when he breathed his last breath. The thought of not ever seeing Clyde again sent a rippling chill down my spine. The tears poured down my cheeks and my chest. No matter how hard I cried it wasn't going to make a difference. But I still cried.

"It shouldn't have happened," I said defiantly. "Clyde should be here with me. He shouldn't be in a grave an hour away from us."

I shouldn't have buried Clyde so far away from us. I know that he said he wanted to be buried in a military cemetery, but he ain't bearing the pain, is he? I am! I should have buried him in Columbus. I should have known better. Clyde didn't know what he wanted. He's dead! He doesn't have to bear this burden.

I drifted into quietness. And I knew that in spite of my pain and anger, burying him in Andersonville was really the right thing to do.

"It is a beautiful place, a sad, but beautiful place," I said.

"He would say it's okay, don't cry Debbie," I said, "It will be all right. God will take care of you. He has never let you down, has He?" I asked myself.

And the answer to my own question was a vibrating "No."

God had never let me down. He always took care of me and my family. I didn't know how, but I knew that our Lord and Savior Jesus Christ would take care of us now. Again, tears fell from my filled eyes. There was nothing I could do but cry until I couldn't cry anymore as I journeyed to the cemetery.

I passed through Buena Vista and I began to smile because I knew I was getting closer to Ellaville. I had only 15 minutes to go.

"I'll be there soon," I said. "I'll be there soon, Clyde."

I felt calmness descend on my face as I prayed to God. I knew He was the only one who truly knew the pain that I was experiencing every day, every moment of my life since Clyde's death. I knew that God wouldn't be angry with me as I continued to pour my heart out to Him. He would help ease my pain. I didn't know how He would, but I knew He would.

As I continued to think through my maze of thoughts, I saw another sign as I neared the Andersonville City Limits. I was overjoyed. I had been traveling for about 45 minutes and finally would be driving into Andersonville Cemetery to be with my husband once again.

Andersonville was smaller than Ellaville with a population of about 250 residents. It took about seven seconds to drive in and out of the city and head toward Highway 49 where the cemetery was located. I coasted to the stop sign and looked both ways, feeling a sense of exhilaration as I turned left. The entrance to the cemetery was only a few yards away. I could feel the tension in my hands build as I gripped the steering wheel tightly. My hands became numb as I anxiously waited to turn right into the entrance.

Soon, I would be standing next to my husband and I would be okay again. As crazy as it might sound, I felt at home in the cemetery surrounded by thousands of brave soldiers and their families. It felt good to be home with my husband again. I passed the Visitor's Center on the left side of the road. There was so much history in this place.

The speed limit dropped to 10 miles per hour, so I slowly turned my car wheels toward the right and swerved in the direction of Clyde's grave. A statue of the state of Pennsylvania cast a shadow over his grave. Nesting straight ahead was the Memorial Pavilion where funerals and other events were conducted. I slowly coasted my car around the circular loop and parked next to the big old oak tree near Clyde's grave. I pulled my lounge chair from the trunk and walked toward his grave to sit next to Clyde during the coolness of the afternoon. It would be Clyde and me. I smiled in anticipation of my time with my husband, the way it used to be.

As I stood at his grave, I felt a gentle warm breeze dance across my cheeks. Petals of dead flowers pranced along the top of his grave. It was a beautiful Tuesday afternoon at the cemetery. I had arrived around 4:00, just in time to sit and talk to Clyde for an hour under the breeze of the old oak tree.

As I sat down at Clyde's grave, I thanked God for letting me arrive safely. "Hello Clyde," I said. "I had to leave work early to see you. I couldn't wait to see you today. I can't explain why I left, but I knew I had come and sit with you."

I felt the breeze beat against my face rather forcibly as I breathed in deeply to capture the moment. My eyes scanned the cemetery and I embraced the thousands of graves lined side by side and row by row as far as the eye could see. I saw white short bricks of mortar flanked row after row along the perimeter. It was a solemn site.

I turned back toward Clyde's grave and touched the small marker that said, "Clyde Slappey, 04/19/1995, buried 04/24/1995." I took a cloth and wiped the dried red clay from the marker. I wanted to make sure that his grave was clean and free of debris, so I took my time to clean it very delicately. I longed to touch his face against mine.

The sun was beginning to hide within the shadows of the grayish clouds that hung low in the sky. The sky was pleasantly quiet and serene, except for a wild burst of wind. The sun would be setting in a few hours. I didn't want to leave, but I knew I had to say goodbye to Clyde eventually.

"I should have stopped and bought Clyde fresh flowers," I said as I touched the dead flowers on his grave. "Next time, I'll bring you fresh flowers," I continued.

"Clyde, I know that you were tired. I know this disease took a lot out of you. But please know that the doctors did all they could. They really tried everything. They never gave up. Not even the pacemaker. I was unsure about the pacemaker, but you wanted to try it anyway, and you did. But it just wasn't enough, Clyde. It wasn't enough. What am I going to do without you? I only know how to be your wife."

I buried my face into the palms of my hands and rubbed them vigorously against my cheeks. I looked up into a tree and followed a leaf as it helplessly fell to the ground, thanks to the afternoon wind. I felt as fragile as the leaf that afternoon.

The wind could have easily blown me away and I wouldn't have resisted it one bit. I wanted to be blown away that afternoon to wherever Clyde was. I wanted to be with him.

The weather was changing. By 4:30, it had cooled off considerably. I felt the chillness of the evening air beat against my arms. I knew it would soon be time for me to go, and I hated the thought.

I remembered being brave and strong at the funeral, but now I was crumbling under my pain. I wanted to go away and hide. From head to toe, Clyde was covered with flowers. I sat quietly and stared at his grave for the next few minutes. I didn't want to utter another word. Words hurt, and I knew nothing I said that afternoon would bring Clyde back to us.

I laid my head down in my lap again and closed my eyes in tears of pain. I didn't know what I was going to do. I only knew that I wanted to spend as much time as I could with my husband, and sitting next to him was the closest I could get.

I begged God earnestly that afternoon to bring Clyde back to me. I wanted to just hear him say, "Debbie, I'm okay. Go on with your life. I'm okay."

I looked at my watch and it was 4:45 I knew that the truck would soon be coming around to let me know that it was time to leave. An hour wasn't enough for me.

"I should have come earlier," I said lamenting. I should have left at noon. "I hope the ground isn't too cold for you, Clyde," I said as I looked at his grave. "Lord, please don't let anyone bother him down there. Please take care of him for me. Don't let anything bother him. Please don't let anything crawl on him."

I stood up reluctantly from the chair, gathering my things to leave. "Lord, I don't want to leave him!"

And then the anger began to build in my voice, "Why did you take him? Why did you take him from us, Lord!? Why couldn't you have taken me if you needed someone? Why didn't you take me instead?" I cried out. "Take me, Lord! It hurts too much. I can't take it anymore! I can't!" I screamed.

As on cue, a white pick-up truck drove by and slowed and I knew it was my signal to leave. I took my left hand and wiped the remaining dried red clay from Clyde's grave marker. I didn't want one speck of dirt left. Everything had to be perfect. As I turned back from staring at the white pick-up truck, I said goodbye to Clyde once again and stooped down to finish my prayer.

"I'm leaving, sweetheart," I said. "I'll be back soon. I'm sorry I didn't come earlier to spend more time with you, but I needed to see you, even for a few minutes. I walked out of the building around 2:00 and I didn't tell anyone."

I took one final glance at Clyde's grave as I folded the chair to walk away.

"Take care of yourself, Clyde. I'll see you the next time, okay. I love you, sweetheart. I love you very much. I'll be back very soon," I said as I walked away with tears.

As the wind began to blow through the trees, I felt very sad. I didn't want to leave, but I knew I had to get back to Columbus to check on Alex Keith. It was almost 5:00 and I would arrive in Columbus around 6:00 if I left that moment.

I picked up the chair and the dead flowers from the side of the grave and walked back to my car. As I began to drive away, I turned and looked over my shoulder and saw Clyde's flowers standing bravely in the breeze of the day with one flower dangling on top of his grave.

"God, please take care of him for me," I whispered softly. "I can't get to him now, but I know you can. Thank you for letting me spend time with Clyde today."

I began to smile as I turned right into the circular drive and took a quick right to exit the park. Clyde was buried not far from the cemetery's entrance.

"I hope my manager doesn't fire me for walking out of the building without telling her," I said, thinking about what I'd done. "But I know she'll understand."

I had spent an hour with the love of my life and all was well. It was absolutely beautiful and I felt better.

As I drove out of the city limits, I felt compelled to turn on the radio to hear some happy music. The first song I heard was *Seal* singing "Kiss from a Rose." I listened closely to the song while driving back to Columbus and fell in love with it. I felt good that evening having spent some time with Clyde. I missed him terribly and knew I could jump in my car at any time and drive to Andersonville and talk with him intimately. Once at the cemetery I felt content.

As the days turned into years, I would frequent Andersonville National Cemetery to visit Clyde during the coolness of the day. As long as I was able, I vowed to keep fresh flowers on his grave.

CHAPTER EIGHT

He's in My Dreams

I wanted desperately to see Clyde again, so I began to dream about him. I wanted to be close to him and the grave was the closest I could get. As the days turned into weeks, my denial gave way to anger and fear; occasionally, the two stages of grief manifested themselves as one. I went back and forth.

I DIDN'T TAKE ANY MORE spontaneous trips to Andersonville. When I felt the urge to see Clyde, I drove the 60 miles to the cemetery on my days off, but most of the time I waited until the weekend. I ached from not being able to talk to or touch Clyde. Grief takes hold of your entire being—your physical and mental capacity, and it shakes you asunder. Afterward, there's not much left. You don't have any energy or stamina.

I would never be the same again in this life. And the burden of living without Clyde was beyond my tiny brain's comprehension. Many days I didn't think I would make it out of bed. The mental and physical pain was so intense and unbearable at times, I was resolved to stay in bed.

He's in My Dreams

I was missing Clyde beyond my senses and so when I began to dream about him, I was grateful. In one dream I found myself falling—no, more like floating down into a dark, cold place. It was awfully dreary, damp, and soggy. There was no light to be seen any way I turned. All I knew was I didn't want to be there. I looked down into the dark dungeon of hollowness and some kind of golden specter appeared to grow closer to me. And then I saw him. It was Clyde. He was wrapped with a solid white satin throw which covered his entire body. I felt as though I was floating aimlessly through the air with no support of any kind around Clyde. I cascaded freely in the air with no consciousness of space or time.

I reached forward to embrace Clyde as he reached for me with outstretched arms. But as I drew closer to him, he drifted off into the darkness just a few feet away from me. The darkness overshadowed Clyde's face and I couldn't see him anymore. And the next thing I knew he reappeared right before my eyes, but this time, his head was lying on a soft cushiony, white satin pillow which matched impeccably with the white satin throw that wrapped snuggly around his body. I kissed him along his brown, warm cheeks and above his eyes to soften the bruise above his right brow. He was warm, but still. And before I could travel my lips down to his face he faded again into darkness and pulled away quickly from my reach. Without hesitation, I reached to cup his hands into mine, but I couldn't hold onto them. I tried desperately with everything in me, but it was all for naught.

I cried out, calling his name, "Clyde, sweetheart. Come back!

"Don't do this to me! Please talk to me, Clyde. I need to talk with you. Please don't leave me! Please don't."

But Clyde didn't respond. There was only stillness. "I need to let you know that I love you, sweetheart. I will always love you. I will love you forevermore. Please wake up for me."

But Clyde didn't wake up. He lay still and didn't flinch or move his eyes.

I cried out again to him, "Clyde! Please don't leave me! Please don't leave me here alone. I can't make it without you!"

I woke up terrified and dumbfounded. I looked around quickly in my bedroom, calling out Clyde's name. But it was a dream. I had lost him again, even in my dreams. I looked at the clock and it read 3:17 a.m., but I knew I wasn't going back to sleep.

I didn't have any more tears left to shed that early morning. I felt bad inside. I was empty, completely desolate. I was tired and worn. And of all things, my head was pounding incredibly from the worst headache I could have imagined. I felt my head was going to explode into pieces any minute from the unrelenting pain. I hadn't had a migraine headache in years.

All I could do was close my eyes and pretend to see his handsome face in my mind. I would have done anything to calm my pounding headache. Nothing made sense anymore to me. I knew that I had God in my life. I knew he would always be with me. But the pain ripped through the base of my being, stripping me of rational thinking. I was alone in my bed that early morning. I saw death as huge and ugly, and I hated it.

Months before Clyde and I were married in 1973 we had visited the Andersonville National Cemetery. I remember how we talked about the mystic calm of the cemetery as we walked the grounds and read the names inscribed on the gravestones. Yet, neither one of us could have ever imagined that Clyde would one day be laid to rest in this hallowed ground. The very brave men and women that he talked about as we surveyed the cemetery some 22 years ago had become his companions in death.

I felt the heaviness in my eyes again, and with welcome arms, I gave way to sleep. In no time I was dreaming about Clyde again. I was close to him again and I was very happy. He lay quietly in the casket with his eyes open.

"Clyde!" I called his name. "Please come back to me. Please don't be dead! Lord, please don't let Clyde be dead. Wake him up for me, please. I can't stand it anymore."

But nothing happened. Clyde was still and he continued to stare straight ahead into hollow, dead space. I turned and lifted my leg to climb into Clyde's casket, but stopped abruptly.

Suddenly, I no longer wanted to climb into the casket with him, but, instead, I turned slowly and pressed my fingers into the moistened red clay around Clyde's casket to climb out of the dark place. Gripping them into soggy clay, I clawed desperately for some traction to continue climbing.

I dared not look back fearing what I would see. I kept climbing, one arm, one foot behind the other, clawing my way to the top to the source of light. My will to resist looking back weakened incredibly as I repositioned my hands to strengthen my grip, but to no avail. And before I could scream for help, I slid back down into the dungeon of hollowness. As I slid downward, my fingers oozed with blood as I continued to fall and bounce off the wet, ragged wall of dirt.

I buried my face as I sweated in endless sorrow. Again, I awoke and looked around in my bedroom—dazed and covered with sweat. Pulling the covers from over my face, I began to recall the dream. I stared over at the clock on the nightstand and it read 4:25 a.m. The dreams were becoming more frequent.

The pain was very intense that morning. I couldn't escape the anguish and the loneliness. I wanted to run away and hide. I wanted to scream, but what for? It wouldn't bring Clyde back. I was too tired and worn and I knew I wouldn't have a good day at work. Lying back on my pillow, I scooped it securely under my hand and pressed down into my now sweat-soaked sheets and fell asleep again. This time I didn't dream and I was extremely grateful.

I woke up the next morning and tried my best to scurry to leave for work. But I didn't make it. Waking up in the middle of the night and dreaming about Clyde had depleted me of all energy. When I dreamed of Clyde from that time on he was dead. And when I tried to wake him he never opened his eyes again. There was only stillness.

It was now July 1995, three months since Clyde's death. I somehow managed to keep working. Believe it or not, work kept me going. It kept me from going off the deep end. Even though I wasn't getting much sleep, I still managed to throw myself out of the bed many mornings when all I wanted to do was stay in the bed, but I kept fighting my anguish and my bewildered days of existence.

It took a while longer for me to stop watching the door in the den. Most evenings around 6:00 p.m., Clyde would arrive home. So, for the first few months I would sit in the den and pray for Clyde to open the door and walk in and say, "Hi Debbie. I'm home." He would walk in and we would hug each other. I yearned to see his face and hear his voice. What I would give to hear him call my name. I had completely lost my appetite. My taste for food, even the smell of it, had deserted me. But I made sure Alex Keith had plenty to eat. Oftentimes, I nibbled on bread and meat, but not vegetables. The agony and pain of death had pretty much destroyed my taste buds.

I learned later that grief is a root cause of many illnesses because of the tremendous amount of stress it wreaks on the body and mind.

As I lay on the bed, I picked up my Bible and attempted to read a Scripture verse or two. But the words wouldn't penetrate through the pages of my mind. I had always read and studied the Bible religiously. I knew where my help came from—of course, it was from God—but I couldn't read a lick because I couldn't concentrate. Many times I would close my eyes and recite the Scriptures I'd memorized in years past. Thank goodness for memories. It would be many years after Clyde's death before I was able to concentrate and study seriously again.

So instead of reading my favorite Scripture, I quoted it from memory: Proverbs 3:5-6.

> *Trust in the Lord with all thine heart; and lean not unto thine own understanding. In all thy ways acknowledge Him, and He shall direct thy path.*

And then I quoted Psalm 31:24.

> *Be of good courage, and He shall strengthen your heart, all ye that hope in the Lord.*

During my first two years as a widow, I thirsted to hear the Scriptures because many times I couldn't read them. Instead, I listened to the Bible on tape and internalized the words as the narrator spoke. Now as the need pressed for me to hear God's word, I would quote the precious words from memory. The stress of grief had overwhelmed me physically to such an extent that I was unable to focus. I had difficulty focusing even when wearing my eyeglasses.

When I was married I became absorbed with my family, and that's not a bad thing. I wanted to be the perfect wife, the perfect mother, but I forgot about me most of the time during our 21 years of marriage. I made time for my husband, my children, and for God, but I forgot to make time for me—Deborah Maxine Slappey. I had to learn to get to know myself and to enjoy life in the present. I knew what to do, but the doing was in the details.

I knew it would be different for me and the kids, but I had no clue of the change that was to come for us.

Suddenly I was faced with living without Clyde, and I had so much extra time on my hands. I didn't know what to do with myself. It didn't take much time to cook and take care of Alex Keith. I was missing being married; I was missing my mate. Nothing made any sense to me anymore. Life didn't make any sense. Work didn't make any sense. And I knew that I didn't make sense anymore either. I kept repeating myself.

My life moved at a snail's pace, it seemed. The summer would soon be over and I would have to face another season—autumn—without Clyde. I didn't want to think about autumn, and I dared not think about the pending winter and approaching holidays. It would mean that Alex Keith would be going to another grade level without Clyde. He would be attending Fort Middle School, the same middle school Clyde Daryl had attended. I would have to take him to the school alone. Clyde Daryl would be classified as a sophomore at college and Alex Keith would be going to the seventh grade, junior high.

I hated the thought that I would have to rear Alex Keith without Clyde. Alex Keith was approaching his adolescent years, and he needed his father's wisdom and guidance. How was I going to help Alex Keith? These thoughts gripped me mercilessly.

My heart sank in desperation. And my head ached constantly from my crying episodes. I kept praying for strength and courage to keep moving forward. I felt I was living but going nowhere. But I kept going because God was carrying me. I wasn't doing anything. It was all God's doing.

On one particular morning, I dropped Alex Keith off at school and drove back home. I didn't have the strength to go to work that day. I wanted to get back home quickly and close the door to the world. Once back home I stepped into the den and ran quickly into my bedroom, shutting my door to the world.

"Lord, I'm hurting. I'm hurting inside...from not being with Clyde.

"Why was Clyde the only one who didn't receive a new heart," I cried. "Clyde Daryl and Alex Keith won't have their father to talk to and smile with. Clyde was only 43, Lord," I said. "He was just beginning to live."

I cried myself to sleep that morning. I only knew I was missing my husband terribly. I could do nothing but lie flat on the light rust-colored carpet in my bedroom and scream in tormenting pain. I didn't have the strength to pull myself up from the floor and turn the television on, so I just lay there. I closed my eyes and prayed for sleep.

I wanted to be alone in the darkened room in the twilight of my grief. I had no strength left in me, not even to pull myself off the floor. I was alone and somehow I had to learn to accept it. There would come a day when I had to face the fact that Clyde had left me in death. But it wouldn't be this day.

"I can't accept it, Lord," I mumbled. "I just can't accept that he's gone. It will kill me if I do. I don't know how to deal with him being gone," I said.

Somehow I managed to calm down and close my eyes to the anguish. With hands and feet outstretched on the floor, I drifted off to sleep.

⌒

I survived the day and picked up Alex Keith from school later that afternoon. After he finished his homework, Alex Keith dashed outdoors to play with kids in the neighborhood. Ten minutes later I heard the screen open again. It was Alex Keith coming back into the house. I was stretched out on my bed watching the news. The sun would soon be setting and I knew he probably would want to take his bath early so he could spend some time playing his video games before going to bed.

"Alex Keith, make sure you close the door securely," I said to him. "We don't want a snake crawling into the house, okay!"

My words instantly took me back in time some 20 years or so when Clyde and I were first married. We were living in our small apartment in Plains, Georgia, Clyde's hometown. Late one summer night we decided to leave the back kitchen door open; after all, it had a screen door and nothing should be able to get in—right. It was a very warm Friday night in 1974, and we locked the screen door. Dogs barked frantically around the neighborhood, but we didn't think much about it since dogs were always barking. Late that evening, somewhere around 9:00, we closed the door and retired for the night.

The next morning, I arose about 9:00, just like any typical weekend morning, to cook breakfast. My morning routine was to open my eyes, lift my shoulders from my pillow, and swing my feet from the warm, cozy bed covers onto the floor and into my velvety soft bed slippers. Our bed was fairly low to the floor so my short legs would find them instantly. I rose from the bed, and as I was about to swing my lower body to the floor, I looked down and was struck with horror.

"Snake! Snake! Clyde, there's a snake," I screamed.

I pulled both feet back and jumped on the bed screaming at the top of my lungs.

"Clyde, there's a snake! It's on the floor…a snake!"

Clyde jumped from the bed, screaming, "What!…Where!… Where is it!"

"It's down there!" I screamed, pointing to the floor where I saw the snake. "I almost stepped on it! It almost bit me! It almost bit me! It was right next to my bedroom shoes!"

Evidently, I had scared the baby rattlesnake with my screaming, because it had crawled back under the bed. Clyde jumped off the bed quickly, grabbed a slender pole near the door, and pulled the snake from underneath the bed. He cracked it hard on the head, killing it. Clyde wrapped the snake around the pole and took it outside. Afterward, he came back to examine my legs for a snake bite. Thank goodness the baby snake had missed my legs. And then our eyes met. If this is the baby rattler, then where's the mama? Panic drowned our hearts with fear like overflowing oceans. "Oh, no!" I said, "Where is the mama, Clyde?"

Clyde looked around the apartment for almost an hour. He peeked into every crevice in the house for the mama snake, but it was nowhere to be found. We drove to Americus, Georgia, to Mom-Mom's house because we knew that she would know what to do. Mom-Mom told Clyde to purchase some alum from the hardware store so he could smoke our apartment. She said that if a snake was still in the house and inhaled the alum it would knock us down attempting to escape from the smoke-filled house. I stayed at Mom-Mom's house while Clyde drove back and smoked the house with alum. We never did find the mama snake in the house, and after a few days, we decided to come back to our apartment. Months later we were still looking into every crevice of our apartment for big mama snake, but we never found it.

I smiled as I remembered the story. More than 20 years had gone by and I still remembered every detail. So, as Alex Keith walked into the house that evening I wanted to make sure he closed the doors shut. I didn't want it to happen again.

"Alex Keith," I rang out. "Make sure you close the screen door!"

Chapter Nine

At the Grocery Store

Even though I knew Clyde was dead, my mind continued to deny it, at least as much as I could. I couldn't fathom the thought that I wouldn't see him again. We had been together for years. How could I ever accept that Clyde was gone. I was angry with Clyde, I was angry with God, and I was angry with myself for not being at the hospital when he died. I continued to beat myself into splinters.

TIME APPEARED TO STAND STILL as I looked at the calendar in my bedroom. Only a few weeks remained in July. I had attempted to push August out of my mind because I didn't want to face our upcoming wedding anniversary, August 10, alone. It would have been our 22nd and I couldn't believe four months had passed since Clyde's death.

"His death still hurts, even after four months," I said silently. "I know it will hurt forever."

I wasn't hungry, but I knew I needed to eat something, even if the food didn't have much of a taste. I had been working for about three months now and I didn't have the strength to leave the office for lunch. From time to time, I brought a sandwich or something from home, and most of the time I didn't eat it. I would forget to eat. All I wanted to do was go to the cemetery and sit with Clyde. Even though I yearned to leave work and drive to the cemetery, I didn't do it again.

I knew I couldn't keep leaving work. I was thankful for my bosses, but I also knew they had to draw the line somewhere. My mind stayed on Clyde as I wrote information bulletins and updated procedure and reference manuals throughout the day. I had composed bulletins for years and could easily write and update documents while preoccupied with my thoughts being 60 miles away.

Since April, I had traveled to Andersonville just about every weekend. I was very lonely, so empty inside without him. I was amazed that I had survived three months without him, but I knew it was God's doing.

It was 5:30 p.m. when I arrived home. I took my purse and work bag from the car and walked slowly toward the back door. As I walked, I looked around at the lawn. Clyde had always kept the yards looking immaculate. I smiled inside as I imagined how the yards missed their master's touch. Clyde certainly had a green thumb, to say the least. Alex Keith and I couldn't take care of the grounds like Clyde. As much as we tried, we couldn't.

"I'm so alone, Lord," I said as I turned to open the door to the den. "I miss him so."

Alex Keith and I were doing the best we could, but there were times when the grass sprouted so quickly, we could only cut it during the weekends. I missed Clyde's smiling face outside pushing the lawnmower diagonally, back and forth; walking up and down the hill to make sure that he cut it perfectly. Our well-manicured lawn had been the envy of the neighborhood.

"What I wouldn't give to see him right now, Lord," I said. "I don't have to talk to him, really, I don't," I said as if I was trying to bargain with God. "I just need to see him, even if it's just for a few minutes."

Sighing deeply, I attempted to blink back the tears as I walked in the house. Alex Keith should be doing his homework,

I surmised, and I didn't want him to see me this way. I tried to shield my pain from him as much as I could, but oftentimes he would see the evidence of my tears in my big puffy eyes. The sinking feeling in my stomach never went away. I carried it everywhere I went.

I had received a raise a few weeks back and was happy as I could be, but when I thought about telling Clyde, sadness filled my eyes. I couldn't. I had no way of telling him about my good news. I knew he would be very proud of me. He always celebrated my successes, either by taking me out to dinner or by buying a thoughtful card.

It wasn't the same without him. I had no one to rush home and tell my good news.

"Hi Alex Keith," I said as I walked into his room.

"Hi Mom. How was your day?" he asked as he stood up from the floor to hug my neck.

"I'm okay. My day was okay. I didn't do much other than update some fields in a reference manual. That's about all," I replied.

I really didn't want to say much.

"Have you eaten yet?"

"Yes, ma'am. I've already eaten," Alex Keith responded.

"Well, I'll check your homework in a little while. I need to get these work clothes off and relax a bit. I'll be back, okay?" I said.

I walked back to my room and closed the door. I was barely able to hold back the tears before grabbing my pillow, crying silently in my unnerving pain. I felt raw, on the edge. I wanted to tell Clyde my good news about my raise, but I couldn't. He wasn't around anymore. I pushed my back against the bedroom wall and slowly slid down to the floor, burying my face into my hands.

After about 15 minutes I walked into the bathroom, pulled my wash cloth from atop the shower pole, and squeezed the water from the wet wash cloth on my face. I looked into the mirror and discovered that my eyes were horribly swollen. It wasn't a pretty sight. I knew that Alex Keith would know instantly that I had been crying again. I changed my clothes and lay on my bed along with my growing stacks of books and mail.

About an hour later, I took a bath and walked to Alex Keith's room and talked a while after checking his homework. He didn't seem to notice my bloodshot eyes.

So many things go through one's mind when dealing with the death of a loved one. Initially, I didn't understand most of my emotions. I had strange feelings. At times I didn't know if I was coming or going. I knew Clyde wasn't physically with me, but I hoped he would talk to me, walk with me, and even hold me.

I knew it didn't make sense, but nothing really made sense to me anymore. Time was relative; everything was simply a moment in time. I didn't understand it, but I knew God did.

I picked up my Bible from the end table to read a Scripture for inspiration, but as before, I couldn't concentrate nor could I read the Scriptures that had meant so much to me in times past. I yearned to read God's word, but I couldn't. I kept praying through the tears. Taking care of Alex Keith and praying to God were the only things that kept me going. God was carrying me and taking care of me now.

For the first year, my life drifted from day into night. My routine was to go to work, come home, check Alex Keith's homework and then go to bed after crying most of the evening. I lived with this regimen for more than two years.

Clyde had died and left us in a world of uncertainty, pain, despair, and, at times, helplessness. Through God's strength,

He brought me back from the brink of insanity. Everything was in God's hand. God gave me the strength to endure my sorrow and despair through my tears.

At the Grocery Store

I went to the grocery store on a Saturday afternoon in July to pick up a few items for Sunday's dinner. I walked up and down the aisles, looking on both sides, placing items into the grocery cart. I looked down the aisle hoping to spot an item on my list and then I saw him. I saw Clyde standing at the end of the aisle looking directly at me.

And without even thinking I yelled out, "Clyde! Clyde!" I ran down the aisle, but stopped momentarily while a lady moved her grocery cart from the middle of the aisle to let me walk through. She sensed my anxiousness and moved the cart rather quickly. I passed her quickly and darted to the end of the aisle, but I didn't see him anywhere. I panicked as I ran to the next aisle, hoping to spot him again.

"I know that was him!" I said very excited, "I know that was him!" I walked to the next aisle, looked to the end of it, but still didn't see him. I looked down the next aisle and the next, but he was nowhere to be seen, so I began to doubt myself.

Had I really seen Clyde? I asked silently. *Was it really him? Or was it someone else—maybe someone who looked like Clyde?* I began to think that maybe my mind was indeed playing tricks on me. My heart was pounding with overwhelming fear and I froze for a moment because I didn't know what to do. I began to feel rather silly.

My body began to shiver as I realized what had happened or what I thought had happened. For a slight moment, I thought Clyde had actually come back to me. The thought sent reels of shock and numbness throughout me. Then I was deeply saddened because I felt I had lost him again. And it hurt to lose him each time. *It's all in your mind, girl*, I said silently. *It's all in your mind.* I began to pray in that very spot in the store. It hit me cold in the face. I knew then I was losing it.

"Where is he? Where is he, Lord? Am I losing my mind?" I cried out in desperation. I walked down the aisle one last time where I first spotted Clyde hoping, even praying I would see him again. But I never saw him in the store again.

"I don't want to lose him again, Lord," I cried. "Please don't let me lose him again."

My hands were shaking. I placed my right hand into my left hand and rubbed it gently, hoping to calm my shaking. I didn't want to leave the grocery store. No matter what I did for the rest of that afternoon, I couldn't shake the feeling that I had seen Clyde and he was staring at me.

Sadly, I started to walk toward the checkout. I had spent an hour searching for Clyde. I turned around one more time, hoping to see him walk up to me, bringing a can of peaches so we could go home and make a peach cobbler. Clyde just loved sweets. I yearned to smell the aroma of his prize-winning peach cobbler. Reluctantly, I turned back to face the cashier and placed my groceries on the conveyer belt, one item at a time.

"How are you doing, Ma'am?" I heard the lady say to me.

"I'm doing okay," I said. "How are you?" I asked, stuttering.

"I'm doing just fine," she said. "Paper or plastic for you, Ma'am?"

"Paper is fine. Thanks so much," I replied to her.

I guess the lady thought I was crazy as I continued to look behind me. I couldn't shake the feeling. I wanted to see Clyde one more time and I guess I saw him in my mind.

I was sure it was him, I thought to myself. *I am almost positive it was him.*

After the lady bagged my groceries, anger began to fuel inside me. "I should've been watching more closely. I should have," scolding myself.

"I probably need to talk with someone. Yeah, I need to...I need to talk to someone. I'll look for someone tomorrow—maybe tomorrow."

I left the store in emotional chaos. I fumbled through my handbag to find my keys as I carried my packages to the car. I was still stunned after the ordeal and felt incredibly exhausted. I'd been in the grocery store for almost two hours!

"Lord," I stammered as I tried to open the car door, "please let me see Clyde again. I just want to see him one more time."

I burst into tears as I placed the groceries on the front seat of the car. "Help me see him again. I'll be looking this time. I really will."

After I closed the door, I walked around the car to the driver's side, staring at the automatic door; hoping Clyde would walk out any minute.

"Oh! I would love to see him walk out of that door, Lord!" I said. "I would rush toward him, jump into his arms, and kiss him all over until we would both fall on the ground."

I waited another 15 minutes in the car, hoping Clyde would walk out of the store, but he never did.

"Debbie, you're being silly," I said. "You didn't see Clyde. You wanted to see him, but you didn't see him. Clyde's gone, Debbie. He's gone. Just accept it and go on with your life. He would want you to. You know he would."

I was shaken for the rest of that Saturday. Even now, as the days have turned to years, I still think about that Saturday afternoon when I thought I saw Clyde in the grocery store. When you want to see someone as desperately as I wanted to see Clyde, your mind can easily slip into a twilight zone of confusion—into a world captured in grey matter where reality and make-believe become one and the same. I believe that's what happened to me in the grocery store.

As I drove home, I wanted everything to be quiet around me. People were living their lives and no one except my family and me were mourning Clyde's death. I know this wasn't the case, but I felt this way at the time. It was as though no one cared except us.

"But Debbie they don't know to care," I said in defense of my own narrow-minded thinking. "How could they? Losing a loved one happens to people every day, and this time it happened to us, the Slappey family. It's as simple as that, Debbie. It happened to us.

"But Lord," I continued, "I wish the world would stop and pay attention that Clyde has gone and left me here, alone. I wish people would stop and listen. I don't want anyone to forget him. I don't want his friends to forget him either, because I won't. I never will. I never will, Lord."

I arrived home about 20 minutes later and walked into the house with the groceries. As usual, Alex Keith was playing with his video game. I never told Alex Keith or anyone about the grocery store event, at least not until now. I thought I was beginning to lose it, and I knew I had better seek professional help.

I would eventually take Alex Keith with me as well. I hoped his talking about Clyde's death would help him deal and talk about his feelings. I knew he wouldn't talk to me because he didn't want to upset me. I had already talked to Clyde Daryl about seeking grief counseling at school. I hoped he would do it.

"Hi Mom," Alex Keith said as I walked into his room. "How was your day?" he asked.

"I'm okay, Alex Keith. I'm a little tired, but I'll feel better in a little while. I'm going to lie down for a few minutes, okay, sweetheart," I said.

I took my handbag and walked back to my bedroom. I lifted the remote from my bed and clicked the TV on. I laid back on the bed and cried in sorrow. I had lost Clyde again.

For the next week, I didn't do much of anything other than go to work, church and chauffeur Alex Keith to his continuing education class. When I had to pick him up from school, I didn't get out of the car. I wasn't ready to mingle in a crowd and make small talk.

One of my greatest fears was for someone to walk up to me and ask me how my husband was doing. I would have to tell them that Clyde didn't make it. He had passed away. I died each time I had to admit that Clyde was gone. I didn't want to explain it to anyone. I had to hear those words vibrate through the chambers of my mind. I would break into shreds whenever I had to say the words.

I kept going to church. I knew I needed to hear the words of God. I also knew that Clyde would want me to continue to do what we did as a family when he was with us. I had to think of Alex Keith now. As I sat in church services my mind wandered many times to the cemetery, thinking about Clyde.

But life moved on, and soon the weekend was over. Monday arrived with lightning speed. I was back at work and then home again to unwind, closing my door to the world. I undressed from my work clothes and lay across the bed to look through my ever-mounting mail. The pile had quadrupled in size. The last thing I wanted to do was open it. It was much easier to simply place the mail in the garage and start over from scratch. The sight of the stacks had become intimidating.

I pondered about whether I had seen Clyde in the grocery store. I remembered looking into his eyes; even if it was for a moment, I saw his sad eyes. *It was Clyde. I just know it was him.* It was all too real for me.

My nights had become tired and drained. The dreams hadn't stopped. I felt light-headed and fatigued and I didn't have the strength to read most times, but still I kept trying. In the stillness of the night my mind began to wander to my sewing machine that was located in the dining room. As a seamstress, I enjoyed constructing ladies dresses, skirts, and tops. I smiled as the memories came rushing back. It had been a long time since I had sewn. Clyde Daryl and Alex Keith were very young at the time. During the late evening I would pull out my sewing machine and would create pretty outfits for myself. I smiled as I remembered how much I had enjoyed sewing.

The telephone rang and woke me abruptly, but I didn't answer it. I didn't feel like talking. I simply wasn't in the mood. I got up and walked to the kitchen to get something to eat.

School registration was scheduled for mid-August. Alex Keith was doing well in the continuing education program at Columbus State College. Soon he would be attending Fort Middle School for the 1995–96 school year. I was very proud of him to be doing so well.

Maybe too well, I thought to myself.

"Lord," I prayed silently as I checked Alex Keith's homework. "Please let Alex Keith be okay, Lord."

We finished working on Alex Keith's homework. He was constructing a storyboard of mathematical terms. It felt good for me to review his homework. I praised him for his excellent work. I walked into the kitchen and washed the few dishes left in the sink before retiring for the night myself. I took a bath and finished opening some of my mail. As I walked back and forth to the bathroom, I kept going back to the incident at the grocery store.

"Lord, am I going crazy? Am I losing it now...seeing Clyde in the grocery store. Was I hallucinating?" I asked. "Please don't let me lose it, Lord. Don't let me slip away. My children need me now," I prayed.

It had been a while since I had picked up my Bible. I'd had a hard time concentrating and seeing words; let alone reading them, but I wanted to try again. I opened my Bible and started reading and it felt quite good, even if it was for a short while. It felt really good.

I crawled into my bed and turned page after page, listening to the ruffled sound as my fingers danced through the pages of the Scriptures.

The Lord is my strength and my shield; my heart trusted in Him, and I am helped: therefore my heart greatly rejoiceth; and with my song will I praise Him.

I read Psalm 28:7 repeatedly on that evening in July. I wanted the Scriptures to sink deep within my brain. The Lord is my strength and my shield… "That's a lot, Lord," I said as I began to recite it in my mind again. "You said that you would never leave me nor forsake me and for this I thank you.

"Lord, I thought I saw Clyde at the grocery store. The man looked so much like him. Lord, you know, I really wanted the man to be Clyde because I miss him very much. I wanted it to be him with all my heart," I said as I began to cry. "I want Clyde to come back to me and for a moment he did. I wanted earnestly to see him again and I thought I did. But it wasn't him. I'm sure of it now. Let me be okay so I can take care of my children."

I opened my journal and began to write…

I lost the only person in this world who could read my mind, who knew when I hurt and when I was in sorrow. I miss his smiling face. We were very close, maybe too close. I guess that's why I'm having a difficult time letting go… I pray, Lord, that one day I can go on with my life…

After I finished writing I said my prayers; pulled the covers up to my elbows and started watching TV, or maybe I should say that the TV was watching me. I knew God would take care of me. He would help me through the sad days, even if I didn't understand exactly what was going on inside me. But I trusted

God with my life. My life was in God's hands and I wanted to run into His arms and hide from my storm. I wanted to stay in His bosom.

"They don't have a father. Why can't they have a father? Everyone else does. Why can't Clyde Daryl and Alex Keith? As the months turn into years, they will begin to miss their father more and more. And he won't be around for them. What will they do then, Lord? The burden is too heavy for them to bear; it's just too heavy for us."

I continued to pour out my soul to God that night, "I know that's the very sad part. Their father won't come back and they both will have to learn to live without him. Lord, I'm sick of this pain...this aching...not knowing what to do with myself...doing things alone...I ache for my children for missing their father as they grow into maturity, Lord. I ache for them. I'm so tired.

"Please just let me sleep for a little while. I can't keep functioning the way I am. I'm tired in the morning, from waking up early in the morning and staring at the walls or watching the weather. Lord, I am so tired of the weather. I need your help! Just help me please, I pray, Lord. Help me please to go back to sleep!"

I would have loved to have some place to take my brain out of my head and put it on a shelf to rest for a while from the aggravation and frustration of grief. But I would remember how God took care of me and my family in times past and no matter how much pain I was experiencing now, I knew he would take care of me. I kept reading and turned to Psalm 30:3-5...

Oh Lord, Thou hast brought up my soul
from the grave: Thou hast kept me alive,
that I should not go down to the pit.

Sing unto the Lord, O ye saints of His, and give
thanks at the remembrance of His holiness.

For His anger endureth but a moment;
in His favor is life: weeping may endure for a night,
but joy cometh in the morning.

I read the last Scripture again…weeping may endure for a night, but joy cometh in the morning…"But Lord," I said, "when is the morning gonna come!? I'm in so much pain. Please help me deal with Clyde's death. Help me deal with it, I pray. I'm weeping desperately, wanting to be close to him, but I can't! It hurts not to be close to him. I can't be close to him ever again in this life, Lord!"

I closed the Bible and held it close to my heart. I wanted to hold on to it as tightly as possible; and I didn't want to let go. As the tears streamed from my soul, I kept repeating the verse in my mind over and over again…*weeping may endure for a night, but joy cometh in the morning.*

I finished my prayers and turned the television to the financial channel. As the months passed, I continued to watch the financial channel and began to learn more about business and finance, which would help me in years to come.

With His wonderful assurance, it didn't take long for sleep to come my way. Sleep was fantastic and gratifying when I had it. God had sustained me hour by hour through my agonizing sorrow. I fell into another friendly sleep with my Bible and journal still clasped tightly in both hands. I don't remember the time, but He closed my eyes from the pain and gave me the strength to go back to sleep. My big teddy bear was close to my side. The dreams continued as I drifted into a deep sleep.

My Dreams Continue

I found myself in a dark, wet place. It didn't have much foundation. I felt as though I was floating in space. But this place was very familiar. I felt I had been here before. As I looked downward, I saw what appeared to be a blackish-golden silhouette. As I drifted closer, the silhouette grew larger and larger.

I knew that it was Clyde's coffin. It was painfully sad for me to look at his coffin again. I touched the walls around me, which appeared to be very narrow. The walls were made of red and black clay, but more red than black. I looked at my hands and saw the dirt, grime, and grass cemented into my fingernails.

It was awful. I didn't want to be here anymore. As before, I didn't see Clyde's face. His coffin was always closed and I didn't want to open it. I quivered to think what I would see if I opened it. I wasn't afraid of him, but I didn't want to see him dead. I only wanted him to rest in peace.

I didn't like the place and wanted to leave quickly. So, I touched Clyde's coffin and turned away, moving closer to the wall to start climbing back toward the light just above me. I could tell that it was a very steep hole, and as I dug my left hand into the reddish, muddy dirt, I turned toward Clyde and waved goodbye to him with my right hand touching his coffin rather delicately so I wouldn't disturb his sleep.

"Clyde," I said softly to him, "I love you very much. I will always love you, sweetheart, always. But I have to leave you, now; I can't take care of you anymore. I wish I could, but I can't, Clyde.

"I need you very much. I wish I could touch you and hold you and take care of you again like I used to a few months ago; but I can't anymore. Only God can take care of you now."

I turned my face back toward the narrow hole and began to climb upward, holding desperately to whatever crevice of earth I could grab. Soggy dirt was embedded into my fingers and my elbows were encased in mush; the hole was filled with slimy mud. But I kept climbing, hoping I would find a dry place to breathe clean air. I didn't look back this time. I was compelled not to look back.

But I kept placing one hand in front of the other, and when I saw a flicker of light not too far in the distance, I climbed toward it. I knew it would take a few more lifts to reach the top. But as my hopes heightened to reach the top, everything quickly faded into one swoop. As soon as I had almost reached the top and was within a stone's throw, I slid down into the grave again.

I watched the blood ooze from my fingernails as I continued to slide downward. I tried to stop the slide, but to no avail. I began to pray.

"Lord, please don't let me stay here anymore," I yelled. "I don't want to stay here anymore. I miss Clyde so much, but I can't stay here anymore with him. Please help me leave this place!"

My eyes popped wide open and I looked around in my bedroom. Sweat poured from my body and I could tell I was no longer in the grave. I turned and stared at the clock and it was 5:52 a.m.

I didn't get up right away. I lay in my bed for another 15 minutes listening to the birds outside in the trees chirping away. The sounds of the birds overwhelmed my thoughts as their singing appeared to redirect my thoughts to their pleasant sounds instead of thinking about Clyde. As I began to hone in on the sound, I reminisced to my adolescent years. I would lie in bed early in the morning and listen to the birds chirp outside my tiny window in the early morning. I smiled as I lay there and listened. The birds didn't seem to have a care in the world. They were carefree.

"Sometimes," I said to God, "it would be nice if I could simply shut off my thoughts and be as carefree as those birds outside. I wouldn't have to worry about anything or think about anything.

"Yes, Lord. I wouldn't mind it at all."

I knew I needed to get up and fix Alex Keith breakfast, so I climbed out of the bed, removed my sweat-soaked garment and said my morning prayers. Afterward, I walked down the hall to wake up Alex Keith and cooked breakfast for him. While in the kitchen, I looked out the window and all appeared serene, typical for early morning. I walked back to my bedroom to take a bath and looked outside my bathroom window. Everything appeared very calm and quiet on that August morning. I took my bath and dressed. Within 30 minutes Alex Keith and I ate breakfast and raced out the door for school and work.

I thought about my early morning talk with God as I drove Alex Keith to school. I had begged God, literally begged Him to allow me to return to sleep and He did. I dropped Alex Keith at the door and kissed him on the cheek before I sped away heading for work. It was a new day for the Slappey family and I was grateful to God. I was happy for Alex Keith because he had something exciting to do during the summer months. He was definitely enjoying his time at college. They would be going to Tuskegee Institute in Alabama, over the next few days and I was glad.

Something changed that day for me. I pretty much went to work, listened to my radio, and worked on my technical writing assignments. But there was something different about the day. Instead of crying at my desk, I chose to deal with my grief in private. I would sob for a few minutes at work in a bathroom stall, dampen a paper towel to refresh my tear-soaked face and head back to my cube to work. But on this day, it was different. I felt very sad as I walked into the building. Previously, during the early morning, I had been feeling okay, though out of sorts, but still okay. I touched my stomach as I began to experience an uneasy feeling in the pit of it. I was feeling very awkward, out of place. It was too early in the morning to be feeling this way, I reasoned.

I couldn't put my finger on what was going on. But I knew something had changed since I came to work. Within minutes I became very apprehensive, even nervous. I walked slowly to my desk and as I turned the corner and approached the outside of the cube, I was overwhelmed with a pain in my stomach. It was very perplexing at first. *Perhaps I need to see a doctor*, I said silently. *With so much going on, maybe I have cancer. Is this an anxiety attack?* I asked silently. I turned and entered my cube and felt a little relieved.

I placed my handbag under my desk and pulled out my Bible to read a Scripture verse. I didn't know what to think nor did I know what prompted the anxiety attack, but I knew I didn't appreciate the feeling and hoped I wouldn't feel it again. I pressed the "ON" button on my PC and instantly became absorbed in my work. During my first year I stayed to myself and I didn't mingle much. I was very grateful for my job because it allowed me to work alone.

I was cordial with my close friends, but I still didn't talk much. I kept my feelings inside and was okay about it, at least during those early months. I was glad to leave the South Center at the end of the day. I said good evening to everyone and walked out the building. As I drove home, I kept pondering about the sick, overwhelming feeling I sensed earlier in the day.

So many things began to roll through my mind. *Had something happened at work? I didn't think so. I hadn't noticed anything out of the ordinary. No, it must be about Clyde's death.* I was sure of it. Every waking hour and even in my sleep, I was thinking of him. As I continued to drive home, I detected a buzzing sound in the backseat. I turned around to see what it was, but I didn't see anything. Still, I continued to hear that deep-pitched sound, so I turned around again, but this time it was not coming from my backseat, it was definitely a sound emanating from outside the car.

Just as I was about to look in my mirror, I saw in the distance a row of red lights, moving rapidly. It was another ambulance! *Not again*, my thoughts raged. That pain deep in the pit of my stomach returned instantly, but this time the feeling was more pronounced than before. I closed my eyes as I remembered the ambulance speeding away with Clyde to take him to the hospital. He had passed out several times while at home. I knew I wouldn't forget the shrieking, awful sound. I pulled to the side of the road and stopped my car. As the deafening sound grew closer, I raised my hands to cover my ears, hoping to blot out the sound. It was happening again to me.

The palms of my hands were sweating profusely as I held onto the wheel. I began to panic and for a moment in time, I was no longer on Manchester Expressway. I had become totally immersed in a swirling tunnel of time, wanting to jump out of the car and run away and hide. I held the steering wheel, trying desperately to keep my grip.

"Lord, please hide me from it! I don't want to hear it anymore!"

And then out of nowhere I heard a horn blow. It could have been several horns blow. I don't remember. Slowly, I lifted my head and unlocked my hands from the steering wheel, turning around in my seat to see what had happened. The shrieking sound from the ambulance had gone away. I could barely hear a faint sound of the siren in the distance. And as before, I was lost in panic and throbbing fear.

And then I heard a buzzing horn from behind me. I turned around and saw several cars behind me. They were blowing at me. *But why?* I didn't understand why. I had managed to park the car on the side of the road, so the ambulance could pass by. I opened my eyes and looked ahead of me, and to my surprise I wasn't on the side of the road; I was in the middle of the road in the outer lane of Manchester Expressway. I was petrified. Evidently, the sound had paralyzed my thinking. During the uproar, I thought I had pulled onto the side of the road, but in fact, I had stopped in the middle of the road as the ambulance approached me. *I could have been killed,* I said silently.

My hands were shaking like a leaf, but I managed to place the car in drive and slowly drove away.

"What happened to me, Lord?" I asked as I pressed my foot on the accelerator. How long was I waiting? Surely, no more than a few minutes, I hope."

The sound from the ambulance paralyzed me and that was dangerous. I froze solid in terror as I heard the siren.

"That's it!" I said, as I gained speed down Manchester Expressway. "That's it!"

"It's our anniversary! Our anniversary will soon be here," I shouted. "That's why I'm feeling sad right now. August 10 is approaching fast."

Clyde and I had spent 21 years together as a married couple and this would be the first anniversary without him. I would be alone this time. It was now crystal clear.

"Oh, Lord!" I said, "how will I make it through our anniversary without him. It would have been our 22nd. Oh, Lord, please help me through it."

CHAPTER TEN

Our 22nd Wedding Anniversary

I would have done just about anything to keep August 10, our wedding anniversary, from coming to pass. Perhaps, I thought, I could bargain with God in some form or fashion to skip our special day so I wouldn't have to deal with the colossal reality that we wouldn't be spending our anniversary together. I knew it wasn't going to happen. I would have to face our anniversary alone.

OUR 22ND WEDDING ANNIVERSARY was nearing. Clyde and I had always done something special for our anniversaries. In previous years we would spend weekends in Atlanta, enjoy a lovely dinner, and do some shopping together at the mall. We always had a wonderful time, but it wouldn't be the same this year. I would be alone. Instead of our wedding anniversary being filled with joy and happiness, it would be filled with sadness, somberness, and grief. I dreaded our special day with a passion.

One evening as soon as Alex Keith and I arrived home, we ate dinner and chatted. Alex Keith knew full well that our wedding anniversary was approaching. He didn't say much about it, but I knew he was thinking of it. By that time it was around 8:30 p.m. Soon after, Alex Keith got ready for bed and said good night and I went off to my room and closed the door.

I was glad that Alex Keith and I had had the chance to chat a little bit. Even though I really didn't feel much like talking, I did it anyway. I needed to make sure he was all right.

I picked up the remote from my bed, clicked on the television, threw myself on the middle of the bed and grabbed one of my pillows to bury my head in it. The tears began to flow, dripping down my cheeks. I knew I wouldn't have another anniversary with Clyde. I missed his love and conversation. It was more than I could handle that night. I didn't have the strength to face it alone. I knew by now that God was simply sick and tired of me crying. I was sick of me crying, too.

Our anniversary was only a few days away and I knew that I had to do something special. I knew that I wouldn't be going to work as I had already asked for the day off. I walked toward the bathroom vanity and looked in the mirror. I was a total wreck, pretty much beyond a total wreck. I took the wet washcloth and wiped my face gently.

From my bathroom window, I heard some children playing, possibly outside in the streets. There were many families with children in our neighborhood. I had noticed that Alex Keith hadn't done much playing with the neighborhood children lately, not since Clyde's death. I guess he didn't feel like playing the way I didn't feel like talking at work.

Then my ears began to listen to the sound of birds moving around in the bushes and trees. Life was going on even without Clyde, and as much as I wanted to stop and scream to let everyone know that Clyde had left me here, I knew it really didn't matter. Life would continue to go on.

I crawled into the bed and pulled the covers over my head. I wanted to shut out the world that night. I didn't want to think about anything. I wanted to close off my sad life, even from myself. But I did listen to the sounds of the night and I was comforted. Maybe I felt sorry for myself, I don't know. But for the moment I wanted to shut the world out of my thinking. I wanted to be left alone to deal with my pain. Our anniversary was fast approaching and I needed all the strength I could muster to get through our special day.

"Clyde, you should have tried harder to hold on," I said staring at his picture. "Why didn't you try harder to hold on for the heart transplant? I was coming to be with you and sit next to your side in the hospital. I was on my way…Lord, why couldn't You let him have a heart? Why couldn't You, Lord? Clyde was so close! He just needed Your help, that's all. He needed Your help that day.

"I wasn't there to help him, Lord. I should have been there with him. I should have," I said as I remembered that terrible morning when they called me to tell me that Clyde had passed out and they couldn't wake him. "Why couldn't You help him hang on a few more weeks, Lord? He tried to do the best to live right and…Why weren't You there for him when he needed You…Oh! Lord, Why couldn't You…Why did You let him slip into a coma? Lord, he never did wake up."

As I wiped the tears with my arm, I turned over onto my left side and pulled the covers from my face, hoping to catch something interesting on the television that would block my thoughts entirely. Unfortunately, there was nothing worthwhile to watch, so I turned it off and wrapped myself into a fetal position and floated off to a quiet sleep. That night had been a very low point for me. Our anniversary and the memories of hearing the ambulance had pushed me to an anxiety attack.

I awoke to beautiful melodies and wondrous morning sounds of birds chirping and singing near my window.

"God," I said, as I began to pray to start my day, "please forgive me for saying those things I said last night. I just felt bad. I hadn't felt that way before. And I do apologize to You."

I sighed deeply as I continued to pray: "I don't mean to be a problem. I am sorry...I know that I'm not the only person who's lost her husband, but I miss him very much. Please forgive me," I begged.

I continued to listen to the sounds outside my window. The dogs were barking—at what, I didn't know. Then I listened closely and heard a cricket; its sound was mesmerizing in my ears. I looked at the clock again and noticed it was almost 5:30 a.m. I lay quietly in my bed and closed my eyes to take in the coolness of the morning. I was very tired from yesterday. All I wanted to do was go back to sleep. I didn't want to think about anything. I wanted to have a blank mind, even if it was for a little while. My spot in the bed was warm to the touch and I didn't want to give it up.

I had been out of work several times but I was extremely worn out. It didn't take much to sway me to stay under my warm covers, so I pulled the covers back over my shoulders and lay down for a few more minutes before getting up to fix breakfast.

"I probably need to find a therapist, someone who knows about grief," I spoke out loud. "I'll do that when I get up sometime this morning—maybe I'll look in the yellow pages."

I didn't go to work that day. Instead of oatmeal, Alex Keith and I ate Rice Krispies for breakfast. I figured it was time for a change. I dropped off Alex Keith at Columbus State and drove back home. Once inside I closed the curtains in my bedroom and shut my eyes to the world. I didn't want a speck of light to invade the darkness. I stayed in bed all day and only left my room to get something to eat in the kitchen.

I watched *Good Morning America* so I could catch up on the news. As I listened closely I found the news was the same as yesterday—people killing each other, people stealing from each other, pretty much the same as before. It was a waste of human life and a waste of energy. My mind returned to thinking about our 22nd wedding anniversary.

I was going to write Clyde a poem to let him know how much I missed him. I got out of the bed and walked around to my closet to get stationery. I began with: "My darling, My Innisfree..."

I told Clyde how much I had missed him and would always celebrate our anniversary as a gesture of our beautiful life together. It would never, ever end. The words in the poem described beautifully our love for each other.

I typed the poem and planned to travel to the cemetery next week to read it to Clyde. I didn't tell anyone about my plans. It was my little secret and I preferred it that way.

⌒

The day passed quickly. I enjoyed being home alone. It was very therapeutic. The phone didn't ring and I was glad because I wouldn't have answered it anyway. I had completed a draft of the poem and I was very excited. I lay back on the bed again to make a few edits to the poem, and after a few modifications, the poem was now absolutely perfect. I knew Clyde would love it.

I had no problem sleeping during the day. It was the nights that bothered me most. I always kept the lights on in my room, the den, and the kitchen. I didn't like the darkness at all.

I pulled out my journal and began to write my thoughts. I had heard that writing in a journal was therapeutic, and I found it to be true. I still have my journal and I read it from time to time to reflect on my journey.

I picked up the Bible and turned to some of my favorite Scriptures. Lately I had been reading more, which was a good thing. I began at Colossians 3:1-4:

*If ye then be risen with Christ, seek those things
above, where Christ sitteth on the right hand of God.
Set your affection on things above, not on things
on the earth. For ye are dead, and your life is hid
with Christ in God. When Christ, who is our life shall
appear, then shall ye also appear with Him in glory.*

Then I read Isaiah 41:10:

*Fear thou not; for I am with thee: be not
dismayed; for I am thy God: I will strengthen
thee; yea, I will help thee; yea, I will uphold thee
with the right hand of My righteousness.*

These words were very comforting to me. I appreciated reading God's words, and even though I was a far cry from understanding my pain and loneliness, I knew that God was taking care of me and my children now. I was thankful to know that He was taking care of me and He had forgiven me for being angry at Him earlier for taking Clyde away from me.

"Clyde belonged to God," I said out loud without even knowing it. I could talk to God openly, and I did.

"Clyde, I know that you are in a better place," I said to him as I looked at his picture. "You don't have to feel any more pain. I know you were hurting all the time. I thank God that you aren't in anymore pain."

It was a beautiful day. Just me and the Lord. I continued to read Scripture and even meditate on it. I was happy that I rested on that beautiful, sunny day in August. Although I don't remember what day it was, I do remember that it was a very comforting day for me. I felt at peace.

Our Anniversary Day

August 10 arrived on the scene in royal colors. As much as I had dreaded the day arriving, I couldn't stop the hands of time from ticking. I knew I needed to face it and that it would take all I had in me, but I also knew that I could face the day with God's help. A Scripture that I'd quoted for many years played a major role in my dealing with our 22nd anniversary. I recited the Scripture numerous times during the first two years, trying desperately to come to terms with Clyde's death.

"I can do all things through Christ which strengtheneth me," I read in Philippians 4:13. I repeated the verse in my mind many times. I closed my eyes and sounded out each word. I knew without hesitation that I could do all things through Christ who gave me strength. He was the only one who could help me.

My emotions were erratic—drifting from sadness to anxiety and then anger again. I took a vacation day on that Thursday so I could drive down to Andersonville and place white roses on Clyde's grave. I wanted to read Clyde's poem to him and was looking forward to it.

"The flowers are beautiful," I said as I gazed toward the rustic, brownstone fireplace in the den. The fireplace was accented with a round, oak-mounted clock with large hands. It was coupled with two octagon-shaped mirrors stationed just to the right side of the fireplace. Centered above the fireplace was the last portrait we took as a family.

I closed my eyes in thanksgiving to Jesus Christ for allowing our family to take our last portrait together. I knew I would cherish the family picture forever and it would always hang above the mantle as an expression of our endless love as a family. Even though Clyde was extremely fatigued that day, he didn't appear to be so in the picture.

I decided to buy 22 white roses for our anniversary, which represented 22 years as husband and wife. White roses represented love and friendship. Since it was around 10:00 a.m., I knew I needed to get ready to leave. I dressed and was soon ready to travel. I made sure the roses were well watered before placing them on the passenger side of my car. I placed two jackets on each side of the flowers to keep the vase from tilting and spilling water in my car.

I was very anxious as I hurried out the door. I looked up at the sky and saw that the sun was beginning to peek from under the clouds. It was going to be a beautiful day. As I began to walk back around to my door, I thought about my stool.

I ran back, unlocked the door and rushed inside to grab it. I wanted to make sure I had towels to wipe Clyde's new headstone, which had arrived in July. As I walked back toward the car door, I decided to unlock the trunk to check and see if I had the plastic container with wash cloths and water to clean Clyde's grave. After a quick check, I was ready to go.

Heading to the Cemetery

I backed out of my driveway and headed for Andersonville. I didn't want to hear any music or anything. I wanted to hear only silence as I drove the 60 miles to the cemetery. I was consciously nervous. I knew I would be all right, but anxiety was forever present, mostly in my hands as I clutched the steering wheel tightly. I kept driving until I arrived in Buena Vista, Georgia, a rather small, quiet town.

Everything was quiet that day because most folks were at work. I quietly passed the service station and the dollar store on the right, just before passing the huge courthouse building to my left. It was relatively serene for most of the drive.

"Lord," I prayed. "Please help me to deal with what I'm about to do. I miss him and I know that you are tired of hearing me say it, but I need you in my life."

I sighed continually as I kept driving down the road. I didn't pay much attention to it. I wanted to get to the cemetery as quickly as possible, place Clyde's beautiful roses on his grave and sit and read to him our special love poem. *He would be tickled to hear me read it*, I thought.

It was a little breezy on that August morning. I pulled into the cemetery, drove around the cul de sac and parked alongside the old oak tree. I opened the trunk and pulled out the plastic container with the water and washcloth so I could clean Clyde's gravestone before placing the roses in front of his grave.

I walked around to the passenger side of my car, opened the door and reached down to pick up the clear vase of soft petal white roses. "They are absolutely gorgeous," I said to Clyde, "I know you like these. Aren't they pretty?"

Clyde had told me on several occasions that he wanted his flowers while he was alive so he could smell them. I bought Clyde flowers from time to time, and now I also wanted flowers to overshadow his grave.

I walked slowly to Clyde's grave as if two 20-pound weights were strapped around both feet. I approached his grave and placed the stool a few feet from it. I kneeled down on the stool and said a special prayer, thanking God for bringing me to Andersonville safely.

I talked to Clyde as I cleaned the grass off his grave. Except for a few sprouts of grass, his grave was still neat and clean, just as I'd left it a few weeks ago. The anxiety soon gave way to peace and calmness as I wiped down his brand new headstone. I had requested special words to be inscribed on Clyde's headstone: *Beloved Husband and Loving Father.* As long as I was alive, I vowed to take care of it and keep lovely flowers on his grave.

As I continued to clean off his gravesite, I looked into the blue sky and felt the uniqueness of God's wondrous love and devotion for His children. I was thankful to Him for blessing our family, and though Clyde wasn't with us physically, I knew he was with us in spirit.

As I read Clyde's poem to him I felt very proud. I folded it neatly and buried it deep in the ground, piling extra dirt over the poem to ensure it wouldn't wash away with the rain. I laid my head down on my knees and cried. I would be spending the rest of my life without Clyde physically in my life. The thought of having to relive this reality for future anniversaries overpowered my soul.

I took my Bible and turned to read Clyde's favorite Scripture. The tears flowed on the pages of my Bible as I read Psalm 24.

The earth is the Lord's and the fullness thereof; the world, and they that dwell therein. For He hath founded it upon the seas, and established it upon the floods. Who shall ascend into the hill of the Lord? Or who shall stand in His Holy Place?

He that hath clean hands and a pure heart; who hath not lifted up his soul unto vanity, nor sworn deceitfully. He shall receive the blessing from the Lord, and righteousness from the God of His salvation.

This is the generation of them that seek Him that seek Thy face, O Jacob. Selah. Lift up your heads, O ye gates; and be ye lift up, ye everlasting doors; and the King of glory shall come in.

Who is this King of glory? The Lord strong and mighty, the Lord mighty in battle. Lift up your heads, O ye gates; even lift them up, ye everlasting doors; and the King of glory shall come in.

Who is this King of glory? The Lord of hosts, He is the King of glory. Selah.

I turned a couple of pages over and read the last verse of Psalm 27.

*Wait on the Lord: be of good courage, and He shall
strengthen thine heart: Wait, I say on the Lord.*

I closed my Bible and placed my hands over it. I looked
around at the trees as the leaves danced in the midst of the
golden, noon sun as I sat on the stool. I closed my eyes and began
to concentrate on the quiet sounds in the cemetery. I heard the
birds and the sound of the wind rattling the leaves on the old
oak tree near Clyde's grave. I listened to the birds sing their
relaxing melodies in the park and I knew I would have to learn
day by day to live with the realities of death. It wasn't going to
be easy, I knew, but it wasn't going anywhere. Death was here
to stay. I had to learn to deal with Clyde's death. I would travail
in my pain for many years to come, but I always kept trying to
find my way back.

I didn't know when, but I knew that God knew. Clyde had
been a very special force in my life for many years. We had
grown up together. We had done special, loving things together
and I was glad that I had known him in this life. I opened my
eyes and stood up from the stool and touched his headstone.
I caressed it gently and started to speak: "Happy anniversary,
Clyde. I will always love you with all my heart. Happy anniversary, my darling Clyde."

Time seemed to stand still for me that afternoon. I sat at his
grave for three hours and knew it would soon be time for me
to leave again. It was already 2:30 p.m. I looked around at the
thousands of graves, all aligned and decorated with the identical
faux granite headstones standing proud in the afternoon sun. It
was beautiful, but sad at the same time to see graves from one
end of the historic site to the other.

I laid my head down in my lap again and sobbed hysterically. I didn't want to leave the cemetery. I didn't want to leave
Clyde again. Each time I came I hated to leave him and it tore
my insides to shreds. Reluctantly, I began gathering my things

as I said my final goodbyes to Clyde. I would visit him many times after and would always bring him fresh-cut flowers, mostly roses.

"Lord, please take care of him for me," I said. "You are the one who can do it now; I can't," I said as I walked back toward the car. "Clyde, I'll see you the next time. Take care. I love you. Happy anniversary."

I placed the stool in the trunk and climbed into the car. I looked back one more time before I drove off slowly. I was thankful and proud that God had given me the strength to come and sit with Clyde for a while. As I drove back home, traveling through Ellaville, Buena Vista and finally into Columbus, I thanked Him for carrying me home.

Driving Back to Columbus

I arrived home around 4:30 p.m., in time to pick up Alex Keith from school. Alex Keith told me about his day's event and I told him about visiting his father at the cemetery for our 22nd wedding anniversary. Alex Keith didn't say much. I knew he was thinking about his daddy, but he never said much. Everyone experiences grief differently. I continued to pray that one day Alex Keith would be able to talk about his father, and for both Alex Keith and Clyde Daryl to go on with their lives.

We finally arrived home and ate dinner together. I checked Alex Keith's homework and we both decided to retire earlier than usual that evening. I was extremely exhausted from the day's events. I perched on my pillow and recounted Clyde's poem in my mind.

"Thank you Lord," I said, "For letting me spend today with Clyde and read his poem to him. I will always appreciate You for it."

Out of the blue, I heard a sound coming from the bathroom window. It sounded like something was scratching on the screen, maybe trying to break into the bathroom window. My heart froze with panic. I wasn't sure if someone was trying to get into my window or something was rubbing against it. I only knew that the sound was real and it was growing louder. I arose from the bed, grabbed Alex Keith's baseball bat next to my bed, and placed it in my left hand. I walked slowly toward the bathroom, pushing the door open while holding the baseball bat close to my side. I wanted to make sure I had enough room to raise the bat and swing hard to knock the daylight out of whatever was there.

I walked closer to the window, and as I pulled the bathroom door toward me, something hit the window from outside and nearly scared me to death.

"Wow!" I screamed, not knowing what had happened. As I looked through the window with the help of a full moon, I saw a black cat prancing left to right through our backyard. I could easily see that the cat was scared out of its wits. Alex Keith came rushing in yelling, "What's wrong? What's wrong, Mom?"

"That stupid cat!" I said, holding my chest in fear. "That cat almost scared me to death! Get away from here and don't come back," I yelled through my window as the cat scurried through the cedar bushes.

"I'm okay, Alex Keith," calming myself. "It was a black cat. That's all. You can go back to bed, son. I'm fine. Good night," I said reassuring him. But that cat had scared me stiff. I looked down at my hands and they were still shaking. I sat down on the commode for a few minutes to regain my composure. I finally calmed down after 15 minutes. I had had enough drama for one night. I smiled as I crawled into the bed. It had scared me, but I was still smiling, almost laughing at the experience. It felt good to laugh again. I said my prayers and to my wonderful surprise, I slept through the night and enjoyed a blissful sleep until around 5:00 the next morning.

"I slept through the night, Lord Jesus!" I said. You would have thought I had won a million dollars.

I was in perfect peace. I was at peace for a moment in time. I knew God was taking care of my children and me. My emotions would run rampant and I knew at any moment I would dive into another depressing time. It was a matter of time and I knew it. But I was very thankful to Him for watching over me and keeping our family safe.

I walked into the kitchen to get some fresh water and returned to check on Alex Keith. He was sound asleep and five hundred Sherman tanks couldn't wake him. Alex Keith slept hard. It was quiet at 5:00 in the morning. With the exception of a few birds chirping in the distance, dogs barking and cats meowing, as well as a few car engines revving up to leave for work, everything was pretty quiet. I crawled back into my bed and looked at the ceiling. I knew I probably wouldn't go back to sleep, but it didn't matter. I was absolutely delighted that I was able to sleep all night.

I enjoyed a very nice day at work. My close friends could even tell I was more at ease that morning. I had survived our 22nd wedding anniversary, and for me it was a major triumph.

Alex Keith and I arrived home around 7:30 that evening. Instead of eating at home, I decided to take Alex Keith out to dinner. We hadn't eaten out in a while and I knew he would enjoy it. Whenever we ate out at Morrison's Cafeteria, Alex Keith would always order chopped steak, macaroni and cheese, and green beans. It was his favorite treat. His second favorite was fried shrimp.

"How are you feeling today, Alex Keith?" I asked him as we sat and dined together. "How well did you do on your math test?"

"I did okay, Mom," he said. "We didn't have too many problems. The teacher just gave us about five, but I did well. She wrote them on the board," he said proudly.

I was happy he was having good days. I had hoped he would do well in the math classes.

"I'm glad you had a great day. I had a pretty good day myself, Alex Keith," I replied to him, smiling.

Alex Keith and I chatted and enjoyed each other's company at the restaurant. It had been a different evening. We had done something totally different and it felt really good. I felt alive. I felt I could make it. I felt good inside and though I missed Clyde very much, I was very thankful to be alive.

August 11, 1995, had been a very pleasant day for me. It had been a very long time since I had felt okay. I watched television and turned to a *National Geographic Special* about snakes, which grabbed my attention immediately. I had always been fascinated with reptiles, especially snakes. Clyde and I had fun watching snake shows together.

It felt good to feel okay and not be crying at the drop of a hat. I was smiling, laughing and concentrating on a television show for the first time in a long time, and it felt good.

"It has been a long time since I laughed, hasn't it?" I asked myself rhetorically. Several months had passed since we buried Clyde and most days the tears were relentless.

I thanked God for a wonderful day and said my prayers to Him. "You think, Lord that I could have two days in a row of a good night's sleep? You reckon?" I asked rather musingly. I was happy I had been able to sleep the previous night. Sleep was priceless, simply a precious jewel to me.

I finished saying my prayers, placed the television on mute, and turned over in the bed, hoping to drift into another deep sleep. It was a comfort to know that God was taking care of us as I drifted into deep sleep. I was sleeping in God's loving care.

Chapter Eleven

Endless Days and Nights

Grieving is a natural response when we lose someone to death. It's the common thread that binds us together as we lament the loss of a loved one. Over the next few months, I learned more about the various stages of the grieving process, and gleaned that there is no one formula for grief. Although everyone experiences grief differently, there are definitely some common characteristics such as feelings of loneliness, abandonment, despair, and physical pain that are universal to most grievers.

As I drove home from work on September 1, 1995, I sensed coolness in the air. The sun slowly cascaded into the shadows of the evening; autumn would soon be arriving. The fall of the year had always been a sad time for me. There was something mystical about the dying of the grass and leaves, and watching the squirrels gather their food for winter. It was a very special season in nature, the harvesting season.

I walked through my backyard looking at the shrubbery that lined the property and spotted a leaf falling from the oak tree. It glided down gently as if in weightless slow motion fighting desperately to hold onto life. The leaf settled lightly on the ground along with other dying leaves; it had come full circle.

It had completed its purpose on earth and now it was making room on the tree for newer leaves to begin their journey. It was the cycle of life and I saw it clearly that warm afternoon.

On a quiet Saturday morning, I was coming back from the grocery store. As I approached the intersection of Milgen and Miller roads to turn left, I spotted a man who resembled Clyde.

"Not again!" I said. "Not again!" I repeated without hesitation. I turned swiftly to my left as I saw the car speed by. The man's head did resemble Clyde's, but it wasn't him. This was the second time I thought I had seen Clyde. I wanted desperately to see him again.

Chest Pains

This incident was the final straw for me. It was time to take some action and seek professional help. The chest pains had continued to bother me, and they seemed to be getting worse. I didn't want to go to the doctor, but knew I needed to set an appointment. I didn't want to die and prayed I didn't have a disease of some kind. I wouldn't want Clyde Daryl and Alex Keith to lose their mother to death too.

"I'll go ahead and see a doctor; that's what I'll do," I said. "I really need to. This time I really will make the appointment."

Later that evening, I decided to look in the telephone book to locate a therapist. Seeing a therapist was very new for me and I really didn't know what to expect. All I knew was that I was in desperate need for help and needed it quickly. I looked under "psychotherapist" in the *Yellow Pages* and found a name.

But first I had to make sure that I was physically fit. I was concerned about my health, as I was experiencing extreme chest pains. The chest pains had given me a scare several times before, so I knew I had better check them out. Sometimes my heart had palpitated as if it was going to burst through my chest. All I could do was lie still and hope that the pain would stop. It would go away, but always seemed to find its way back home. I recalled the time when I felt a stabbing pain situated in the middle of my chest while driving to work one morning. I placed my hand on my chest and rubbed it vigorously, hoping the pain would subside, and thank goodness it did. I didn't tell the children about my chest pains. Clyde Daryl and Alex Keith had lost their father and I certainly didn't want them to worry about me.

Near the end of September, my doctor gave me a physical and assured me my heart was okay. She sat me down and explained that I was suffering from depression, I was grief-stricken and the stress of dealing with Clyde's death was affecting me physically as well as psychologically. She prescribed medications to help me sleep better. She also suggested I purchase multivitamins and mineral supplements to enhance my overall physical well-being.

I was very grateful to her and felt somewhat assured after listening to her explanation about my chest pains. The cardiologist told me that grief can be very stressful on the body, even debilitating. I was determined to fight grief, and within days of seeing my cardiologist I made an appointment for the first Thursday in October to see a grief therapist.

It's Time for Grief Therapy

Ms. Thelma Arrington was very nice, caring and kind. I don't know how I was able to find Ms. Arrington, but she was exactly the kind of person I needed in my life to help me come to terms with my grief. I prayed to God she would be able to help me. I desperately wanted the therapy to work.

I would be seeing her in about a week and knew I would be very nervous about going to her office for the first time. I hoped she didn't think I was crazy or something.

I remember walking into Ms. Arrington's office and telling the receptionist my name. She smiled and told me to have a seat on the sofa and that Ms. Arrington would be with me soon. I don't remember the color of the sofa or the paintings on the wall. I guess I was somewhat preoccupied about seeing a therapist, and all I could do was to wait in anticipation of seeing her.

The room was pleasantly inviting and comfortable. Nervously, I waited for about 20 minutes before I heard a door open and two ladies came out of the back room. One of the ladies said hello and the second lady said goodbye as she walked out the door.

"Hello. My name is Ms. Arrington," she said, extending her hand.

"Hi, I'm Deborah Slappey. I'm happy to meet you, Ms. Arrington," I replied nervously.

Ms. Arrington asked me to come with her and I obliged, following her into one of the rooms to the left of the reception area. I was very nervous and I'm sure she knew it.

Ms. Arrington made some small conversation and then came directly to the point. She took her pad out and began to ask me a series of questions. I instantly felt at ease with her. She had a very soothing effect on me. Instead of feeling nervous, I felt calm in her presence.

She asked about our children and what had happened to Clyde. As I began to speak, to my surprise, the words began to pour from my lips in a desperate tone. I saw the tears began to bubble in her eyes as I described Clyde's last few weeks at the Mayo Clinic. I could tell immediately she was passionately involved with her patients and she journeyed with me in my pain. She connected with me that afternoon.

I appreciated her being there at that very moment. She felt my pain and the torment I faced each day since Clyde had passed away. I talked about our two children, and told her how Clyde Daryl had returned to college and that I was very proud of him. I told her that Alex Keith was showing no evidence of grief, which concerned me.

Ms. Arrington listened very attentively and wrote notes on a yellow legal pad as I described my sleepless nights. I was very glad I'd found her. To this day, I hold her in very high esteem and have recommended her to other people over the years.

"Mrs. Slappey, you've gone through a lot with your husband, learning about his sickness and now dealing with his death. It's quite a bit to handle, and all of this happened within a five-month period. You're not going crazy. No, you're not," she said.

Ms. Arrington told me I was experiencing grieving episodes. She also told me that I had to work through my grief and that it wouldn't be easy, but she would help me work through it. Ms. Arrington described grief as work, and it was the first time that I'd heard anyone refer it that way.

Each person, she said, experiences grief at different stages, different ways. Some people grieve for months, some for years. There is no one formula for grieving and dealing with grief. I listened to her attentively as I didn't know that much about grief, only that I was grieving.

As I wrote in *I Feel Okay*, I had lost my grandfather, even some very close friends, but nothing as traumatizing as losing my best friend, my husband, to death.

My conversations with my therapist were very intimate. I shared everything with her. I remember talking to her about my teddy bears that I had purchased and placed in the middle of my bed, surrounded by four soft pillows for comfort. Up until Clyde's death I kept a couple of teddy bears in the living room, but that was about all. Lately, my teddy bears had become my source of comfort while lying down and they meant the world to me.

Ms. Arrington gave me an explanation for my newfound behavior. She said the cuddling was my connection with Clyde and I had transferred my need for belongingness and my loneliness to my teddy bears. It made sense to me and I had no reason to doubt her explanation. I was relieved I wasn't going crazy.

"Mrs. Slappey," she asked, "are you angry at Clyde for leaving you here alone?"

"Yes," I responded quickly to her. "I know Clyde couldn't help he died and if he had the strength he would have held on. I know that." I hesitated and added, "He was tired." The amyloidosis had become systemic throughout his body and he had weakened considerably at the end of his life.

"But I don't blame him anymore. At first, I was very angry with him for leaving me here. I wanted to take his place, I really did. But I know that God makes those decisions about who lives and who dies. As much as it hurts, I know that Clyde is in a better place. He was in serious pain most of the time. It doesn't seem fair that it had to happen to him, but it did. It happened to me, it happened to our kids, it happened to a brother and a brother-in-law, a cousin, a brother in Christ and a friend. No matter what I say, I still miss him terribly."

I remember her face as I did my best to answer her question and described Clyde's passing-out episodes. When I told her how I wanted frantically for him to open his eyes as they removed the breathing apparatus from his mouth, I saw the tears flow and I knew she had connected with my pain and agony. Ms. Arrington reminded me of the folks I met at the Mayo Clinic. I told her I wanted everyone to remember Clyde and not to ever forget him. I didn't want his memory to go trailing off in the sunset in five years.

I kept talking about our good times and how our family of four had enjoyed our family vacations together. I even told her about how the Slappey family saved "summer money" every year so we could travel to Panama City Beach or somewhere in north Georgia or a Florida beach. We dubbed our vacation money as 'summer money' and we had a ball spending it. I smiled, even giggled a time or two when I described the great family fun we had, spending four, sometimes five days enjoying the breathtaking sunsets, Ceylon blue skies, and ocean while on vacation. The kids absolutely loved our trips together, and even now Clyde Daryl and Alex Keith speak highly of our fun summer vacations together.

I described our family fun times as we played in the sand, scooping the sand under our feet and tossing it everywhere. We would wiggle the sand between our toes and play for hours before going in to shower and experience the delectable steaks at Angelos, an absolutely fabulous steakhouse in Panama City, Florida. It was a beautiful time for me as I reminisced about our wonderful trips together.

Our family would never, ever be the same and I didn't know what I was going to do without Clyde in our lives. I was lost without him. I had many questions, but no answers. I remember Ms Arrington saying that it was going to take time and that I couldn't push Clyde out of my mind in a puff. My world had changed forever, she said, and it would take time to heal. Life was more complicated than that.

Her words allayed my fears and I appreciated her calming nature. I didn't have to rush out and get rid of all of Clyde's clothing just because he was no longer with me, as some people suggested.

I kept talking, and I guess she wanted me to do so. I had held the pain inside for months. This was truly the first time I was able to sit down with someone and talk about the horror of losing Clyde and watching him breathe his last breath in the hospital room. It had been devastating.

I used every fiber of my being to keep going while Clyde was at the Mayo Clinic; I had no choice in the matter. But when Clyde died, I told her, I didn't know how to stop going until months after his death. I wanted to do everything right because I knew he would have wanted me to do so. I had placed such pressure on myself to make everything right that I began to fall apart at the seams, physically and mentally.

And my depression was exacerbated after I spoke to the nurse at the Mayo Clinic. I screamed in pain when the nurse told me that every patient had received a heart, that is, everyone except Clyde. He hadn't survived to receive a life-saving heart. I held my head down in despair. We had suffered extraordinarily as a family.

I told Ms. Arrington that I would have done anything for Clyde to ease his pain, even take his place. I was very upset with Clyde's local doctors, particularly the one who had treated him for years and had completely misdiagnosed him. It was a tragedy of unparalleled proportions. The doctor would take the responsibility of Clyde's death to his grave. Tears flowed as I continued to speak.

"Have you spoken with any of his doctors locally since April?" she asked me.

"No, I don't want to talk to them," I replied, staring straight ahead of me. "I don't want to even hear their names," I continued as my voice elevated with anger.

I told Ms. Arrington about the local doctor who had diagnosed Clyde with primary amyloidosis and told him that he was dying of an incurable disease with no family member present. He simply didn't care, I told her. We had been waiting all day to see the doctor. He didn't care, not for his patients; not for anyone! He was a callous man and what he'd done was absolutely unforgivable.

I could see the horror on her face as I described the doctor's actions. I told her everything. My pain bubbled to the surface as I confided in her. My words poured freely from my mouth.

I didn't spare much or hold back anything. I was angry, very angry. I didn't hold back one blink. I told her about one of the local doctors who initially had turned Clyde away because he didn't have time to add him to his precious schedule. They didn't have time to fool with him. One particular doctor in the clinic did listen to Clyde and worked him into his schedule. I would always remember the doctor who came to Clyde's rescue. He saw him, and because of his compassion, Clyde eventually traveled to the Mayo Clinic two months later.

I knew why Ms. Arrington had plenty of tissues in conspicuous places around her office. She was a grief therapist and she knew exactly what to expect. As I began to describe the doctor who told Clyde about his incurable disease, I saw by her face that it had "struck a cord" with her. Ms. Arrington identified with my pain that evening and I won't ever forget her.

She hung on to every word out of my mouth. She made me feel I mattered, Clyde mattered and someone was listening to me. I had missed having a conversation with an adult. Since Clyde had passed, I had limited conversations to close family, people at work and my sisters and brothers in Christ. I spoke with Mae often, as well as my sisters and brothers. I had missed having a conversation with Clyde when I arrived home from work. I had missed our long talks about politics.

Clyde and I had many wonderful and entertaining conversations over the years and I longed to have them back. I longed to see Clyde walk through the double doors in the den. Now, I found myself talking my heart out to a perfect stranger, even if she was a therapist. I told her that I prayed to God repeatedly for relief from my days and nights of despair. I also told her how much God meant to me and how he had soothed my anguish many times during the last few months. There was so much hurt in me. But I didn't know how much I was hurting until I began to share my feelings with Ms. Arrington.

I dreaded that my one hour-session would soon be over. I wanted to stay and talk with her for hours on end if I could. I knew she had other patients, and even though I wanted to keep talking with her I knew she needed to help other people as well.

I didn't tell anyone that I was having therapy. I was ashamed at first, so I kept it to myself. But I learned as time passed, it was okay to seek professional help. God always made sure that his children received what they needed to keep going in this world. For spiritual wants and needs, he gave us His Son and for our physical needs, he gave us physicians and therapists to help our minds and bodies heal.

I looked forward to my next session with Ms. Arrington. I couldn't wait to arrive the next week at her office again and sit in her comfortable sofa. Her office reminded me of a warm, cozy den. It was relaxing and conducive for therapy sessions.

Ms. Arrington asked me about our two children. She was very concerned about Alex Keith, I recall. I told her Alex Keith had turned 12 years old one week before Clyde passed out for the last time. Her facial expression ignited as I described my conversation with Alex Keith as we walked through St. Mary's Hospital in Rochester, Minnesota. I tried to explain to Alex Keith about his father's comatose condition. I told Alex Keith that his father was not getting better.

It was painful for me to say it, but I had held it in and now it was coming out in seas of despair. I wanted to tell it all to her. I wanted her to hear every sad story. When I talked about Clyde's local doctors she heard the anger in my voice once again, when I called their names. I experienced varied emotions during that time. I was angry, sad, and regretful. Many other feelings surfaced during my first two years of living with grief.

I had a plethora of feelings, and at times, I didn't know how to manage them. Different feelings would emerge; they would come and go, and I did my very best to hang on for dear life as I experienced a multitude of emotions.

I remember telling her about the time I was about to leave Clyde in Rochester, Minnesota, at the Kahler Hotel and how he pleaded for me to go and take care of Alex Keith. I felt good though when I told her I didn't leave Clyde that Sunday morning. I left a voicemail with my manager to inform her that I wouldn't be back in Columbus on Monday and would be staying with Clyde until physicians made a decision about adding him to the heart transplant list. I was very happy that I had stayed with Clyde. I was going to take care of him with everything that was in me. And when I told Clyde that I wouldn't be flying back to Columbus, he, too, felt relieved and we enjoyed the rest of our breakfast together in the hotel.

And then my smiles would turn to sadness again as I described to her another scene in the hospital. I told her about the time Clyde was at a hospital in Atlanta, Georgia, how he passed out on the bed after a phlebotomist irritated him while drawing blood.

There were many stories to tell, too many to tell at any one session; so many sad moments to share with her—but she listened anxiously. It would be months before I told Alex Keith and Clyde Daryl about my grief therapy.

Everyone will have to decide about seeking professional help during their time of grief. It is a decision that you should weigh carefully. Even though I didn't take any medication, such as anti-depressants, there is medication available that will help along the way. If I had to do it over again, I would opt for the medication. I know that seeking professional help was one of the best things I could have done for me and my family.

I had three individual sessions with her and during the third meeting she recommended I join one of her group sessions that was currently in progress. Initially, I felt very uneasy about talking about my personal life in front of strangers. Going to therapy had been a giant step for me, and now she wanted me to get in front of a group of people and talk to perfect strangers about my husband—no way. *Spill my guts in front of a crowd of people I don't even know. I don't think so.* One-on-one therapy was just fine with me. Eventually, though, I agreed to attend one group session, but if I didn't like it, I would return to my individual session. Of course, I never did.

My Second Therapy Session

One week later I arrived at Ms. Arrington's office. During my second visit, I gazed at her very nice wall color that danced with a soothing pastel peach color, accented with tiny square patterns on the ceiling. Ms. Arrington would always ask me how I was doing and ask if I had been dreaming about Clyde again. I told her about my recurring nightmares of falling down into Clyde's grave and fighting to climb out of it. She listened attentively and kept writing notes on her legal pad as I continued to describe the scenes.

"How do you feel when you slide back down into the grave with Clyde?" she asked.

"Well, I have mixed feelings, sort of," I said. "There's a part of me that wants to stay in the grave and there's another part of me where I'm overwhelmed to get out of the grave. I try my best to climb out of the grave, but as much as I attempt, I can't seem to climb out of it. In my dream I know I have to take care of Clyde Daryl and Alex Keith, so I must come back to them. Clyde would want me to do so."

Ms. Arrington didn't respond. She kept writing and listening to me. Time passed too quickly. Before I knew it, the hour session was over and it was time for me to leave. Sadly, Ms. Arrington walked me to the door and we said goodbye. I appreciated her time and as I walked out of the door, I looked up at the sun. The sun beamed bright against my face. It was warm, even though it would soon be going down. For a brief moment, and for the first time in a long time, I felt I would make it through my days of agony. I had needed someone to listen to my pain.

"God," I said to Him, "you've been trying to tell me this all the time that I will make it. But, Lord, I don't have the strength in me to utter the words. Please give me the strength to hold on...please," I pleaded.

Hopeful and grateful, I opened the door to my car. The effects of the wind gently bending the trees captured my attention. I climbed into my car and drove home. But as it always did, the pain of death soon found its way back into my heart. I was alone again, without Clyde, without the love of my life. And I felt very sad and worn.

Alex Keith Starts Middle School

I arrived home around 7:00 p.m. School had started and Alex Keith was no longer in elementary school. He was enjoying being in middle school. Alex Keith was tickled beyond reason about his newfound status—a pre-teenager!

Alex Keith had scored a homerun when he took the two math classes at Columbus College the past summer. I wanted him to take as much mathematics as possible. I'd seen the future of industry and I knew that society would have a need for computer specialists, engineers, and other science professionals, so the earlier he was exposed to math and science, the better he would be able to survive the ever-changing technological world.

As I look back on my assumptions some 12 years ago, I was truly in awe that my assumptions were dead on the mark. The country, even the world was in a constant flux to recruit computer and engineering professionals. As much as Alex Keith had enjoyed the continuing education classes, I knew he was even more thrilled to be returning to school.

On that rather brisk Thursday evening in late September, I was very contented with reviewing Alex Keith's homework. The homework assignments were stretching me a bit, to say the least.

I paid closer attention to his algebra assignments. When I was in school I had enjoyed algebra, so checking over his homework brought back fond memories. But my strongest suit was language arts and Clyde's was math. I knew I couldn't take his place, but I tried my best to check Alex Keith's homework the way I thought Clyde would have. As Clyde checked his boys' homework he always shared one of his tall tales with them. They enjoyed them very much. I didn't have a tall tale, but I could check Alex Keith's algebra homework. We had a few laughs as I checked his work, and it was refreshing.

As usual, Alex Keith took his bath around 9:00 p.m. and went to bed. Of one thing I could be sure, he always got his 10-plus hours of sleep every night. I was the one who didn't sleep much. Over the last few nights since the start of therapy I was sleeping better. Before retiring for the night, I walked into the den for a final check to make sure the screen door was locked. It had been a quiet autumn evening and even the birds weren't whistling in the trees.

I had been feeling rather triumphant over the last few days, but slowly the euphoria of the grief sessions were dissipating into shallowness as the darkness swallowed the daylight. I went ahead and took my bath and sat on the bed. Tonight, I only wanted to see the weather, but a good movie without someone crying or dying would be great too, I thought.

"I would love to find a John Candy movie!" I said. "Where are the John Candy movies when you need them?" I asked rhetorically. I flipped the channels, moving from channel to channel, hoping I would pinpoint something outrageous to watch on TV. I didn't want to think tonight. I didn't want to think about Clyde because I knew I would end up crying again. This was one night I wanted to laugh out loud to chase my pain away.

As I kept flipping through the channels I found *Hogan's Heroes*. Soon the night trapped the dusk of the evening and all that was left was the echoes of the night. I lay in my bed and listened to the sounds as each cast a shadow of a thought in my mind. *Hogan's Heroes* went off the air at 11:00 p.m. and I decided to lie across my bed and concentrate on sounds of the night.

Just outside my window, I was able to make out a frog. "Erp! Erp! Erp!" I heard it say. At least I thought it was a frog. Then I heard chirping, probably of several crickets. The chirping sounds were everywhere. I closed my eyes so I could clearly distinguish between the sounds of the night. And as I closed them, the chirping became much louder. Next, I heard the birds. I hadn't heard them sing all evening.

Next, I heard scratching on my window screen. At 11:00 at night, any scratching sound would get my attention. I stood up and walked toward my window, pulling back my curtain and shade. There in full view was a moth with its wings caught in my window screen. It was flapping its small wings and trying to escape from the tiny holes, but didn't seem to be doing so well. I knew I couldn't help him, so I let go of the curtain and walked back to the bed to settle down for the night.

It had been one of those rare, special nights and I knew I was blessed. I picked up one of my teddy bears from the bed and held it close to me as I finished watching an episode of *Beverly Hillbillies*. My smiles soon turned to laughter as I watched Jethro and Granny.

I thanked the Lord Jesus for a beautiful day and for letting me hear nature as I had that night. I checked the house over one more time. As I walked into the den, I looked down at the gold carpet and remembered how Clyde always loved to lie down on the floor and roll around with his boys.

Walking through the kitchen, I stared into the dining room. Everything was peaceful and quiet, all in its place. I walked toward the gold English style mirror in the dining room. It was as beautiful as the day Clyde and I hung it on the wall. He would always carry his 200-lb tool box; it weighed that much at least. He purchased every tool on the planet it seemed. He called it the jack-of-all-trades toolbox.

I kept staring at the well-hung mirror, still just as elegant as when we first hung it on the wall. I walked toward it and was rather surprised to see several wrinkles lining my face, eyes, and forehead. Over the past six months I had aged considerably from the stress of grief. My eyes were drawn back into my head and the folds between my eyebrows were deeply wrinkled.

I stared into the mirror and looked around at the furnishings in the living room. It was my favorite place to sit. I sat on the sofa and caressed it. It was a very beautiful paisley sofa with special highlights of olive green, maroon and black, and speckles of orchids dancing through the Victorian style couch. It had been a showcase of comfort, inviting a person to relax and to sit awhile.

As the months passed into years I would visit the living room at the hint of dusk and sit on the sofa and look through the double-pane windows in the front yard, hoping to spot a squirrel scurrying up and down a pine tree holding a nut in its little paws. It was a special time of day as I took quality time alone, sitting in the living room and enjoying a quiet evening. The house was filled with pleasant memories and I knew I would take my beautiful memories with me to my grave.

I looked at the Truetone stereo in the corner of the room. Clyde and I had purchased the stereo while living in Spartanburg, South Carolina in the 1970s. The stereo came standard with an 8-track system that was second to none back in the day. Clyde wanted to keep it just in case it became an antique. I still have that stereo today.

I smiled as I remembered him saying, "Debbie, we better hold on to this stereo. It really hasn't been touched at all. It might be worth something one day."

The window treatments were arranged with soft octagon-shaped panels of English Rose carnations captured and surrounded by beautiful green lily pads. The floral panels were highlighted on each side with virgin notes of English Rose damask fabric with a sprinkling of rayon blend.

It was a beautiful room and I was always touched by the peacefulness and serenity it evoked upon entry. I closed my eyes and began to pretend that Clyde was sitting next to me. He would sit down with me on the living room sofa and I would lie in his loving arms. We would talk very quietly for hours, hoping Clyde Daryl and Alex Keith wouldn't hear us. We always tried to steal a moment for the two of us.

It was a very special moment. And as I remembered lying in his arms, I began to lie back against the back of the sofa and froze that special moment in time in my mind. It was just Clyde and me. I didn't want the moment to flee. I wanted to hold onto it as long as I could. Even if it was my thoughts, I cherished the moment in memory.

"How I long, Lord, to be with my husband. How I long to touch his smiling face and hold him close to me. I only need to touch him…just to touch his smiling face, Lord. I just want to touch him and see if he is all right."

The tears ran down my face, and as much as I wanted to hold back from crying, I cried anyway. I pushed back the tears as I tried to fight my way back to my thoughts of Clyde sitting next to me. I wanted to go back. I wanted to stay in my mind and pretend he was near me. So I pulled one of the green chenille pillows from the sofa and rested my head against it, turning my thoughts once again to Clyde sitting next to me.

I began to smile as my mind found Clyde again. I had found him once again in the crevices of my safe place, my mind, and I wanted to drown in the circle of my memories as they hovered around me. I wasn't going to let him go this time. I enjoyed our time together as memories flooded into many special moments. It was all I had that night—my pillow, my thoughts, and my tears.

Part Three...
Learning to Live Again

Chapter Twelve

Working Through Grief

I was experiencing a multitude of emotions—sadness, anger, and depression—all mixed into one oversized soup bowl. My life was turned upside down and my foundation was shaken. I knew I needed to talk to someone and I thanked my Lord for giving me the strength to seek professional help from a grief therapist.

I was learning more about the effects that grief inflict on the body. I wanted to learn about my condition to help my sons, my family, myself, and maybe one day, others. It's what I needed to do.

GRIEF THERAPY WAS THE BEST THING for me. Up until then my life was routine: going to work, picking up Alex Keith from the college, going to church on Wednesday and Sunday, and going back home again. Once I returned home, I closed the door to the world. I didn't feel up to doing much of anything else, let alone work because I didn't have any energy.

When I first decided to go to grief therapy, I was extremely nervous because I didn't know what to expect. After about three visits, she recommended that I join her grief group. I'd never been a part of a group session, so you can imagine my nervousness.

"Lord, I pray that I'm able to attend the group therapy thing. I don't know what to expect, but please give me the strength to put one foot in front of the other and go on with it," I prayed. "Please help me with this."

I continued to pray to God in silence. I wanted to go, but I was very apprehensive about it. The things I was feeling—having teddy bears in my bed and choking pillows to death were so unlike me. I prayed that it was related to grief. I didn't want to lose myself; I needed peace and quiet, but I prayed I wasn't going crazy.

My first group therapy session would be held Thursday after work at 5:30 p.m. By Tuesday I was very nervous about it. I had embraced my first three weeks of individual sessions, but talking in a group setting was a scary thought. I didn't want others to see me weak and in pieces.

Ms. Arrington felt I would be fine and she told me it would be very good for me. "Just try it out for size," she said. "And if you don't like it, we'll go back to individual therapy," she continued.

"Debbie," I said. "The group session will be okay. It really will. You have nothing to fear. There will be many people in the room who have lost loved ones. They know what you are going through," I said, trying to reassure myself. "Ms. Arrington said that it would be good for me to listen and talk to other people who had lost spouses, children, and parents."

"It really will be okay," I said, trying to reassure myself.

Well, I decided to give it a try. I went to work that Tuesday morning in early October, hoping to push the thoughts of the group session out of my mind, at least for a time. I had begun to concentrate a little better at work and was very happy about that.

I still didn't talk much at work. I wanted to keep working as much as possible. Lately, I hadn't had an urge to rush out to the cemetery. I had only experienced it a couple of times during the first few months, but I was now trying to wait until the weekend to drive down and spend some time with Clyde.

I continued to work on my bulletins and manuals, and the next thing I knew it was 5:00 p.m. My day at work had passed quickly. I was glad to know it was time to leave the office. Before going home, I stopped by the grocery story to get some items for dinner for the next day. I had called Alex Keith to let him know I would be stopping by the store and if he needed anything, I would pick it up. As always, Alex Keith wanted something sweet.

I knew I would eventually get Alex Keith into therapy, but I felt I needed to get myself emotionally situated first and then have Ms. Arrington recommend someone for Alex Keith. He seemed to be doing well, but I knew deep down he had pushed away his feelings about his father. Whenever I brought up the subject about Clyde's passing, Alex Keith would quickly change the subject and tell me that he was going outside to play or to play with his electronics toys. Alex Keith simply didn't want to talk about his father's death, and I knew this was not a good thing. Eventually, he would need to talk about his feelings that were buried deep down.

I arrived at home around 6:45 p.m. I prepared baked chicken, green beans, and mashed potatoes for dinner. Brother Clayton had called to check on us. He did so often and I appreciated it very much. Brother and Sister Clayton always made sure we were doing well.

I was thankful to Brother Allen, an elder of the Church of Christ, for inviting Alex Keith and me to attend the renowned Tuskegee-Morehouse Game in October. I remember it well. I was very grateful to him and was looking forward to going somewhere other than work and church. It was very ironic that Clyde and I had lived in Columbus since 1988, but we hadn't attended the big game, as many called it. Clyde and I had planned to attend many times, but never did. I remember one time when Clyde and I came very close to attending the game, but unfortunately, he was summoned to work, so we didn't attend.

Alex Keith and I didn't go to many social activities outside church and school, so I thought that attending the weekend football game would be a welcome diversion for both of us.

Group Therapy Begins

Thursday arrived and I was more than anxious. You might say that I was borderline hysterical at work as I waited in anticipation for group therapy. The therapy session was in the same building as my previous counseling, so I knew exactly where to go. I didn't know if I would be comfortable talking to strangers about my personal thoughts, but I was very curious to see what actually happened in a group.

I walked into the building and the receptionist greeted me. She motioned me to go to the room that was in the far back corner, a few more steps down the hall from where Ms. Arrington and I had met. I walked into the room and saw a circular cluster of chairs in the middle of the room. I knew that was Ms. Arrington's doing.

"Wow!" I said silently, "I'll have to face these folks and I don't even know them!"

Shyly, I looked down at the carpet as I walked toward the middle of the room. When I walked in I saw only three other people sitting in the room, a white man and two women—one black, one white. My therapist introduced me to them and they were very cordial. I'm sure they could tell I was nervous, but they seemed to be at ease. Ms. Arrington pointed me to a chair to sit, but I declined and chose to sit in the far center chair across from the door. That way, I surmised, I would be able to see everyone in the group easily.

I didn't mind listening, but talking was simply out of the question. Ms. Arrington had already told me to listen, and I was more than content to do just that. I watched people come in one by one, and the only word that I could utter was "hello." Soon the chairs were all taken and Ms. Arrington was ready to start the session. I waited with nervous anticipation.

Ms. Arrington welcomed everyone to the session. And without batting her eyes, she turned to me and asked me to introduce myself to the group. I hadn't planned on saying a word other than hello, but her eyes prompted me to say something. I began to introduce myself with a very noticeable nervous quiver in my voice.

"Hello everyone," I said, clearing my throat. "My name is Deborah Slappey. I...ah...I lost my husband, Clyde Slappey, a few months ago. It was in April."

That's all I could say, and thank goodness Ms. Arrington rescued me from having to say more. I wasn't ready just yet. She told everyone I had lost my husband to a very rare disease and that he was very young when he died.

Ms. Arrington then turned to one of the ladies in the group and asked, "Don't you want to talk tonight, Jane?"

Jane nodded her head and began to speak. As I listened to her words, horror and an avalanche of empathy flooded my soul for Jane and her family. Jane was only 34 years old when it happened. Her husband, 36, had been admitted into the hospital for a seemingly routine procedure, but complications developed after the surgery. She said they had two young boys.

Even to the doctor's surprise, Jane's husband died a few days later. She told us her husband didn't have a will. Since they were very young they didn't think it was a big deal not to have a will. Jane described the horrific reality of dealing with the Probate Court with no will. *I'm very familiar with the Probate Court*, I thought silently. According to the courts she had no claim on the assets. Jane had to bid on her own property, along with everyone else at the estate auction because nothing was in her name. I was horrified by her story.

I was blessed that Clyde and I planned ahead in the event one of us died. We had made the tough decisions early in our marriage to write a will and hoped we would never have to face it, but unfortunately we had. Jane continued to describe her ordeal and how she coped with losing her husband. She began to cry and we all cried with her.

Ms. Arrington broke through the silence when she turned to a male member of the group and asked, "Don't you have something to share with us tonight?" I didn't hear his name because I was totally consumed in Jane's words.

At first the man began to speak in a whispered voice. He described his wife of 20 years who had been gravely ill suffering from cancer. He said his wife's last seven months had been excruciatingly painful for both of them as he watched her suffer helplessly. No one could help her. The cancer had metastasized and the only solace she experienced was lying on the living room sofa for respite. She slept on the sofa until her death. Since then, he told us, he had been unable to walk into the room where she died.

He dropped his head and the room became deathly silent. The man wanted his wife back, but she wasn't going to return. Clyde wasn't ever going to return to me either. I knew exactly what he was feeling. It was pure unadulterated pain and there was nothing either of us could do to change the fact that our spouses had died and their footprints were no more on the earth. I began to cry for him and myself. I had been trying to understand death, even make sense out of it, but there is no such thing as making sense out of death. Death was death and there was nothing we could do about it. I guess that is what I had been trying to do for months.

I won't ever forget Jane and the man who shared his story with us. I'm sure others had heard it before, but it was my first time and it imprinted an indelible mark in my mind after hearing their painful ordeals. When the 90-minute session ended I was surprised that the time had passed so quickly. I was touched by everyone's honesty with expressing their innermost feelings to others without a thought. This was very remarkable to me.

"I could never do that, Lord!" I said very emphatically as I was driving home. "How do they talk in front of strangers like that? I don't want everyone to know about my business! I can't do something like that!

"I admire them for having the guts to speak about their loved ones that way, but that's not for me. I don't feel comfortable speaking in front of strangers about my deepest feelings. It's not for me," I said shaking my head. "It's not for me."

Ms. Arrington scheduled another group session for the next Thursday. I knew I had to come up with something so I wouldn't have to be there. The one-on-one session was okay, but I wasn't comfortable with the group thing.

I didn't have much of a social life because I refused to go anywhere alone. I couldn't fathom the thought of going to the movies without Clyde. I really didn't have the energy to do much else but go to work, church and now therapy. I didn't know at the time, but I was suffering from depression and my therapist was creating a group environment where eventually I would feel comfortable talking about my loss and sharing it with others who were dealing with the same thing. I learned later that the best therapy for grief is talking about it. I made progress in my group grief sessions.

As I lay down for the night my mind drifted to Jane's words about her husband. You never know where death is. Her husband went into the hospital for a routine procedure and died.

"You know, she is in worse shape than I am, Lord," I surmised. "She doesn't even have the financial means to take care of her own family because everything was in her husband's name; not both, as it should have been. I'm sad for her and the children."

I was thankful to Clyde that we had planned for unforeseen events. We had our home and cars in both of our names with Rights of Survivorship. I was in much better shape than that lady. I was thankful to God for helping me to be okay financially, at least for the time being. Jane had no money and couldn't get her hands on their assets initially because everything was in her husband's name. Thankfully, she was able to retain her home and vehicle, but it was a weird situation for her and the family. The law was very black and white when it came to death and taxes.

I remembered her words at the session: "A word of advice," Jane said to everyone. "Have a will. It's the safest thing you will ever do to protect your loved ones."

I thought I had it bad until I listened to those two people earlier in the evening. I prayed for Jane and the man before going to bed. I saw the pain in their eyes and heard it in their voices. For the first time, I was praying for someone else's pain and not just mine.

"Lord," I prayed, "Please help Jane and the man. They are both in worse shape than I am. I feel their raging storm of sorrow and despair. They're hurting inside, really hurting. Please help them find their way. Please Lord, help that lady. She's so young to lose her husband. Please help her children. They must be devastated. Lord, please help Jane with her situation.

"And please help that man, too," I continued. "I don't know his name, but you do. His pain is amplified. His tears—he's in so much pain. Please help him find his way back."

After I prayed, I lay back on my bed and picked up my Bible to read, but couldn't. I couldn't concentrate or make out the words because they were blurry.

Around 11:30 p.m., I lowered the television volume to say my prayers and hopefully fall asleep. I yearned for my life back.

"Lord, I just want my life back," I prayed. "I want to be normal again. I want to smile and laugh at Clyde's jokes. I want our family to all be sitting at the dinner table with Clyde telling one of his favorite stories. Clyde Daryl would talk about his classes and how well he was doing in college and Alex Keith would talk about his fun times at the baseball game. I miss my family being together; laughing and talking together. I miss it and I want it back."

I took my sleeping gown and wiped away the tears, puffed up my pillows and took the television remote to switch the channel from the Weather Channel to anything but weather. *Anything but weather tonight,* I screamed inside. I flipped through the channels, hoping to find some show that would make me smile and laugh. I yearned for something to make me forget. I kept flipping through the channels and to my surprise located an old *Green Acres* rerun, starring Eddie Albert and Eva Gabor. I remembered how everyone on the show was funny, the whole town, and the pig was truly the best of the characters.

I watched every minute of the show until after midnight. It felt good to laugh at the crazy old pig. I laughed out loud a time or two, and it felt good. I was thankful for *Green Acres* that night. Even though it lasted only 30 minutes, *Green Acres* was my dose of medicine to drift into wonderful sleep. I finished praying to God, pulled the covers close to my neck, and thanked my Lord for giving me the strength to make it through another day. Before I knew what was happening, I slowly drifted into tranquil sleep.

The next morning was Friday and I heard the clock sound off at 6:30 a.m. Slowly, I pulled myself from the bed and walked into the kitchen to fix oatmeal and coffee. Within an hour or so, Alex Keith was walking outside to the bus stop and I was getting ready for work. I didn't say much to Alex Keith that Friday morning except good morning and hello, listen to your teacher, and do your work. I was excited about the Saturday evening football game which was scheduled to start at 6:00 p.m. *Alex Keith and I will arrive about an hour earlier so we can get good seats,* I thought.

Then my thoughts returned to the group session. I remained in deep thought as the group session echoed in my mind.

"I just don't know, Lord," I said. "It's so tragic. She lost her husband in a moment. He was admitted to the hospital for a routine surgical procedure and he died from complications. Just how do you deal with something like that?

"I knew full well about Clyde's prognosis. I knew what the doctor had told us. I knew it could happen anytime. And I had hoped it wouldn't happen, but it did. But she had no idea." I kept thinking about Jane throughout the work day.

As I completed my assignments, my thoughts raced back and forth as I listened to Jane's story in my mind. I remembered her tears and felt her pain. I dropped the pen down on the steno pad and closed my eyes in despair as I replayed Jane's tragic story in my mind. She would miss her husband forever. Then I felt my own pain of missing Clyde. I laid my head down on my desk for a few minutes. And for those five minutes or so, the pain of losing our mates connected.

At the end of the day, instead of going directly home I decided to do something very different. I traveled to the Parisians store. It felt very odd as I pulled into the parking lot because I hadn't shopped in a long time. While Clyde had been sick I only bought clothing to wear for our trips to Rochester, Minnesota, to soften the wintry mixes of snow and ice and the fierce cold, cold air.

I was barely able to open one of the heavy metal glass doors at the side entrances to Parisians. Thankfully, a gentleman approached the door as I was fighting to open it and he let me in.

I could sense autumn had arrived. The air was cool and crisp as I felt the gentle breeze dance against my face with a tender touch. As I walked into the store, my eyes were mesmerized by the beautiful soft earth tones of browns, creams, oranges, and soft corals of blouses, jackets, and sweaters on display. I was amazed that people had started wearing white and creams beyond September, practically year round now.

Once inside, my automatic pilot switch activated, leading me directly to the shoe department. Even as a teenager, I adored shoes, but I didn't have the money to buy them. I remember my mother taking my sisters and me to Kress Department Store to buy our Easter shoes. Mae made sure we all had shoes to complement our Easter outfits. It was a very fun time in my life. All I wanted to do was peruse the shoe styles for the season and if I found a pair, I would buy the shoe in several colors.

I picked up a beautiful navy blue sling back with a stunning three-inch heel. I kept browsing and trying on shoes for almost an hour, and I was enjoying myself immensely. I wanted to do something else besides go to work and home, and I did. I wanted to break my routine. I tried on a dozen pairs of shoes, but nothing fitted my feet. After about an hour or so I didn't see any shoes I liked, so I moved to another passion of mine—handbags. Shoes and handbags were my thing. If I couldn't find shoes, I could usually locate a handbag to satisfy my wants.

As I admired the store displays, I looked at every handbag in the store, but not one struck my fancy. And it was okay because I had accomplished what I'd set out to do. I had changed my routine, and it felt good. It felt more than good; it was more like chocolate cake dripping with semi-sweet chocolate syrup. I walked over to the fragrance section and was delighted with the enchanting aroma of potpourri sprinkled nonchalantly around the display cases. "Thank you so much, God," I said under my breath. "I appreciate you giving me the strength to shop today."

I walked around to the lingerie section and browsed through the racks of beautiful gowns and sleepwear delicately wrapped around the display hangers. Everything was precious, soft, and silky. I pulled a soft, flannel gown next to my face and imagined sniffing the enchanting aroma of fresh plucked roses embroidered on the front of the gown. I admired the embroidery. It was well stitched and added a sense of purity to the gown's fascia, so I bought it.

I also purchased underwear and a soft pastel pink short gown with highlights of pink and blue carnations in the front sewn just above the bodice. With my bag in hand, I walked proudly out of the store. I felt as if I had triumphed over Goliath. It was the first time in a very long time I felt special, walking into a store and buying something for a change. I felt extraordinarily empowered that I had accomplished something big.

I opened my car door and slung the packages on the front passenger side. As I drove home, I looked into my mirror and was overwhelmed by a breathtaking, stunning sunset. At 6:30 p.m., the sun appeared to sink into the sky leaving a trail of orange-scotched hues of yellows, reds, and streaks of apricots against the outer parameters of a cloudless blue sky. The scene was beyond breath taking. I can only describe it as infinite beauty from God's holy place.

I arrived home around 7:00 p.m. Alex Keith was in his room playing his games. As I walked in, I had a smile on my face and Alex Keith easily spotted it as I walked into his room.

"Hi, Mom!" he said. "How are you doing today?"

"I'm fine Alex Keith. I just stopped by the store to grab a few things," I replied with a smile larger than life.

I didn't want him to know I was beyond joy after shopping. But I was beside myself.

"How did you do today, Alex Keith?" I asked.

"Just fine, Mom. I made an A on my homework assignment. The teacher told me I was doing good with my lab journal, too."

"Well, I'm glad, son. You have been working very hard on that assignment. Just keep up the good work and you'll be fine."

I changed clothes and tried on my new lace-trimmed gown. It was a perfect fit. *I needed another gown anyway*, I thought silently. My other sleepers had worn. I wrapped my robe over my gown and walked into Alex Keith's room.

Alex Keith was a very intelligent young man. He was very good with mathematics and was now taking pre-algebra and catching on quite well.

"You certainly got your math skills from your daddy, because you didn't get it from me," I complimented him. "Your daddy was the math whiz, not me."

Alex Keith's face lit up when I said that.

"Yeah, Dad sure was pretty good with math, wasn't he," he replied with a huge grin on his face.

"Your dad was very smart with figures. He was always calculating something on a notepad, going back and forth and double checking his figures," I added.

Then the conversation turned silent. I knew Alex Keith was thinking about our good times together as a family, and so was I. I couldn't say much else after that. I dropped the subject and started talking about something else.

"So, have you gone to the planetarium yet?" I asked him, hoping to switch the subject.

"No, not yet, Mom. Our teacher said that we would be going in a few weeks. I'm really looking forward to seeing the inside," he said, hesitating for a bit. "Mom, you remember when we all went to the planetarium? Everything was very dark and you couldn't see your hands in front of you. Now that was dark, but it was cool," Alex Keith grinned, remembering our visit years before.

"Yes, I do remember that night. It's been a long time. You have a good memory! I forgot about that time we all went together. You were rather small, but you still remember that time.

"Time passes by quickly, doesn't it?" I added.

"Well, I've finished checking your homework. You better get ready for bed. Have a good night, son."

My eyes popped open widely and immediately I stared at the clock. It was 3:00 in the morning again. My pain cried out that early morning. I had been feeling very strong; I had it together, I thought.

"Did I have a dream? Did I dream about Clyde? Is that why I'm feeling the way I do?" I asked.

But as I tried to remember, no memory of a dream surfaced in my mind. Yet I felt like crying, crying hard inside. I thought I was doing better. I really thought I was, but here I was in the middle of the morning awake once again.

"What happened, Lord?" I asked as the tears rolled down my cheeks. "I thought I was doing okay. I'm going to therapy. Why am I feeling this way? What happened? What happened? I was doing so well.

"Lord, will the pain ever go away? Will it ever leave me alone? I'm so tired, Lord, of the pain, the agony. Please take the anxiety away," I begged.

I knew I wouldn't be going back to sleep, so I grabbed my journal from underneath the mattress and began to write my thoughts. I kept trying to understand the intense anxiety that stirred my soul and I finally remembered that I had been dreaming about Clyde.

In my dreams we were happy, sitting in our den enjoying the ambiance of the beautiful fire. The boys were sitting in front of the fireplace and Clyde and I were sitting comfortably on the sofa. Clyde had his arm around me and I felt the warmth of his love protecting me from the outside world. Everyone was doing well and I was happy. My dream of having a loving and caring family had come true. God had blessed me with a wonderful family, a dream I had described in my 1972 *Senior Moments* while in high school. I thanked God because I knew it was all his doing.

Then I drifted into another scene. Clyde Daryl and Alex Keith were sitting in front of the fireplace and I was sitting on the sofa, but Clyde was no longer sitting next to me. I looked around for him and even called out his name, but there was no answer. I stood and walked into the kitchen, calling, "Clyde! Where are you, darling? What are you doing? Please come back and sit down. The fire is warm and spectacular. It's so peaceful. Please come back and sit down with us!" I cried out in desperation.

But Clyde didn't answer. I walked into the dining room and Clyde was nowhere to be found. I walked into the living room, the foyer, calling for him. Next, I walked down the hall, brushing my feet against the golden beige carpet.

"Clyde!" I yelled. "Where are you my love? Where are you, sweetheart? Come back so we can enjoy the rest of the fire. It's beautiful."

The door to our bedroom was closed. I opened the door very slowly and drew my head through the very tiny crack of the door.

"Clyde," I whispered softly. "Where are you, sweetheart? I'm here. I need to be with you!"

I was finally able to get my head through the door, but I didn't see him. He was nowhere in sight. I opened the door and entered slowly into our bedroom.

"Clyde!" I called out. "Where are you? We are all waiting for you. Where are you, darling?"

I walked around our queen-sized bed, hoping maybe to see Clyde in the bathroom shaving. I saw the light on in the bathroom.

"That's where he is," I said. "He's in the bathroom!"

As I walked closer to the door, I reached out my hand to knock on the door.

"Clyde, we're waiting for you, sweetheart," I said. "The fire is divine. Come back so we can enjoy the fire together."

Clyde didn't say a word, so I knocked on the door again. And still silence.

"Clyde, are you okay?" I asked. "Are you okay in there?"

I opened the door slowly, and because our bathroom door swung inward, I felt a strong resistance as I pushed to open the door. I pushed hard against the door and I saw Clyde's feet sprawled across the bathroom floor. Startled, I squeezed through the opening in the bathroom and found Clyde lying unconscious on the floor. I didn't feel a pulse, nor did I detect any breathing.

I screamed, almost at the top of my lungs, "Clyde! Oh, Lord! Please let Clyde be all right! Please don't let him be dead!"

The dream unfortunately was real. Clyde had passed out and didn't regain consciousness. One moment we were a happy family and the next moment, Clyde was gone, and the entire family was in shocking pain. As I remembered the dream, I closed my eyes to smother the tears.

"Lord, have mercy!" I said stuttering my words, "I miss him so much. Why did he have to die and leave us here?" I kept seeing Clyde sprawled on our bathroom floor.

It was now around 4:30 in the morning and I stopped writing in my journal. I turned over to my right side and stared at the television. I wanted only to stare at something and try to forget everything. Amnesia would have been a welcomed reality for me that morning. But for the first time in a long time, there was some excitement in the air—Alex Keith and I were going to the game of all games on Saturday.

The Tuskegee-Morehouse Game

I was looking forward to the Tuskegee-Morehouse game. I prayed that it would take my mind off things. And it did. The game didn't start until 6:00 p.m., and by that time the wind had begun to stir 15–20 miles an hour. The temperature was forecasted at 65 degrees, but when we walked into the stadium, I was convinced the wind chill was approaching 45 degrees or less. I wrapped my jacket around my body and scrunched my hat over my ears because I didn't want to catch a cold. As the evening rolled into night, the temperature dropped even more and the wind began to howl. It was cold in those bleachers.

My eyes panned the bleachers and I didn't spot many people I knew, but I watched the game with interest and enthusiasm. As the wind blew even fiercer, I wrapped my heavy green jacket even tighter around my body and pulled my black hood over my ears even more. I wasn't really watching the football game, but I thoroughly enjoyed both the marching bands. I had enjoyed watching bands while attending Clark College in Atlanta back in the early 70s.

The bands' performances brought pleasant memories and warm thoughts of my days at college as I would listen to Billy Paul singing *Me and Mrs. Jones*. I enjoyed watching the drum majors' charismatic performances as they stepped high into the sky with their swirling batons in hand. They marched around the field as if they owned every inch of it. Alex Keith enjoyed the game. He cheered for Tuskegee, and wouldn't you know, Tuskegee won.

As the years passed, Alex Keith and I decided to make attending the Tuskegee-Morehouse an annual event. We even added Albany State, my alma mater, to the list to attend as an annual event. It was something different to do, and because the two of us hadn't done much since Clyde had been sick, it was a welcome change for both of us. Going to the game was one of several turning points for me as I began to acknowledge the reality that Clyde had gone; it had been six months. Alex Keith and I left about 15 minutes before the game ended to avoid the snarls of traffic. We had a good time.

Soon the weekend ended and I was back at work on Monday. I would be going to my group therapy, and for some reason I was eager for Thursday to come. I felt a tremendous need to be around other people who understood my feelings. I was happy; even if it was short-lived, I was happy for the moment.

Thank God He was watching over me. Whatever it took, even if it was from a tiny cricket, I was very grateful I was able to close my eyes and sleep. I felt myself slipping away into nothingness that early morning as I held onto God's unchanging hand by a meager string. We had a great time at the game. It was a welcomed relief from our weekend routine.

The afternoon at work was almost delirious. I was very sleepy and hardly could keep my eyes open in front of my PC as I pecked away on the final points to prepare an information bulletin. I had had a meeting earlier in the day in the conference room to discuss the information bulletin with my business analysts and all went well. I thanked God I was able to work in spite of my lack of sleep. I had been doing the job for four years, since 1991, and because I knew my job well, writing a bulletin or even updating software manuals was pretty much routine. But I functioned at work as best I could under the stress I faced daily.

I finally added the finishing touches to the information bulletin and handed it off to the editor for review. *For sure*, I thought to myself, *she will find some issues here and there with this bulletin. Lord knows, I've done all I can on this one. My brain is tired and my body aches.*

To my surprise there were very few corrections, so I updated the bulletin and reprinted for a final review before printing and distribution. I looked at the clock and it was almost 5:30 p.m. As soon as I cleared my desk, I walked out of my cube, and within minutes I was passing the receptionist desk. I waved goodbye and darted out the door, fumbling hopelessly to find my keys at the bottom of my purse.

I approached the exit door of the building, sighed, and pulled my car keys out of my handbag side pocket and raced to my car. I couldn't wait to drive home. I had had a full weekend and was ready to dive into my bed and sleep in quiet peace. I was thankful to Brother and Sister Allen for giving Alex Keith and me a rare opportunity to enjoy a wonderful game and for a moment in time to feel normal again.

CHAPTER THIRTEEN

Lord, Help Me Find My Way Back

I wasn't angry at Clyde anymore. I knew I needed to internalize God's love and reach for His hand to lift me out of my valley of grief. I closed off the rest of the world when I began to sink deeper into depression. But a whisper of light caught my eye and I began to reach out to God again. He planted my feet onto dry land and helped me find my way back to Him into His marvelous light.

WHY DO PEOPLE HAVE TO DIE? I asked this question many times while growing up. As a child I used to cry at the thought that one day Grandnanny (my grandfather), Mom-Mom, and Mae would die. I didn't want any of them to die, and just thinking of it made my body ache all over. I remember walking out into the field hoping no one would see my tears. But Grandnanny did die in 1974 and Mom-Mom died in 1998. I wasn't able to stop either of them from dying.

When I heard the tragic news that Dr. Martin Luther King, Jr. was assassinated in April 1968, I remember asking the same question. And before we had any time to recover, Bobby Kennedy was struck down in June 1968, two months after Dr. King. I was petrified, and at age 13, those incredible scenes remain indelible in my mind.

Now, I faced an even greater challenge in my life. I had to learn to live without the love of my life. I had always prayed for God to protect my mother, grandmother, and grandfather, but I had no idea that facing my husband's death some 30 years later would turn out to be incomprehensible.

As I sat on the edge of my bed on that beautiful fall evening in October, I couldn't help but reflect over my life. I had had a good life. I'd always studied hard and made good grades. I tried to do the right thing. Mom-Mom skinned me and my four sisters alive if we didn't do what she asked. Mom-Mom didn't sit us down and talk to us individually about life's lessons. No, she didn't have time. She reared us to be self-supporting. Instead, she talked to us about life's lessons while we were worked in the fields—picking peas, cucumbers, okra, and squash. Mom-Mom didn't beat around the bush. She was always blunt with her words. She never told us she loved us, but we knew she did. We felt and sensed her love all around us.

As I continued my journey down memory lane, I thought about words I had written in my high school memory book back in 1972. My goals after graduation were to obtain a master's degree, marry a handsome man, have a child, and live in a big mansion and happily ever after. I smiled because I knew I had realized all those goals. I had married a handsome man and instead of one child, we were blessed with two.

The house we had purchased was very nice indeed. It was our special home, our very own mansion. I smiled as I thought about our life together and what we'd accomplished. I lifted myself from the bed and walked into the living room and sat on the sofa. I looked around at the furnishings. Everything was very nice and decorated and the living room furniture was practically new because we never spent much time sitting on it. We spent most of our family time in the den, kitchen or bedrooms.

As I stared into the room, I began to drift into pleasant memories of Clyde and me sitting on the paisley green and black sofa with diagonal purple stripes running through it. Towering over the sofa was an exquisite painting, highlighting a scene in a garden of peace and tranquility as if it dipped into the ocean.

I smiled as I looked around the room. Over the years Clyde and I had collected some beautiful things. Our house had a warm, loving atmosphere and it really made me beam with pride.

"Clyde, we really did good," I said as my eyes scoured the room. I grabbed one of our many pictures on the coffee table and held it close to my face. "My mind hurts without him. My heart hurts, too, Lord…I miss…him…so. I'm not going to cry," I said to myself. "I don't want to cry Lord, not today."

I dropped my head into my lap and screamed in agony. I fought desperately to keep from crying. I jerked myself from the sofa and stood in front of the window, looking through the window panes, trying desperately to focus on anything but myself. Then my eyes followed three birds dancing along the edge of a pine branch. I watched and listened inquisitively as the birds sang their beautiful melodies. I was taken away to their place of refuge as I listened to their sweet sounds. I walked back to the sofa and sat down, stretching my neck back and listening to the different sounds. I went to sleep before I even knew it as I sat and concentrated on the birds' melodies. Thankfully, I didn't cry.

My Dreams Continue

I wiped back the tears as they escaped from my eyes. I was missing Clyde beyond comprehension, and many times I could hardly bear the torment. Trying to shake away the memories, I grabbed the remote and started flipping through the TV channels, hoping to find something that would help me take my mind off the memories. I picked up one of my pillows along with the flannel blanket that was resting on top of the sofa. I draped it over my legs for warmth.

Early November was sneaking close. I couldn't believe it had been six months since Clyde's death. I dreaded thinking about the holidays and didn't want to imagine Christmas without him. I pushed that thought away.

As the first few months passed into history, I was learning to push things away in my mind as protection. If I didn't want to feel the anguish or the sorrow, I changed the scenery as quickly as I could. One time when I was flipping through a magazine, I saw a sad picture of a child who had died in a hit-and-run accident. I read the first few lines of the article and quickly dropped the magazine to the floor. I didn't want to feel the sorrow, so I had to let it go.

It's Time for Group Therapy Again

The day for group therapy arrived and I left work promptly in anticipation of the session. I still didn't know many of the attendees' names. I could only remember Jane's. We all arrived about the same time around 6:00 p.m., so I had a few moments to talk casually with everyone and talk about our children and work.

Ms. Arrington always started the session by asking how everyone's day had been and whoever answered the question first started the session. I didn't remember seeing Jane that evening. She had such a profound effect on me the last time and I wanted to see her again. For the first time I was listening to the pain and heartache of other people. I wasn't alone. Grief was hovering all around me.

I knew I wasn't ready to talk about Clyde in front of the group. I wasn't ready and I believe Ms. Arrington also knew because she could see it in my eyes. But I knew one day I would do it. I didn't know when, but it wasn't going to be tonight. Ms. Arrington had such good wits and intuition about her. She understood me plainly. I knew I could trust her and appreciated her wonderful words of kindness and encouragement. She knew everyone sitting around the circle was as fragile as glass, and it wouldn't take much to push any of us over the edge.

A woman spoke first and described her sleepless nights and I could definitely relate. She talked about visiting her husband's doctors because he had had multiple health issues and how her physician had prescribed medication for her chronic insomnia. As I listened to her, it further validated that I wasn't crazy. My insomnia of anguish and despair was normal in the grieving process. I breathed a sigh of relief. The feelings I had experienced with Clyde were also being experienced by other people.

And then another lady began to speak. She didn't seem as distressed as the rest of us. As she began to speak she told us that her husband had passed away a few years ago. She talked about her two children and the first two years of living without their father. She talked about her situation during the first six months and how she began to unravel at the seam as reality began to sink in that her husband was gone. I listened to her intently and was amazed by her story.

At that moment, I couldn't fathom how time could ever ease the pain and sorrow of losing Clyde. She warned us not to make hasty decisions, especially during the first year, but to hold off a while. She stated that the mind had to catch up with reality, and it wouldn't be easy.

Years later, I remembered her words as she described grief. The lady was exactly right. I didn't make any major decisions for a year. Thank God I didn't. I would have made some major mistakes had I done so. As the years passed, I told others about the lady's words. I also warned others to be very careful of people attempting to take advantage of them during the most vulnerable times of their lives. Unfortunately, there are people who prey on widows and widowers — from excessive home repairs to illegal financial scams.

I was able to see beyond my pain and acknowledge that someone else had truly traveled the same road I was traveling and had made it to the other side. I was very thankful to her for being at the group session that night and for her words of encouragement and perseverance. The lady stated that group therapy had been the turning point for her and her children to move forward with their lives again.

I was glad I came to the session and knew I would never forget her priceless words about learning to live again. Her words soothed me. The session ended as quickly as it had begun. As before, I didn't want it to end. I felt connected to everyone in the room, even though I didn't know most of them. Death was the common thread that bound us together.

People were incredibly real. There was no distinction of color, race, or even sexual bias. Everyone was real. The common thread that bound us was death and grief. The more I listened, the more I began to see the significance of group therapy. It was a place for everyone to come and talk and share our stories of loss—a place of healing. We were supporting each other.

After Ms. Arrington talked briefly for a few more minutes, she said good night to us and we left for home. We parted our session with genuine warm hugs for each other. We were experiencing a bond together and it never ended. I still have a genuine affection for everyone who suffered with me during the early years. Even though our grief sessions ended, we continued to pray for each other along our respective journeys. We also learned in time that even though the group sessions would end, grief would always be a part of our lives.

Building the Habitat House

I remember it well. In November 1995, TSYS began to build a Habitat House for a local family. I volunteered to assist in building the home for a lady and her children. I didn't have much energy, but I still wanted to work, so I assisted with the house construction on a sunny weekday afternoon. I wore my jeans and even though they were hanging loose from my waist, I traveled to the Habitat House and began to work.

I was willing to help out in anyway I could because I wanted to make a difference. I nailed aluminum siding and painted the exterior of the house. I was willing to assist wherever they needed me—even carrying bottles of water and snacks to everyone. We worked hard and enjoyed every moment of that afternoon as we built the house together.

It had been a long time since I had felt truly part of something worthwhile, and while TSYS dedicated the home to the family on an early morning in mid-November, I smiled. We had made a difference in the life of a lady and her children. And as TSYS team members stood around to dedicate the new home and hear the TSYS executives words of accomplishment, I felt proud.

Changing My Bedroom

I had been toying with the idea of changing my bedroom around. I don't know why something as mundane as changing my room around would help, but I was willing to try just about anything at this point. Clyde and I had a relatively small bedroom, so changing the bed pretty much changed the entire appearance of the room.

On a sunny Saturday in late November 1995, I decided to change my bed so it would face the door. I had an idea how I wanted everything in my mind, so Alex Keith and I made it happen. For 45 minutes we slid the bed one way and moved the heavy double dresser the other way. We moved the night-stands to each side of the bed, and to my unexpected surprise my bedroom had been transformed into a special little haven just for me. I liked it.

I never dreamed that rearranging my room would make a difference, but it did. My bedroom now felt like mine. Clyde and I had shared our bedroom together for 21 years and now it was just mine. We rolled the television stand to the left side of the bed next to the double-sided pine bark dresser. That way, I could watch TV from any angle from my bed. I smiled with confidence as I placed my four teddy bears alongside the stacks of mail on the bed between my pillows.

Alex Keith even liked my rearranged bedroom. "It's cool, Mom," he said. "It's really cool."

For the past six months I had kept everything just as Clyde had left it. I hadn't moved anything from his dresser, not even on his side of the closet. I wanted to keep it the way he left it before he passed away. But I knew one day I would be changing things around, and this was a good day to start. I felt I had accomplished something and I said out loud, "Clyde, you really would be proud of me. I changed our bedroom. We changed it, sweetheart—just Alex Keith and me. But we didn't change it too much. Thank you for understanding, Clyde. I needed to do it; please be proud of me. I am."

CHAPTER FOURTEEN

The Holidays Without Him

*The holidays were approaching and I dreaded facing them. I was
learning to function one day at a time, but the onslaught of
Thanksgiving and Christmas brought on an entirely different
kind of anxiety that I didn't expect.*

I DIDN'T KNOW WHAT TO EXPECT as the holidays
approached. Thanksgiving and Christmas had always been a
special time for the Slappey family. Though tiring and hectic,
we had managed to enjoy the blessings of the season. Clyde
and I had always cooked the Thanksgiving dinner together.
It had been a long-standing family tradition. I would prepare
the turkey with all of the fixings and Clyde would entertain the
family taste buds with his delectable smoked turkey and ham,
and a pork roast as an added bonus on several occasions.

Clyde would get up early Thursday morning and prepare
the smoker for the all-day event of smoking the meat for the
special dinner. I don't mean to be biased, but Clyde smoked the
best turkey on this side of the Atlantic. It was all good and I
knew I was blessed with an incredible man who loved me and
would do practically anything to please me.

As I looked out the kitchen window into the streets, I shook my head as my memories soon faded into sadness. I didn't know what I was going to do as the holiday approached. I didn't feel like traveling, nor did I have the energy to cook. All I wanted to do was crawl in a hole and never come out again. My mind was paralyzed at the thought of our family having Thanksgiving without Clyde. But I knew it was coming and I had to learn to deal with it somehow.

I had already gone through Memorial Day, Father's Day, Fourth of July, and even Labor Day. Now Thanksgiving and Christmas would soon arrive and I knew these last two holidays would be the most difficult of them all to deal with.

"How do I fathom being without Clyde on two of the most special days of the year for our family, Lord? How do I do it? You said I can do all things through You who strengthen me. I definitely need Your strength with this one. Please help me with this one," I pleaded.

But my mother made it easier for me and the kids. She suggested that everyone come to Columbus for Thanksgiving. Mae knew it would be very difficult for us to be away from the house without Clyde. I wasn't in the mood for holidays. But I also knew that God wanted me to keep going forward; I didn't know how, but I had confidence that He would see my family and me through the holidays.

⌐

I had another opportunity to go to grief therapy before Thanksgiving. It appeared that every week new people joined the group. Everyone had been nice and supportive. Ms. Arrington did her usual introductions at the session. Instead of looking around the room to have someone start the conversation for the night, Ms. Arrington looked directly at me.

"Deborah, would you like to share your story with everyone tonight?" she asked. And without even thinking, I replied, "Yes, I will."

I knew that it was time for me to talk. I couldn't believe that the words were coming out of my mouth, but I knew it was time. I looked around at everyone and began to tell my story—Clyde's story. I don't remember my exact words, but I do remember describing our trips to three hospitals, hoping to find someone who would help Clyde find a cure for primary amyloidosis. Everyone listened attentively. The room fell deadly silent as I began to describe Clyde's battle with the rare disease. It was very quiet, so quiet that you could hear a cotton ball land on the low-piled carpet in the room.

As usual, the tears traveled down my face, neck, and chest. Reaching for a tissue, I wiped the tears from my eyes and continued to tell Clyde's story.

"When Clyde died in St. Mary's hospital, I died as well," I continued. "I became numb inside and outside. I felt disconnected from my source of strength and I didn't want to leave him in the cemetery. I knew God would take care of him, but I wanted to take care of him too, as I had done many times in our years together. I didn't want our journey to end as it had on April 19, 1995.

"I knew inwardly that our journey had ended, but I didn't want to stop. I wanted it to end like the many fairy tales I'd read during my childhood. You know the ones—where you live happily ever after. It's not supposed to end in death, not like this. But I couldn't change this outcome no matter what I did or even what I said. Clyde had left me forever, and I knew I wouldn't ever be the same again."

Again, the tears dripped from my lips. Ms. Arrington asked me how I felt when Clyde died. Of course I knew what she was doing; she wanted me to keep going…to keep talking about it. I knew she wanted me to empty myself of the pain, sorrow, and despair I'd held onto for months.

I continued, "I dream about Clyde's death and it's not pleasant at all. I dream that I'm floating in a hollow space, in a time continuum of some kind. I'm a science fiction fan, so that's the best way I can describe it. I continue to float down until I land on a smooth, satin-like object. It's oblong and I really don't know what I've landed upon until my feet touch the wet, black dirt that sticks between my toes and I know I'm near Clyde. I sense his presence. I don't want to leave him. I try my best to open the casket and don't know what I'm going to do when I open it, but I want to open it desperately. I attempt to spring the lock, but I'm quickly pulled away and begin to float upward to the top of the hole. But I don't want to leave him.

"As soon as I'm almost to the top of the opening, my hands give way and my body turns lopsided. I find myself falling back down again into the deep, dark hole with Clyde. My fingernails are clawed and bloody red with wet, dark earth. The blood oozes from my nails as I unsuccessfully attempt to lessen the impact of my fall.

"Each time I dream this dream, I float higher and higher, close to the top of the hole, but I never reach the top to the beaming light, just ahead of me."

I paused for a moment and looked. From their faces I knew they hadn't heard of the primary amyloidosis disease. It was ghastly quiet. I could see that everyone was hanging on my every word.

I continued, "I dream the same dream that Clyde is dead."

I stopped talking and turned my head in the direction of the clock. To my surprise, I had been talking for about 20 minutes, and to my surprise, I didn't want to stop; but I knew I needed to so others could speak as well. This was the first time I had spoken in public to anyone other than Ms. Arrington about

Clyde's death. Everyone in the room had connected fully with my pain. Our bond would last forever.

After two other people spoke, the session ended. Not wanting the evening to end, several of us stopped by a local restaurant to eat a bit. We talked about our husbands, wives, and children. We kept talking and enjoyed each other's company for about an hour or so before going home. It had been a pleasant, unforgettable night as we shared our grief together. It felt good to smile and socialize again.

Thanksgiving Day

As the Thanksgiving week rolled into reality, I was extremely nervous with an awesome sense of dread. If I could have wiped November 23, 1995, off the calendar, I would have. I didn't want to go through the holiday without Clyde. It would mean that he truly was dead and I didn't want to think about it. That evening I lay on my bed and cried myself sick to the point my head began to pound unnervingly into a heart-wrenching, throbbing headache. I took two Tylenol tablets and slowly drifted to sleep. Because of a pounding headache I stopped crying and eventually fell asleep.

This year I didn't have the strength or the will to cook the holiday meal without Clyde, so I decided to order our turkey dinner.

As I lay down that Wednesday evening, Thanksgiving Eve, I prayed to God. I felt disengaged, troubled, and dripping in despair. I didn't want to acknowledge that Clyde wouldn't be here with us for the holiday. I couldn't.

"Lord," I prayed, "please help us to get through this holiday. I miss him very much. Sometimes I can't stand the anguish. He's not with me. I can't talk to him; I can't smile with him; I can't listen to his crazy jokes. Oh Lord, I can't do anything with him anymore. I don't want to face this holiday without him."

Clyde Daryl had arrived home the Tuesday before Thanksgiving and I was very thankful and happy to see him. I could tell he'd lost some weight. We all needed each other to get through Thanksgiving. I knew he was glad to be home as well.

I awoke around 8:00 a.m. on Thanksgiving morning and turned to Clyde's side of the bed. I knew he wasn't there, but I had to look anyway. I didn't hear Clyde snoring on his side, nor did I hear him rise early in the morning dew to start the fire in the smoker for the turkey. He wasn't here; no matter what I said or did. I would never smell the charcoal, wood-burning smell escape from the tiny vent of the smoker as the aromas swelled with the mind-penetrating scents of spiced garlic and rubbed Italian pork seasonings emanating from the turkey, pork roast, and ham.

But all was not lost. Clyde Daryl decided at the last minute to take on the tradition of smoking our turkey for Thanksgiving. He arose early on Thursday morning and smoked the turkey. I was glad he wanted to carry on his father's tradition, and after several hours, the turkey was ready. I took small pieces of skin from the turkey, and the taste was impeccably a Slappey tradition. Clyde Daryl's smoked turkey had managed to live up to Clyde's and I knew he would have been proud of him.

The family arrived around 1:00 p.m. In addition to the smoked turkey, I also ordered a complete turkey dinner. I wanted to make sure we had enough food. Mae and my sisters, Anne, Ruth, and Phyllis brought food as well. We had more than enough for sure.

L.C., being the eldest, gave the blessing, and as soon as we warmed the food and placed the trimmings on the dining room table, everyone ate heartily, except for me. I didn't have much of an appetite, but I wanted everyone else to enjoy the dinner. I nibbled on pieces of smoked turkey and ate a small amount of dressing and scrapings of sweet potato soufflé.

I wanted everyone to feel comfortable. I even tried to take part in the conversations, but I knew I wasn't much company. All I wanted to do was rush back into my bedroom and scream to release the pain and agony of my new reality.

As everyone continued to enjoy the occasion, I closed my eyes tightly, hoping to force back the tears. While everyone was busy laughing and talking I walked quietly to my bedroom, closed the door, and walked over to the photo on my end table. I touched his face with my finger and traced the painful lines of stress on his face, holding the picture close to my chest. Clutching the picture tightly, I rested my head against the pillow. It saddened me to know that the closest I could get to Clyde was to hold his picture in my hands and remember. I closed my eyes to see his face in my mind and visualized his award-winning smile. I smiled as his face became visible…but before I could savor the moment, I heard a tap on the door.

"Come in," I said, taking my right wrist and rubbing it against my cheek. It was Mae. She'd noticed that I had slipped out of the den.

"Are you okay, Debbie?" she asked.

"I'm okay, Mae," I replied. "I came back here for a few minutes to get off my feet," I said. Hoping to change the subject I asked, "Have you had enough to eat? There should be plenty of food left," I continued. "Get as much as you want, Mae, to take home for you and L.C. because Clyde Daryl, Alex Keith, and I definitely can't eat all of it."

"The food was absolutely delicious!" Mae replied, puffing up one of the pillows with her hands on Clyde's side of the bed. "I just wanted to check on you." She hesitated. "You know, Debbie, Clyde would want you to be okay. He wouldn't want you to be sad."

I hesitated for a moment. "Yes, I know he would Mae," I said as I picked up the remote control to turn on the TV. "I know he would. I'll be all right. I just want to be alone for a few minutes. I'm okay. Come on and sit down on the bed with me," I said.

Mae sat down next to me and we talked for awhile. I appreciated her concern. I guess I didn't need to be alone that afternoon after all, and was glad my family had come to surround us with love and attention and spend their Thanksgiving Day with us. I really appreciated them coming to Columbus. Even though I didn't cook much, I wanted to make sure everyone enjoyed themselves eating, talking, and just having a good time. "Let's go back in, Mae," I said to her as I lifted myself from the bed. "I'm really okay," I added, touching her shoulder.

"Debbie, I know it's a hard day for you, but Clyde would want you to be okay, you and Clyde Daryl and Alex Keith," she said reassuringly, touching me on my shoulder.

"I know he would, Mae. I know he would."

"So, let's go back and join everyone, okay."

As we left the room, I straightened my upper body, raised my shoulders, and walked behind Mae out of the bedroom, wiping my tears with a tiny piece of tissue paper found on the vanity. Forcing a smile, I walked back into the den to join everyone as they all eagerly watched the Thanksgiving football game. My two-year-old niece, Jasmine Nicole, was busy playing with one of her toys. I sat down with the rest of the family, making small talk. Alex Keith and Clyde Daryl were busy washing the piles of dishes and utensils left from dinner. My sisters Phyllis, Anne, and Ruth were busy chatting and L.C. and my brother, Timothy, were in the backyard talking and enjoying the autumn breeze.

It all seemed to be a very typical, normal day. The feel of fall was in the air, giving us a beautiful, sun-filled day. The leaves had deserted the trees, falling to the earth with colors of golden amber, burgundy, even purple-rain-stained leaves, and every hue of the rainbow one could imagine. I could see the leaves fall as I peeked out the French doors in the den. It was a gorgeous day and I was thankful to be alive. I thought silently, *Clyde would have made sure everyone was comfortable and was having a good time.*

I walked to the storage house adjacent to the house and pulled one of the double white doors open to look around the room. My eyes spotted Clyde's tool box that seemed to be in the same spot where he had left it a year ago.

"Just look at all these tools," I said. "I bet Clyde has just about every tool they make in this chest. He can give several away and still have plenty left over," I continued, caressing his shiny hammer.

I should have known that Mae wasn't too far behind me. I heard the scraggly sound from the screen door as it opened wide. She found me digging through Clyde's tool box.

"Clyde had a lot of tools, didn't he?" she said to me, smiling.

"Yeah, he did. He just loved his tools. I remember he would be so excited to visit Sears and purchase another Craftsman tool. It was a big deal for him. I even remember purchasing a few tools for him myself, mostly for Father's Day gifts. I could always count on the tools being a big hit with him.

"Clyde Daryl and Alex Keith can keep them; they have their father's tool chest. They'll appreciate them in years to come," I said.

"That's good," Mae replied. "They need to keep them and don't give them away. Clyde would want his boys to have them."

Mae and I continued to walk around the house, staring at the exterior. I could tell the house trimming was getting a little worn, so I knew I should have it painted soon. Clyde didn't get the chance to repaint it before he fell ill. I knew I could find someone at church to do it. I would ask Brother Clayton about recommending someone. Overall, the house was in very good condition. Clyde had made sure of that. Before he got too sick, he would make sure the lawn was cut and manicured and the bushes trimmed. Many times I had helped Clyde clean the yard. I even planted most of the shrubbery in the front and side flowerbeds around the house. I had always wanted a beautiful, immaculate lawn for our home, so we all pitched in as a family to make it happen.

About a year or so after we moved into our house in 1989, we decided to re-sod the front yard with Tifton Bermuda. The previous owner had removed most of the sod from the front yard and replaced it with straw. We preferred grass. The entire family worked all day on that beautiful Saturday and ended up totally exhausted, having laid sod practically on the entire front yard. By the time we finished, we had emptied three truck loads of sod in the front yard. It was absolutely beautiful, our labor of love. Our neighbors still talk about our nice yard today.

"Clyde really took care of the house," I said to Mae. "He always was working on something. Always busy."

"Oh, yes. His home was his pride and joy," Mae responded.

"We've been here for about six years now and we'd done so much to the place. But we did it together and I'm so thankful we did. It really shows. Clyde was very proud of our home. We all were."

I dropped my head in silence. I didn't want Mae to see me crying. I knew she would start to worry, and I didn't want that. We walked back into the house to see everyone watching football. Time seemed to fly quickly on that Thanksgiving afternoon. Before long it was 4:00 p.m., and everyone prepared to leave. We hugged and waved goodbye as they backed out of the driveway. It had been a full afternoon and I was happy we spent the holiday with family.

Day After Thanksgiving

I woke up early the next morning with the birds singing wonderful songs of joy. Their songs penetrated deeply within me and I wanted to hear more.

"They seem very happy, almost overjoyed," I said silently.

"Lord, they sound peaceful as if they don't have a care in the world. And they probably don't." I smiled. I continued smiling as I listened to the birds' melodies.

I looked at the clock and it was 7:30 on Friday morning. Back in the day, I would be shopping all day long. The day after Thanksgiving was my day, my holiday kickoff shopping time. It was just me, the Peachtree Mall, Kmart, and Walmart, and I had a ball!

I would leave Clyde, Clyde Daryl, and Alex Keith in bed as I trotted off to store after store, spending practically the entire day shopping.

"Boy, I enjoyed myself," I said loudly. "I miss it. I really miss it, Lord. But I really don't feel like doing it today."

I grabbed the remote from my pillow and turned the volume down because I didn't want to hear the noise of the television. All was quiet in the house. Clyde Daryl and Alex Keith were fast asleep, and other than the birds' chirping, the morning was quite peaceful.

I spent the majority of the day in bed. I didn't want to go anywhere, especially shopping. Most of the time the TBS station would have special televised programming on Clint Eastwood or John Wayne throughout the day for holiday viewing, but not this Friday. Thankfully, I was able to find an animal show on one of the nature channels. Anything was fine except love stories. I couldn't handle them right now. Around 11:00 a.m., Clyde Daryl and Alex Keith decided to head off to the mall.

The house was very quiet and I was glad. I appreciated being alone. I never wanted Alex Keith to hear me crying, so when I was alone I could cry out loud without having to suppress my emotions. I reached out for Clyde's picture on the night stand and held it to my chest.

"Lord, I really miss him," I said starring at the picture, "I miss you Clyde...so very much. It hurts me because you aren't with me, not close to me. I try my best, Lord, to keep going. I really try, but there are times when the pain is so unbearable. It's so aggravating to the point I can't think anymore. It's like someone is stabbing me in the stomach repeatedly. It feels like someone is stabbing me in the face again and again and I can't escape it."

My head was pounding and my neck was aching. I buried my face in Clyde's picture and wiped back the tears. I couldn't bear to think that Clyde was in a grave some 60 miles away. I buried him in Andersonville because he told me he wanted to be buried in a military cemetery. Since he couldn't be buried at Fort Benning, Andersonville was the next logical choice.

I cried most of Friday afternoon and stayed in bed most of Saturday, too. I knew that lying in bed was one of the worst things I could do, but I didn't care. I was very happy to have Clyde Daryl come home. He would be leaving on Sunday traveling back to Wake Forest and I would be sad to see him leave. Clyde Daryl was doing his very best to take care of the family. He always checked on me, making sure I had everything I needed.

"I know you miss Dad," Clyde Daryl said that Friday evening after shopping. "I miss him too. It doesn't seem like Thanksgiving without him, does it?"

"No, it doesn't, Clyde Daryl. No, it doesn't," I repeated. "But I know Clyde would want us to keep going, and so we will," I repeated in a determined voice.

We hugged each other and Clyde Daryl went into the room to see what Alex Keith was up to. I was helpless at that moment, and I'm glad I didn't start crying in front of Clyde Daryl.

Soon Sunday morning arrived and Clyde Daryl left around 10:00 a.m. It was a good trip for him and I was glad he came home. He would have another two weeks before finals and would soon be completing his third semester at college. I was extremely proud of him.

Monday morning arrived sooner than I had imagined and I was back at work. I was glad Thanksgiving was over. I continued to carry out my work as best as I could. Staying busy at work had helped me tremendously.

I didn't have another grief session until the following week. We met one more time before the Christmas holidays. I detected a pit in my stomach when my thoughts focused on Christmas. Thanksgiving was bad enough, but Christmas would be worse. I began to pray.

I wanted to push Christmas out of my mind. I knew God was with me and I was very grateful He was taking care of me and the kids. I certainly wasn't able to do so myself. I sat at my desk and became immersed in my work assignments.

Thank goodness, I thought silently, *I have something to do.*

Quitting time came quickly the Monday after the Thanksgiving holiday. Looking into the bluish sky that late afternoon, I felt empowered as I left the building. I felt as if I could reach up and poke my finger into the center of the clouds and they would shrink to cotton candy. The sky was a shimmering sight to see. I knew Clyde was in heaven with God and with Jesus.

"I bet Clyde wouldn't want to come back here, even if he had a chance to." I smiled. "I know I wouldn't want to come back," I said as I approached my car and unlocked the door.

It was a delightful afternoon and the sky was almost perfect. I was thankful at that moment to God for giving me the opportunity to know my husband. After a brief moment, I climbed into my car and drove out of the South Center parking lot, heading for home.

December arrived before I knew it, and I wasn't doing well at all. My anxiety increased as the first week of December rolled into existence. I felt totally out of sorts; I'm sure it was because of the holidays.

At the last group session of the year, Ms. Arrington told us to be aware of the holiday blues and the rise of depression. I'd noticed I was more apprehensive lately, but I didn't understand why. She stated that holidays triggered heightened episodes of grief, despair, and anxiety. Ms. Arrington said it was important to surround ourselves with family and friends. I listened to her advice closely and understood what she was saying. I had been dealing with Clyde's death for the last eight months, but I was feeling angry, betrayed, and abandoned. I had lost my way again; I wanted to run away and hide in a deep dark place.

For many the holidays are a happy and joyous time of year, but for some it's a time of sorrow and pain. We had always enjoyed the holidays, but it would be different this year. Clyde wouldn't be with us and I was sad.

I believe we all cried in the group that evening in December. It was a blessing for me to be part of the group. They meant the world to me, and I was grateful to be surrounded by people who knew exactly what I was feeling. We talked, laughed, and cried together. I realized it was the talking about our tragedies that helped move our paths to healing. Ms. Arrington provided the forum to induce healing.

I arrived home that evening around 7:00, and walked into Alex Keith's room.

"How are you doing today, Alex Keith?" I asked him. "Did you have a good day?"

"Oh Mom," Alex Keith responded. "You know how it is. We worked on math and science and English, and do I have to continue?" he asked with his big smile.

"Yes, you have to continue, Alex Keith," I responded. "It sounds like you had a pretty good day. Did you take out the trash that you forgot last night?"

"Yes ma'am. I did. And I cleaned the trash container, too. It smells really good now, Mom."

"Okay! That sounds like a winner," I said.

Alex Keith and I continued our conversation as we walked into the kitchen. After warming my supper, we sat at the table and talked about everything from today's events to his schoolwork. It had been a long time since we had sat down at the table and talked. I enjoyed it very much, and before we knew it, the antique clock on the kitchen wall struck 8:30.

Thirty minutes later, Alex Keith hurried to take his bath and said good night. I walked into my bedroom and began my ritual of getting ready for bed, which I'd observed for some eight months now. I was grateful to Sandra Smith, my friend for telling me about taking calcium tablets prior to going to bed. Sandra told me they would help me sleep better and she was right. I was sleeping better and wasn't waking up as much as I had done during the first six months after Clyde's death. This was a tremendous improvement for me and I was grateful.

Christmas Arrives

I wanted to stop Christmas from coming, but it was steadily approaching. No matter how hard I cried and screamed at the top of my voice, it didn't change one thing—Christmas was coming just as Thanksgiving had.

I made myself buy a few gifts for the kids, but that was about all. I didn't have the will to do much shopping for family and friends. In years past, I would wrap gifts as we sat under the golden glow of the fire popping in the fireplace. It was absolutely wonderful to be surrounded by family. Clyde was responsible for one gift—mine, and he even had the store wrap it for him.

Before I knew it, it was Christmas Eve. Clyde Daryl was home for the holidays and he and Alex Keith were busy decorating the Christmas tree. In past years, Clyde made sure a beautiful, well-lit tree stood in front of the double-pane window in the living room. Clyde would pick out the tree with the children and the men of the house would decorate it.

Clyde Daryl and Alex Keith were very busy putting the finishing touches on decorating the tree. They were determined that we continue our tradition. I walked into the living room and picked up a red satin ornament and placed it gently on the star-studded Christmas tree. The young men had done a fine job.

"Clyde," I said. "You would really be proud of them. The tree is beautiful and they are carrying on the tradition with you in spirit, my love."

Even as I lifted the ornament and placed it on the tree, I didn't want Christmas to come. I didn't want the clock to strike midnight because I would have to admit to myself that Clyde wasn't with us and he wasn't coming back. I didn't want to think about it.

As we finished decorating the tree, I thought about placing fruit and candy on the living room sofa as I'd done in years past for the kids. This was another family tradition I had started years ago when the children were small. I wanted to make sure Clyde Daryl and Alex Keith had their fruit because of my grandfather's long-standing tradition of placing piles of fruit on the living room sofa for his grandchildren. Around 11:00 p.m. while everyone was in their rooms, I took a couple each of apples, oranges, tangerines, and some orange candy and made two piles on the sofa—one for Alex Keith and one for Clyde Daryl. I smiled when I was finished.

"This is just what the living room needed," I said, looking around the room.

I said good night to Clyde Daryl and Alex Keith and walked back into my bedroom. It was time for me to face what I had dreaded for months, watching the minutes tick down to Christmas Day, though it wouldn't be easy. I hated the thought, but it was going to happen no matter what I did. As the time ticked away, I felt very anxious, but more flustered as I watched 1995 slip into history.

"Lord, there is nothing I can do to stop Christmas from coming, is there?" I asked him.

I watched the clock change to 12:01 a.m. And when it happened I looked over at Clyde's picture. "Merry Christmas, Clyde," I said to him. "I hope you are okay. I miss you very much darling, and I wish you were here with us. Merry Christmas!"

The day I had dreaded for months was now reality. I cried under my pillow that night. There was nothing else to be said or talked about. I would have to learn to live without him, even at Christmastime. No matter what we said or did, it wouldn't change this fact: Clyde was gone.

I flipped through the channels, hoping to find something that would take my mind off my reality. I found the original *Jaws* movie. Even though I had watched it countless times, I was more than happy to watch it again. As I watched the final scenes and my eyes found sleep, it was the best thing that could have happened to me on that early Christmas morning. I wasn't thinking about my sad life, and for a few hours, the motion picture *Jaws* helped me to forget about everything.

No sooner than I thought I had drifted off to sleep, I heard Alex Keith coming into my room. Barely opening an eye, I looked over at the clock and it was past 6:30 a.m. I had slept for five hours.

Alex Keith came into the room and was very excited about Christmas. He always was. He wanted me to come into the living room, as we had always done. But this time, we were doing it with only the three of us. Slowly, I pulled myself from the bed and wrapped Clyde's robe around my waist. By that time Clyde Daryl had joined Alex Keith in the living room. I walked up the hall and into the living room, hoping to see Clyde sitting comfortably on the sofa, waiting for us to join him. I wanted to burst into tears, but I held them back for the sake of the children. I didn't want Clyde Daryl and Alex Keith to see me crying. I sat on the sofa in Clyde's robe and hair curlers stuck in my head, hoping they wouldn't look directly at me. It was real. Clyde wasn't coming back. I knew it was real, but I had to keep saying it to myself over and over again.

Help me, Lord. I screamed silently. *Lord, please have mercy on me. Help me smile for my sons right now. Please help me!*

I knew they saw the pain in my face. I was barely able to walk down the hall into the living room. I was in deep despair as I watched them open their gifts one by one.

We took pictures as we'd done numerous times as we opened our gifts. I was lethargic from the despair that pulsated within my soul. We did a group hug after opening our gifts. I knew Clyde Daryl was trying to do what he knew his father would have done. I knew my sons were missing their father. We came together and hugged each other one more time before clearing away the ripped paper from the floor.

As their mother, I couldn't ease their pain. At ages 19 and 12, Clyde Daryl and Alex Keith had to live without their father in a cruel, careless world. I helped them pick up the remaining pieces of paper and walked back to my room, closed my door and screamed in sorrowful pain.

"Lord," I asked Him, "how will they go on without their father? I have done all I can for them. They need their father now, not me. I can't give them what they need to be men. I can only give them a mother's love. It's so unfair for them to live in this world without their father."

I placed the pillow over my head and cried. I didn't want Clyde Daryl and Alex Keith to hear my screams. But no matter what I said or did, nothing would change the reality that Clyde was gone. The crying didn't help and I knew it wouldn't, but I cried anyway, holding his pictures close to me.

"You didn't come back Clyde. I thought you would, but you didn't. I just want to see you. That's all."

Time seemed to pass quickly on Christmas morning. I went back to bed and I didn't get up again until noon. My stomach had started to growl, so I knew I had to eat. I had catered the holiday dinner so we would have an abundance of food throughout the holidays. It was very hard for me to pass by our kaleidoscope of family pictures in the living room. I wanted to be alone with my memories of good times together as a couple and family. We all made small talk around the table, but we all knew.

I knew it was extremely difficult for Clyde Daryl and Alex Keith. I knew they were trying to be strong for me, but I wanted them to let it out. I wanted them to scream, cry, and beat their fists against their chest. Anything to acknowledge the hurt and pain that paralyzed them inside. Little did they know I was doing the same thing for them. I was holding back my tears for them.

Clyde Daryl and Alex Keith cleared the table after we finished eating. They always did their chores together. I was glad they were close and prayed they would always be close to each other as they grew into strong men. Clyde told them to stay close and take care of each other.

Clyde Daryl and Alex Keith decided to go to an afternoon movie, so I gave them two discounted movie tickets. As soon as they left, I crawled under the covers of my bed. This time I didn't turn on the television. I yearned to hear the silence in the house. I lay back on my pillow and closed my eyes to remember the good times once again.

"I won't ever be the same, I know that. I won't ever be complete again without Clyde," I said to God. "I want to remember our time together this day. Help me to remember the good times we had together, not the sad times. There are plenty of sad times; I want to remember our happy ones—like when we laughed together when our children were born. That's what I want to feel right now, Lord. Please help me to remember our times together."

I closed my eyes and began to see the photographs of our memories align one by one in the corners of my mind. We had many happy times. Lying down in our bed, I began to smile as I watched reels of memories flood my mind. I concentrated on the happy scenes that flashed before me and smiled. And a time or two, I actually giggled.

"Clyde was just as crazy as they come. He had a wonderful sense of humor," I said as I smiled, wanting desperately for the memories to keep coming. I watched the precious memories scroll one by one in my mind.

"I'm thankful Lord that you've given me the opportunity to know this man. Thank you."

As the words flowed from my lips, I closed my eyes, eased my shoulders off the stacks of pillows, and slowly sank easily into a much needed nap. For a little while, I felt no pain.

A Brand New Year

I have always been amazed at how everything literally stops during the Christmas and New Year's holidays. Nothing much gets done on the planet during the last two weeks of December nor the first week of the new year. I experienced it first hand when Clyde was in the hospital.

I was on vacation the last week before the new year, so I kept myself busy gathering clothes to donate to Goodwill and Salvation Army. I dreaded the coming year; I didn't want to leave Clyde in 1995. I felt I had abandoned him and I wanted to stay with him. I knew there was nothing I could do to stop time. I had been unsuccessful with holding back Christmas, so why did I think I would have any control with holding back the new year? I knew my thoughts were just wishful thinking, but if I could have stopped time, I would have that night.

$\approx$

"Mom, are you okay?" Clyde Daryl asked me as I folded the clothes carefully in the donation box.

"I'm okay, Clyde Daryl," I replied. "I was just thinking. You know how it is."

"Dad really loved this sweater, didn't he?" he said, pointing to one of Clyde's favorites.

He had always worn his short-sleeve striped peach and blue-colored shirt. He loved to wear the shirt with his relaxed khaki slacks.

"Yes, he did, didn't he!" Clyde Daryl chuckled as he remembered his father wearing the shirt.

"He wore that shirt all the time, Mom," he said laughing. "It looked good on him, too."

"Yeah Clyde Daryl," I said. "Clyde was very particular about his clothes. He would always ask me about his color coordination."

A rush of sadness filled my eyes and I blinked my eyelids to shelter the tears. Clyde Daryl saw my tears and touched me on the shoulders.

"Mom, it's going to be all right," he said. "I miss him, too. I really miss his smiling face."

Trying to change the subject, Clyde Daryl picked up Clyde's cap that he wore to work during the freezing days of winter.

"Mom, do you remember this cap? Dad would pull it over his head and snap it under his chin. He looked so funny in that cap," he said with a big grin.

I began to laugh as well. "Yeah, I remember that old cap. Clyde should have been ashamed of himself, pulling that cap down over his ears like that. But you know what, he wasn't ashamed. He just wanted to keep warm. Clyde is a character. He's truly a character!"

Clyde Daryl and I had a good time that evening reminiscing about the good old days. Alex Keith joined us later and we all smiled and even laughed as we took turns telling some of Clyde's old jokes. We had a good evening together as a family, unlike any other night since Clyde had left us. We felt right at home, telling wonderful stories about our loving life together.

We all laughed out loud when Alex Keith told the story about when he and Clyde traveled to Kmart. Alex Keith always knew he could get away with just about everything when he was around Clyde.

"I always wanted to go shopping with Dad because he would buy me a toy. I remember one time when Dad took me to Kmart and I wanted this toy airplane I had spotted on the store shelf. I really wanted that airplane," Alex Keith said with a big smile. "I remember Dad telling me that he wasn't about to buy me another toy because I had plenty, but he always bought it for me. I was thrilled to have the toy airplane. That's why I always wanted to go shopping with Dad instead of you, Mom," he chuckled. "I could get just about any toy I wanted with Dad."

We shared stories and laughed together about our special memories. I enjoyed it very much because we were laughing and enjoying the conversation. As the evening wore on, we knew it would end in sadness. No matter how much we laughed that night, eventually the reality settled over us like a dark cloud. I said good night to the boys that New Year's Eve night and retired to bed around 11:15 p.m. I didn't want to let go. I didn't want to leave Clyde in 1995. I wanted to carry him with me into the New Year. I watched the last few minutes of 1995 slip into the past.

"Lord, no matter what I say or do, you're still going to let 1996 happen, aren't you?" I asked. "Can't you stop the time? I don't want to leave Clyde in 1995," I pleaded.

I watched the New Year's coverage and everyone was smiling. They were all with their special someone. I watched the ball slowly descend from the sky on the TV as the last few seconds ticked away, I knew time wouldn't ever stop until God said so. As the clock majestically changed from 11:59 p.m. to midnight, I knew I had lost my Innisfree forever in 1995. I couldn't bring him with me. He wasn't coming back to me, ever. I battled with my new reality numerous times during my first few years.

"Please take care of him, Lord," I said as I fell on my knees in despair.

Clyde Daryl and Alex Keith came knocking on my door.

"Hold on a second," I said as I walked into the bathroom to bury my face in water to wash away my tears.

"Come on in," I said, wiping the tears. This time they saw my bloodshot eyes and the tears didn't stop.

"Happy New Year, Mom." Clyde Daryl and Alex Keith came rushing toward me with their arms stretched wide open for a big group hug.

"Happy New Year!" they said again.

And choking back my tears with a sniffle, I hugged them back and said, "Happy New Year, my sons! Happy New Year!"

CHAPTER FIFTEEN

Coping with Reality

*Initially, facing reality was extremely difficult for me, but I knew
eventually I had to face the fact that Clyde was gone. I was starting to
cope with my new reality and appreciating what I'd learned about grief.
I knew it wouldn't be easy, but I wanted to try to keep going, for my
children, for my family, and for myself.*

The first days back to work after the holidays
were welcomed. I was glad I didn't have extra time on my
hands at home. I had kept busy gathering clothing to donate
to several local charities, but not Clyde's. I was glad that I
had been with my family and that Clyde Daryl had spent two
weeks at home. The Lord knew we needed to be close to each
other. School had started again and we were all trying to get
back into our routines. Clyde Daryl had left a few days later
to Wake Forest.

During the holidays, I scheduled grief therapy for Alex Keith.
I had a few more group sessions and soon would be consid-
ered a graduate of the program. Since most of Ms. Arrington's
therapy was geared for adults, she recommended someone else
for Alex Keith.

I had learned through my group interaction that it was important to talk about my feelings and to keep a journal. I had started one long before I started seeing Ms. Arrington, but it was good to know I was doing the right thing by writing down my thoughts. I had also suggested to Clyde Daryl that he seek group therapy in Winston-Salem. He said that he would.

I arrived home one cold afternoon in January 1996. We had experienced some very wintry days since the holidays had come and gone. At home, I had continued to sift through my closet bulging with clothes, hoping to give away more of them. I stared at Clyde's clothes and saw that everything was still neatly arranged just as he'd left it months before.

"I'm not ready to take Clyde's clothes out of the closet," I said. "I'm not ready, Lord."

I couldn't even bear to think of giving his clothes away. I wanted them to stay on his side of the closet, right where he left them—intact, undisturbed.

"Alex Keith," I called. "Please come and get this box and place it in the den."

He walked into the room and grabbed the box.

"Mom," he said, "what do you have in this box, an elephant?"

"No, son, but almost one," I said, smiling back at him.

"Just place it next to the door and we'll take it to Goodwill tomorrow."

Hoping to capture Clyde's scent, I pulled one of his grey suits out of the closet and buried my face into it. Even now I could still detect his scent, and I was delighted. Sadness filled me and I cried inside because I knew eventually that his scent would fade away.

"Lord," I said, "Please let me keep his scent to remember him. I don't have anything else of him. Let me keep his scent, Lord," I pleaded, looking up toward the ceiling.

Again, there were no answers. Clyde had been gone for nine months now. The months had passed too quickly for me. I held on to his shirt, slacks, and even his suits. I wanted to close my eyes and feel his presence. So I stood near the closet for a few moments, enjoying what was left of my dear husband's physical presence.

I pulled one of his short-sleeve shirts, the khaki-colored one, to my chest and took in a deep breath, but was barely able to detect his scent. It's amazing the things that you remember when the person isn't around you anymore. I didn't think I paid much attention at the time, but special moments played back in my mind. The way Clyde used to shave and pull up his lips to shave his face was absolutely fascinating and funny. I remember one time while Clyde was shaving when he pulled and folded in his lips and nose and managed somehow to cut his face while clowning around with me in the bathroom. I giggled as I remembered his crazy antics. I smiled as the memories unraveled in my mind. He didn't let much get him down. I remembered our long talks together and how much we laughed and had fun.

"Clyde, you know, we had beautiful moments together, didn't we?" I said sadly. "It was just you and me in the beginning. We had a hard time financially, but it made us both stronger. Thank you sweetheart...thank you so very much."

I walked back to the bed with Clyde's suit and draped it over my body. It was the last suit that he bought and he never had the opportunity to wear it. I continued to stare at it, spreading both sleeves over my face.

"Lord, please let me remember him tonight, please."

I sat on Clyde's side of the bed and breathed deeply into his suit, praying to God to strengthen me so I could to travel the rest of my life journey without him. My breathing became shallow as I longed to capture his presence one last time. The chest pains had been relentless, so I promised myself I would see a doctor soon.

I fell asleep with my arms wrapped around Clyde's suit. I felt safe and warm and away from the cold night. Before I went to sleep I pressed the television remote to mute. As I wrapped myself into Clyde's suit, I felt safe and calm on that cold, dreary night in January and didn't have any trouble sleeping.

Therapy Resumes in the New Year

I was glad to be going back to group therapy. As mid January 1996 rolled into existence, I was enthusiastic about attending the session. The first session of the year brought in new people including a middle-aged lady who had lost her mother and husband within months of each other.

After the session was over, I walked over and hugged her. I told her about Clyde's tragic death to a very rare disease and she hugged me back. I told her she had given me strength to keep going as I listened to her talk about her situation and I would continue to pray for her and her family.

I knew I wasn't the only person who had lost a loved one, but when I listened to others describe their pain, I learned quickly that we all had pain to bear. All of us. After the meeting several of us gathered in the parking lot and talked a while before leaving for home. I thanked God for his presence in my life. As I walked into our home, I went straight to Alex Keith and hugged him lovingly and asked him how his day had been. I felt good inside. No, I felt alive.

As always, he said, "Mom, I'm doing okay. I'm just playing with my *Game Gear* right now.

"And how was your day, Mom?" he asked, looking over at me with his dark brown eyes.

"I'm doing okay," I replied. I felt this was as good a time as any for me to talk to Alex Keith about grief therapy.

"You know, Alex Keith, I've been going to grief therapy with this group. I enjoy being with the people and sharing my thoughts with them about Clyde." I hesitated for a moment for it to sink in.

"I think it would be a good thing for you to do as well. But not the therapist I'm seeing. I believe it would be a good thing for you to talk about your feelings, son...about your dad. You don't talk about him much and I believe it would be a good thing if you did."

"Oh Mom," he replied. "I'm okay. I'm really okay. I don't want to talk to anyone. I'm really all right talking to you and Clyde Daryl about dad. Really I am."

"I know you are, son. I just feel you need to talk it out. I know it won't change anything, but at least, let's look at it together, okay," I responded, stroking him on his shoulders.

"Oh, well, okay," Alex Keith said reluctantly.

Alex Keith had managed to keep his feelings buried. I wanted him to talk about Clyde, and even though he hadn't talked about his father with me, I prayed that he would talk to someone else—a professional. Brother Clayton spent some time with Alex Keith and I was thankful. I knew it was important for him to interact with a father figure and Brother Clayton was that and more. As the months turned into years, I knew he would grow to miss his father beyond words as he matured.

I was glad he didn't push against seeing a grief counselor. I knew in the end it would be good for him and it would be good for me as well. The next week I spoke with Ms. Arrington and she recommended someone for Alex Keith.

Diagnostic Test at St. Francis Hospital

"Mrs. Slappey, you are fine. You've gone through a lot with your husband. You just need to take it easy," Dr. Dannell said to me as she patted me on the shoulder at St. Francis Hospital. Dr. Dannell performed a heart catheter and found no heart abnormalities. I was relieved I wasn't having a heart attack and appreciated her reassuring words that I was physically okay. Dr. Dannell had a beautiful, calming spirit about her and

I would always appreciate her caring attitude and genuine concern for me. I never told Clyde Daryl or Alex Keith about my visits to the doctor and my having severe chest pains. I didn't want them to worry.

⌒

The first few weeks of the new year passed quickly. Alex Keith and I attended grief therapy. I felt we were making good progress. He was talking about his feelings with the therapist, and I was glad. The days turned into weeks, and before I knew it, it was mid February. I was still going to bed around 11:30 p.m. and waking up around 4:00 a.m., but it was better than 2:00 a.m.

I was in dire pain one early morning in mid February. Sleep had simply deserted me once again. I glanced over at the end of my bed and reached over and grabbed my Bible by its end, dragging it behind me into the bed. I hadn't read in a while, so I ruffled through the gold-edged pages, skimming for my favorite Scriptures.

Feeling a bit restless, I kept flipping through the pages until I found these words from Psalms 30:1-5:

I will extol Thee, O Lord; for Thou hast lifted me up, and hast not made my foes to rejoice over me. O Lord my God, I cried unto Thee, and Thou hast healed me. O Lord, thou hast brought up my soul from the grave: Thou hast kept me alive, that I should not go down to the pit.

Sing unto the Lord, O ye saints of His, and give thanks at the remembrance of His Holiness. For His anger endureth but a moment; in His favour is life: weeping may endure for a night, but joy cometh in the morning.

The words pulsated in my mind: *weeping may endure for a night, but joy comes in the morning.*

"Oh Lord, I pray, let it come. Please let joy come in the morning."

Pulling the pillow close to my face, I drifted slowly back into quiet sleep as I whispered the words: *weeping may endure for a night, but joy comes in the morning.*

I didn't wake up again until about 6:30 a.m. I took a deep breath and prayed to my Lord silently. Alex Keith and I moved rather quickly to leave the house that morning. I reflected on my almost one year of sleeping without Clyde. Whether I liked it or not, I was learning to live without him. As much as I had struggled against it, God was still carrying me on. The calcium tablets had actually worked. They had helped me sleep better.

"Lord," I prayed, "I'm trying to live every day without Clyde. Many days it hadn't been easy. Please help me keep going and take it one day at a time. That's really all that we have, Lord, is the present in time."

I prayed earnestly to God urging him to give me the strength to keep going. It was time for me to go, so I grabbed my handbag and rushed out of the house. I knew I would be late for work, but hopefully, I wouldn't be too late. My saving grace through the many months of turmoil was going to work every day. I didn't think so at first, but working as a technical writer, especially with the analysis and research aspects of my job, had helped me to focus better. I was thankful for my job; I was thankful to God. I was thankful to my teammates and my managers for lending me a helping hand during my darkest days of living in the shadows.

Alex Keith and I were attending grief therapy together. The doctor felt that sharing in our group therapy might work out better for Alex Keith. Eventually, Alex Keith would participate in one-on-one therapy. I was glad we had taken the step together.

It would take time for us to deal with our tragedy and one day we would smile again.

On the last night of group therapy, I said goodbye to Ms. Arrington and everyone. I told her I would always appreciate her thoughtfulness and kindness. She was the epitome of a loving, caring professional and I would miss her very much. Ms. Arrington holds a soft place in my heart and throughout the years, I have recommended her services to others.

My Trip to the Mayo Clinic

With group therapy behind me, I wanted to focus on taking care of myself better. I kept having the chest pains and even though I was examined by one of the best cardiologists in Columbus, I still felt a bit unnerved about my pains and my diagnosis of stress. So, I decided to get a second opinion and chose the Mayo Clinic. I chose Jacksonville instead of Rochester, Minnesota, because I didn't have the strength to return to the place where Clyde had died. I trusted the Mayo Clinic to examine and give me their professional opinion about my chest pains and general health.

I called the receptionist and scheduled an appointment for Monday, March 18, 1996, only a few weeks away. Mae agreed to come up to the house again and stay with Alex Keith while I was away. I would be gone for about a week. I would drive down to Jacksonville instead of flying since it was only a five-hour trip. I had a lot of respect for the Mayo Clinic and I prayed that the branch would live up to its parent's reputation in Rochester.

"Jacksonville will be fine," I said. "They should have about the same treatment and reputation. At least I really hope so."

Soon March 18 arrived, and as I was about to pull out of the driveway that Monday morning, I read the concern on her face.

"Debbie, you be careful, here," Mae said. "I really hate to see you drive so far alone."

"I'll be okay, Mae. Truly I will. I'll drive slowly. You see," I said pointing to my map. "I have my map in hand. I'll be okay."

"I have to do this, Mae," I said, hesitating for a moment. "I need to go and get myself checked out. That's all. I'll be okay...Really I will."

"I know you will," she replied. "Just let me know when you arrive. Call me, okay," she said with that concerned look in her eyes, hugging me tightly. I knew what she was thinking.

"Okay. I'll give you a call as soon as I check in. I love you, Mae. I have my car phone, too, so everything should be fine."

I waved to Mae as I backed out the driveway. It was around 11:00 a.m. when I left home. Waving to her one more time, I placed the car in drive and sped down the road. I had prayed about the trip and had asked God to take care of me as I drove away from home. I also asked God to take care of the family while I was away. Earlier that morning, I had talked to Alex Keith and hugged him before he left for school.

"Lord, please help me to be safe and please protect me from those crazy people on the road," I said as I cleared Interstate 185 and drove onto Highway 280, heading toward Albany, Georgia. The morning was crisp and cool and it was serenely quiet on the road. The drive gave me plenty of time to think about things and it was good for me to do so.

I had five hours to drive from Columbus, Georgia, to Jacksonville, Florida and I would make the best of it. I would enjoy the captivating scenery along the way.

"Lord," I said, driving down the road. "I really want my heart to be all right. I don't want anything to happen to me. Please let me be okay for my children and myself. I need to take care of them."

I was glad I could speak to God. He was my driver that morning. As I drove toward Cusseta, Georgia, a dense fog settled in front of me, seemingly out of nowhere. I slowed down a bit and flipped on my lights. For a mile or so, I couldn't see 100 feet ahead of me.

After about 45 minutes, the fog lifted and I felt much better. Minutes later I drove into Dawson, Georgia. I remembered the quaint little town so well. Back in the 1980s while living in Albany, Georgia, we would stop at the chicken place where the rooster stood proud and tall above the building's roof. I chuckled as I remembered Clyde's words: "the only clean thing in that building was the rooster on top." I smiled even now as I remembered.

Based upon my travel time, I estimated I would arrive in Jacksonville no later than 4:00 p.m., right smack in the middle of rush hour traffic, unfortunately. Why I decided to drive down to Jacksonville alone in March 1996 is beyond me as I think about it now years later. I guess somewhere in my mind I felt I needed to prove to myself that I could take a trip alone, without him. It was all I could think of at the time.

So, I kept traveling down that lonely road. Spring was just around the corner, and even though dogwood trees were blooming, most of the grass on the side of the road was still dull grey, at least in sections along the highway.

"Lord," I whispered, "I don't know, Lord, whether I'm really having major issues or if it's the grief that's giving my body a fit, but please let me be okay, Lord. I pray in Jesus' name. Amen."

In no time I was headed for Albany, Georgia. I was enjoying my drive back to my old hometown and felt good inside.

Soon, I was seeing familiar statues that dotted Highway 280 as I inched closer to Dougherty County. Clyde and I had lived in Albany for 10 years before relocating to Columbus in 1988. Clyde had been promoted to Parts Specialist at the Georgia Power Company and I was very proud of him. I worked as a marketing and business education instructor at Albany Technical Institute at the time. But when Clyde received his promotion I didn't hesitate to quit my job and relocate with him to Columbus. I had a great job that paid quite well, but when it came to a choice between work and family, family always won hands down. So, we packed up the house and moved to Columbus.

Clyde relocated to Columbus in July and the rest of us joined him in late August. We wanted to make sure Alex Keith started kindergarten in Columbus rather than in Albany. Since it was late in the school registration process, we had to register Alex Keith at Gentian Elementary for his kindergarten year. But the next year when he entered first grade, I was determined to register him at Waddell Elementary, his assigned school. Our kids were growing up quickly. Clyde Daryl would be attending Fort Middle School in the seventh grade.

The memories took center stage in my mind as the tires wound down Highway 280. I looked over to my left and saw the old Lilliston Corporation building, at home among the towering pine trees in the background. While working at M&M Mars for six years, I had visited Lilliston numerous times to pick up the company quarterly newsletter. I smiled as I thought about the many times I left M&M Mars on Oakridge Drive, and drove to Lilliston Corporation to pick up the newsletter. I had managed the *Snacktivities* newsletter for two years before leaving M&M Mars in 1985.

Albany had always been very special to us. We had many family members and friends, and especially our brothers and sisters at the Church of Christ on U.S. 19 South. As I edged closer to the city limits, my smile widened as I noticed the progress on the outskirts of Albany. Dawson Road was scattered about with many new buildings, including several anchor stores including J.C. Penney and Dillards at the Albany Mall. As my eyes panned each side of the road, I was spellbound by the many thriving retail businesses that lined the perimeter of the mall. The growth spurt had occurred in a measly seven years.

I kept driving through the city, but slowed a bit to enjoy the scenery. I was well ahead of schedule. From Dawson Road, I turned right onto Slappey Drive and took a left onto Oglethorpe Boulevard, passing Highland Magnet School, Clyde Daryl's old elementary school.

As I turned left onto Oglethorpe Boulevard, Highway 82, I couldn't help but peek out of the passenger window and see the old apartment complex where we lived when we first relocated from Spartanburg, South Carolina, in 1977. The apartment was still standing, but barely. Surrounding the dilapidated apartment building were overgrown border bushes encircling the apartment, and it was all overshadowed by a makeshift auto shop. "That old shop is still there." I smiled in amazement.

"And this was our home, Clyde, for almost two years," I said with a smile. "God was surely very good to us when we bought our first home on Colquitt Avenue." The sun's brightness beamed on my face as I continued to drive down the highway. I felt calm and at peace with myself as the warm glow of the sun kissed my cheeks and arms. For safety's sake, I purchased some pepper spray and placed it under the rug on the passenger side of the car.

Lord, I thought silently, *I just hope I don't have to use it.*

I felt privileged and blessed to be assured that God was doing the driving for me. He was the driver and I was the passenger. I thanked Him again for giving me the courage to drive down alone. I recited 2 Timothy 1:7 from memory as I kept driving.

For God hath not given us the spirit of fear;
but of power, and of love, and of a sound mind.

My grey Oldsmobile cruised on down the road. I felt empowered that afternoon because I knew I had triumphed over another obstacle in my life as I learned to handle things on my own, even driving. It was a bright and sunny afternoon with a brisk cool wind flying on the wings of the afternoon sunshine. As I neared my destination, the adrenaline began to build in my hands and I felt them tingling with exhilaration. I didn't want to miss the exit, so I clenched my fists around the steering wheel as I neared it.

As God always did, he took care of me. The sign appeared on the horizon and I moved to the turning lane. Within minutes, I rounded the exit road onto Interstate 10. When I saw the sign: *Lakeland and Jacksonville, Florida*, I felt relieved.

"I did it, Lord!" I said rather excitedly. "I did it! Thank you so very much."

I knew I wouldn't have to take another turn until I arrived in Jacksonville, and so far, the trip had been uneventful.

I was glad I was driving down to Jacksonville on my own. I was absolutely euphoric. I finally calmed down and kept driving toward Lakeland, gawking at the breathtaking scenery that only the State of Florida could encapsulate. The landscape was picturesque; on each side of the road were trees like none I'd seen before. The trees were very tall, similar to the tall cedar trees at home, but much prettier.

In addition to the beautiful palm trees stood rather statuesque pine trees that layered the sky with their billowing branches. About 30 miles out of Lakeland I drove into a protected forest reserve. The virgin forest seemed to stretch some 20 miles or so and cast an eerie calm upon me in the middle of nowhere. All kinds of flowers were growing on each side of the road and trees stood magically waving their branches in the wind as if they were welcoming me to Florida.

As I drove through the reserve, I felt the hair stand up on the back of my neck. I couldn't explain it, but the feeling was real. For about 20 minutes I felt horribly alone. The drive through the forest was whisper quiet. Occasionally, I met another car and was extremely grateful. It felt very creepy as the sun hid behind the clouds at times while I continued to drive toward

Jacksonville. For the next 20 miles it felt as if I was the only one alive as I drove through the Robin Hood-like forest.

As I neared the city limits of Jacksonville, I became very excited once again in anticipation of my arrival. I had driven for five hours without any interruptions until I arrived in Jacksonville, right in the middle of rush-hour traffic. I sat in snail-creeping traffic for almost an hour before traffic began to move again. Using my directions, I drove directly to the Mayo Clinic located on San Pablo Drive. The clinic was located on the east side of the city near the beach, and when I turned left onto San Pablo Drive, the scenery was beyond my expectations. The campus was a stunning canvas of unimaginable serenity.

Instead of traveling around the city on Interstate 95, I chose to drive through downtown where I saw a beautiful lake situated in the middle of the city. It was a beautiful city. "I could easily live here," I said. "Easily."

The population of Jacksonville was about half a million people. Automobiles were everywhere. I could tell from the construction that the city was growing very rapidly. I was jubilant to have finally arrived in the city and felt I had triumphed over a sleeping giant in my life, traveling alone and learning to function without Clyde.

The scenery was breathtaking and the entrance into the clinic was accented with every beautiful flower that you could imagine. I couldn't help but fall in love with the tranquil setting of the evening sun. As I drove into the entrance, I noticed the towering oaks trees and beautiful magnolias outlining the campus. They had the truest evergreen tree leaves I've ever seen.

During my planning for the trip, I had reserved a room at the Marriott Courtyard Hotel. The receptionist told me that the hotel was near the clinic, but I had no idea that the hotel was inside the campus. So when I drove into the entrance, my mouth dropped when I saw the campus.

It was remarkable, beyond enchanting and even alluring. I was mesmerized by the tranquil setting peeking serenely through the trees. Its regal presentation of flowers towered over the landscape and the flower beds reminded me of several garden settings that so attractively adorned Callaway Gardens near Columbus in Hamilton, Georgia. I was instantly put at ease by the magnificent splendor of the décor. It was more than a clinic I thought as my eyes toured the campus. It was a welcome respite for me.

"This is very nice," I spoke rather loudly. "I like this setting, Lord. It's peaceful; it's quiet. I'm glad I came here. Thank you."

As I continued to immerse myself in the splendor of the campus, I looked over to my left and read a sign that directed me to the next turn to Marriott Courtyard. Nestled within the towering trees was an off-white stucco-like building, the hotel. I was awed by the different kinds of trees that surrounded the hotel, enveloped by palm trees. Dogwoods sprinkled the perimeter of the woods around the hotel entrance as well.

After a much needed stretch I walked into the hotel lobby. Directly in front of the hotel was a kidney-shaped lake filled with a family of ducks wobbling in and out of the water.

The lobby was tastefully decorated with some of the same flowers I'd seen near the campus entrance. The scent reminded me of beautiful, fresh-picked flowers. I checked into my room, and as soon as I opened the door, I placed my suitcase on the bed near the door and collapsed on the other bed next to the double window. A few minutes later, I pulled my tired body from the bed, dropped to my knees and prayed to Almighty God to thank Him for bringing me to this spectacular place of refuge.

"I really needed to be here," I said. "It feels good to be here.

"Lord, I thank you…I thank you for giving me the courage to drive so far away from home. I needed to do this, Lord, and

I know You know what I mean. I thank You for letting me come down here. I needed to see it for myself.

"Help the doctors, I pray, as they check my heart. I pray it will be okay, Lord. I pray for this; it just hurts so much, Lord. Please let it all be all right, but not my will, but Yours be done."

I was elated and apprehensive at the same time and wanted everything to be okay. As soon as I finished praying, I called Mae to let her and Alex Keith know I was all right and had made it to Jacksonville. I didn't want them to worry since they hadn't heard from me since I left home early that morning.

I talked with Alex Keith as well, and he was busy doing homework. I told Alex Keith I loved him and would be heading back home on Friday. Friday, March 22, 1996, seemed light years away as I hung up the telephone. I had worked up a ferocious appetite, so I decided to take my bath and get something to eat. I didn't want to eat alone, but I knew I would have to do it eventually.

The room was very comfortable. It was tastefully accented with furnishings contemporary in design. The room's décor was highlighted with a very comfortable brown leather chair matching closely with the square table attached to the wall. Each bed was covered with a beautiful chenille comforter accented with ribbons of silk strung around evergreen leaves merging into the center of the comforter.

The drapes covering the sliding door were constructed of the same contemporary colors of gold, green, and rose on silk fabric, but more damask-like, which added a more elegant, finishing touch. I was pleased with the bathroom as well. It was equipped with a white double vanity, encased with marble-like tile and four light fixtures tacked across the wall. To further enhance the décor, the same wallpaper continued the theme from the room into the bathroom, but with the addition of a contrasting stream of powder blue and rose border wallpaper with tiny dots of yellow hues piercing the center.

Eating Alone

I walked into the restaurant and looked around at the beautifully decorated eating area. "I just hope the food is good," I said to myself.

I had no intentions of driving away from the hotel as the sun was just about to set, and it would be dark soon. It was either the hotel restaurant or the vending machines for me. I was unusually uncomfortable about eating alone. I had avoided doing this back home, but now I had no choice.

"Debbie, you need to do this," I said. "You can do this."

I walked closer to the attendant and before I could say my name, she spoke to me.

"Good evening," she said. "Ms…"

I hesitated, but finally uttered, "Hello, my name is Deborah Slappey…"

"Are you dining alone, Mrs. Slappey?" the waitress asked.

I stood frozen by her question. I really didn't want to answer it. But I was dining alone. Clyde wasn't here to eat with me. He never would be eating with me again. That was the sad truth, no matter how much it hurt me to say it.

I choked back the tears as I repeated my own words in my mind: "Clyde isn't coming back. We won't ever sit down together and eat again."

"Yes…Yes, I am," I finally stuttered, "Yes, I'm alone."

"Well right this way, Mrs. Slappey," she said, ushering me to follow her.

This was the first time someone had asked me, "Are you dining alone tonight, Mrs. Slappey?"

"Is this okay, Mrs. Slappey?" the waitress asked me, stopping in front of a small table..

"Yes, it's fine." I stammered.

Why was she asking me these questions? I asked. *Did she know about my husband dying and that I would be eating alone? Did she know?* I wondered.

Calm down, Debbie, I thought silently. *It's okay. She doesn't know about Clyde. She couldn't know. You haven't told her anything.*

"Is this table okay, Mrs. Slappey?" she asked again, interrupting my thoughts.

"Oh, yes, it's fine. It's really fine," I was finally able to respond to her question.

"You seemed to stare at the table. I thought maybe you wanted another place to sit," she replied.

"No, it's quite all right, Ma'am. It's fine," I said as I pulled the chair back from the table and sat down.

The waitress gave me a menu, but I knew what I wanted already.

"I'll bring your beverage," she said before walking away.

"Thank you so very much," I replied to her. I felt so out of place for a moment. I heard her words echo in my mind again: *Are you dining alone, Mrs. Slappey? Are you alone?*

I didn't want to think about it. The thought just sliced into me as if with a dull butter knife. I hated being alone. I hated being a widow. I hated that Clyde had died and had left me here to deal with the pain of being alone. I hated being in the restaurant alone. I couldn't even remember the last time I had eaten alone in a restaurant.

"Lord, I pray, please help me with this," I began to pray. "Please help me deal with being alone tonight in this strange place."

Soon another waitress came and was very nice as well. She took my order of baked chicken, mashed potatoes and broccoli, and before long she brought me a mixed green salad. I was starving, so I immediately began to eat my salad as I looked around the restaurant. The room was filled with beaming chandeliers, which radiated their glow over the white silk-rayon tablecloths. It was a dazzling representation of brilliance, coupled with an amazing light show. My eyes followed the light brilliance as I spotted other people dining not far away.

I ate my salad and it was very good. I took my time and ate my meal rather slowly. By now it was about 8:00 p.m., and I didn't want to eat too fast, hoping to avoid heartburn. Forty-five minutes later, I had finished my meal and was heading back to my room. Since I didn't know anyone at the clinic, I wanted to get back to my room quickly and lock my door.

I had resolved to walk around the campus during the day-time, but not at night. I walked into my room, locked the door, and placed the arm of the chair underneath the doorknob so no one could open it. I didn't want any surprises. I lay on the second bed in the room, the one closest to the double window. I always felt safer in the second bed, not the first one. I checked the local listing for specific television shows, but I didn't see much to look at. I pretty much ended the evening by watching the local and national news.

After watching for a while, I lay my head back on the pil-low and began to reflect on the day's journey. I really couldn't believe I had driven all the way to Jacksonville alone. This was a big deal for me as Clyde, for years, had driven me practically everywhere. But now I was learning to do things on my own again. I promised myself not to ever be dependent on anyone else again, at least not that way. I was tired as the evening unfolded. The room was very quiet and the serenity spoke so quietly that soon I felt my body giving in to sleep. I changed into my night clothes and rolled my hair and retired for the night. I kept most of the lights on and the TV as well.

As it had been a very busy day, I turned over to my side and listened to the local news in Jacksonville. Before going to sleep, I wanted to look over the paperwork I'd received from the clinic to make sure I had the papers filled out correctly. My appointment was scheduled for 6:30 a.m. I set the alarm clock for 5:15 a.m. so I would arrive at the campus by 6:00. The time was nearing 10:30 p.m., and I longed for sleep. So, I turned down the television, said my prayers and then rolled over to my side to fall asleep.

To my surprise, I didn't wake up until close to 3:25 the next morning. It was a blessing to be able to sleep in a strange room far away from home. It had been the first time in a long while I hadn't cried.

First Day at the Mayo Clinic

I went down to the lobby around 5:45 a.m. to eat the continental breakfast and to catch the shuttle. As I made myself comfortable in the lobby on one of the sofas it didn't take long before the shuttle appeared outside to take us to the clinic. I was rather nervous as I hurried out of the hotel to catch the shuttle bus. As I approached the building, I noticed its off-white bricking. The shuttle pulled into the entrance, where I observed several other patients waiting at the entrance. *Wearing my sneakers was a good idea,* I thought. I remembered the long walks with Clyde at the Mayo Clinic, so I knew I'd better wear comfortable shoes.

I walked into the lobby and it too was nicely decorated with modern furnishings throughout the large lobby area. As I panned the room I noticed several lines of people standing in front of customer service windows. I walked to the line that had the fewest number of people and waited my turn.

I listened to the conversations as we waited in line. In no time I was at the front of the line waiting to be called.

"Next!" the lady said rather loudly.

I approached the window.

"Good morning," I said. "My name is Deborah Maxine Slappey. I have an appointment with the clinic."

"Did you complete your paperwork the clinic sent you, Mrs. Slappey?" she asked.

"Yes, I did," I replied to her, pulling out the documents from my packet and handing them to her. "Here is my completed information."

"Thank you," she said. "I need to see your insurance card."

I opened my purse and pulled out my wallet and handed my card to her. "Here it is," I responded, handing it to her.

She reviewed my paperwork and circled certain items on each page. Then she typed information from the documents into the computer. I stood waiting for her to finish. She paused and asked me questions from time to time. After a few minutes I had registered. She returned my paperwork and directed me to take the elevator to the Cardiology Department and give them the paperwork. I thanked her and turned to step onto the elevator with other people headed for cardiology. I wondered if the clinics were basically centralized or autonomous. I knew I would soon find out.

Soon I heard the beep from the elevator, letting me know I had arrived at my floor. Unlike Rochester, the room was practically packed with people. Looking around the room, I was able to locate a few empty seats at the back. I walked toward the receptionist and told her my name, handing her the paperwork I'd received from the receptionist downstairs. She looked over my paperwork and told me to have a seat while she created my itinerary for the next few days.

I remember Rochester being full, but this office is bursting with people, I thought. There was barely a place to sit down. I walked to the back of the room and for a moment, felt I was back in Rochester. I sat down on the left side of the receptionist desk and waited for her to call my name. She took my paperwork, pulled my name up on the computer, and started typing from the documents.

I looked around at the crowd. Everyone had a book, crocheting tools, or something in their hands to pass the time. It seemed they knew something I didn't know—it was going to be a very long wait. As it was still 7:30 in the morning, I didn't feel like reading. I propped my left elbow on my chair and laid my head against the chair and waited.

I pulled my purse under my arms tightly and closed my eyes.

No sooner had I had found my comfort spot on the chair than I heard my name, "Mrs. Slappey...Mrs. Slappey." I looked up and saw the lady turn her head from side to side, hoping to spot my silhouette from the crowd. "Mrs. Slappey..." she repeated again.

"Here I am," I said, walking toward her.

Tucking my purse under my arm, I walked quickly to her, because I didn't want her to skip my name.

"Yes, Mrs. Slappey. We have your schedule worked out. Now, let me go over it with you, okay," she continued.

I was scheduled to see several doctors, including the cardiologist. I remembered from Rochester that they were always thorough with their patient workups and wanted to make sure everything was okay physically. Mayo Clinic took a well-rounded approach to patient care. I liked that and was looking forward to my visit.

CHAPTER SIXTEEN

Learning to Live Without Him

I didn't know what to expect as I walked into the cardiologist office. I prayed that my heart would be okay. Over the past year I had been suffering from some incredible pain. I didn't know it at the time, but I had entered into another phase of grief, which was acknowledging that Clyde was gone and learning to restructure my life without his physical presence. In other words, I was learning to live again.

M Y FIRST STOP AT THE MAYO CLINIC would be with the cardiologist, who would oversee my entire visit. So far, he had scheduled me for lab work to include an EKG, an echocardiogram and other stuff I couldn't pronounce. My appointments were scheduled through Friday morning, which was good because I wanted to leave for home on Friday.

The receptionist indicated I would be called back as soon as possible. The doctors were already behind that morning and she told me that it might take up to an hour or so to see the doctor.

Since it was going to be a long wait, I browsed through magazines from the rack next to the table near the receptionist desk and strolled back to my chair. Unfortunately, someone else had already taken my seat, so I sat on the opposite side of the room and waited for them to call my name again. *This Mayo Clinic is even more impressive than its parent,* I thought. Their equipment was state-of-the-art. But as in Rochester, most of the information was entered into a computer. As I sat there for about two hours, people were slowly being called back into the examining rooms. I must have looked through dozens of magazines. I pulled out my notepad and started writing about my trip. This helped to pass the time.

"Well, Clyde," I said quietly. "Here I am down in Jacksonville waiting for a doctor to see me. Isn't that ironic? I was there with you every step of the way. But now I'm waiting for the doctor to see me. And I'm alone."

It was strange for me as I waited. I hadn't taken the time to see about myself while Clyde was sick. I wanted to make sure he was okay, but it was now time for me to take care of myself. I wanted to be here for my children.

"Mrs. Slappey." I looked up and saw a lady dressed in pink and white standing near the left side of the receptionist desk calling my name.

I stood up because I didn't think she would see me coming from the opposite side of the room. It took me a few seconds to walk to her. Again, I didn't want her to miss me.

"Here I am," I said as I walked quickly toward her.

"Hello, Mrs. Slappey. How are you doing?" she asked.

"I'm doing fine. Thank you for asking," I replied.

"I'm so sorry that we are running so far behind. The doctors have many patients to see this morning," she told me.

"There are so many people here," I replied to her. "My husband, Clyde, my late husband, was at the Mayo Clinic in Rochester, Minnesota, and I don't remember seeing as many people as I see down here. You have a lot of patients."

"Yes, we do," she said. "We are seeing Medicare patients, so we get a little behind from time to time," she told me, pointing at the door for me to enter.

She ushered me to a tiny room and pointed to the small couch. The room was an exact replica of the one in Rochester, except for the color. The color scheme was light cinnamon, not shiny, but with a matte finish.

"The doctor will be in to see you momentarily," she said as she walked out of the room and closed the door.

"Thank you so very much."

I looked around the room and it was truly déjà vu. The layout was the same as in Rochester. They had the same layout, which was very reassuring to me. Out of nowhere the door swung open.

"Good morning, Mrs. Slappey. How are you doing? I'm Dr. Jeff Jones," the doctor said, extending his right hand to me.

"I'm doing fine, Dr. Jones, and you?"

"I'm just fine. Thank you so very much for asking." He hesitated as he sat down at the computer desk.

"And what brings you to the Mayo Clinic, Mrs. Slappey?" he asked, looking at me with anticipation of my answer.

"Well, Dr. Jones," I started. "I've been having some pain in my chest. It's right under my left breast," pointing my right hand to my middle chest.

He asked me to describe the pain and I told him it felt like a thousand stabbing needles pricking under my skin. The stinging pain occurred every three or four minutes. I told him that it didn't hurt all the time, but it was very uncomfortable when the pain began to radiate across my chest cavity.

"My doctor in Columbus seems to think that it's stress related because I lost my husband about a year ago...Dr. Jones. I just want to be sure. I need to be sure."

"Tell me about your husband, Mrs. Slappey. When did he die?" he asked.

Dr. Jones listened to me intently as I described the amyloid disease that killed Clyde. He didn't know any specifics about the disease, but had heard about it. He then decided to add another appointment to my schedule—a psychologist. Of course, I knew why he did it. He would be checking my physical heart but he also wanted the psychologist to check my state of mind. I knew exactly what he was doing. Dr. Jones seemed very concerned.

Dr. Jones didn't examine me and I really didn't think he would. Pretty much, he followed the same procedures as they had done at Rochester with Clyde...fact finding and then determining the best regimen of treatment over the next few days. As I walked out of the door, Dr. Jones shook my hand and told me that he would see me later in the week. Indeed, I had come to know that this was the protocol at the clinic. Over the next few days I would be going to various physicians and completing a regimen of laboratory and other diagnostic treatments.

I walked out of the room and handed my now crossed-out schedule of appointments to the nurse. She asked me to sit down for a few minutes so she could make adjustments to my schedule. By this time, the room had almost emptied. I was able to sit close to the reception desk so she wouldn't forget me.

As I waited for the nurse, I thought about my conversation with Dr. Jones. Very few physicians were aware of primary amyloidosis. Since it was a killer disease, I was determined to bring more awareness about the disease. At the time I didn't know what, but I prayed I would have the strength one day to speak before groups about primary amyloidosis.

"Mrs. Slappey." I heard the nurse repeat my name as she looked around for me.

"Yes."

I walked toward the reception area.

"Mrs. Slappey, let me go over your schedule with you, okay? It has changed quite a bit."

Dr. Jones wanted me to start with diagnostic tests within the hour. The nurse had already called ahead so I would be able to go directly to the laboratory. Next, I would have an appointment with the cardiology department in the afternoon. I was scheduled for other diagnostic tests, such as the echocardiogram and EKG. The last change that Dr. Jones added was for me to see a psychologist on Tuesday afternoon.

I sat back down and waited for the nurse, and finally after another 10 minutes or so, she returned and said that Dr. Jones would see me for my final appointment at 10:00 a.m. Friday. The nurse gave me the directions to the laboratory and off I went.

As I walked through the corridor of the clinic, I noticed their building structure was a little different from that in Rochester. They didn't have many tall buildings; the facility was spread out horizontally rather than vertically like the Rochester campus. I walked from building to building instead of traveling up and down elevators. Also, each building was a different color and had a building number permanently affixed on the wall of the building entrance.

The laboratory was located near the main lobby entrance. I checked at the desk and sat down on one of the nice leather recliners to wait my turn. As I had witnessed upstairs in the cardiology department, there were many people in front of me. It would be a long wait, so I picked up a magazine and made myself comfortable. I felt I would be waiting at least an hour, maybe less.

The wait took about an hour before I was called into the back room for them to take my blood. Here I was, hundreds of miles away from home sitting in a very comfortable, cushiony soft chair, waiting for them to draw my blood.

I tell you, Debbie, you really have some nerve, girl. You really do, I said silently. But I didn't think it was nerve; it was a reckoning. I wanted to prove to myself that I could do this alone, without having someone to drive me down. I had prayed to God for strength. God knew better than anyone else what I was trying to do. I was declaring independence.

I left the laboratory at around 1:30 in the afternoon. Patients walked briskly to and fro, earnestly trying to maneuver around the campus using maps. I darted to my next appointment, back to cardiology.

I walked into the reception area, where once again the room was completely full. I checked with the receptionist and spotted an empty seat. Moments later I was flipping through a *Money* magazine while waiting. Folks didn't talk much as they waited for their names to be called.

After about two hours my name was finally called. They performed two tests of my heart, an EKG and an echocardiogram. Since I was only able to pick up some crackers from the dining area between appointments, I was famished by the time I finished the last test.

As I walked out of the campus building around 4:00 p.m., I felt the warm light of the sun permeate my face. Within minutes, I felt revived by the warm glow of the sun's rays. It felt good to be alive. As I closed my eyes to take in the moment, I sensed harmony, perhaps for the first time in a long while. I was transported to a special moment in time as I saw myself pushing Clyde in the wheelchair at the Mayo Clinic in Rochester. By this time, Clyde's body had weakened to the point that he was unable to walk. We were enjoying our time together; learning about the Mayo brothers and their enchanting legacy.

I smiled as I remembered our special moment together. I knew I would carry those special moments with me to my grave. We were filled with hope as I pushed Clyde in his wheelchair and locked it securely so he wouldn't fall out while reading the statue.

I spotted the shuttle ready to take patients back to the hotel.

"Ma'am," the driver said to me, "wouldn't you like a ride to the hotel?"

"No thanks. I'll just walk. It's such a beautiful day," I said to the gentleman. "Thank you for asking...Have a wonderful afternoon."

I wanted to see the campus. Everything was explicitly dazzling around me. I was captivated by the view as I walked on the path that led to the hotel. Flowers lined the walkway to the hotel. Since it was March, I didn't think all flowers had bloomed, but in Florida practically every flower was in full bloom. The flowers were just beginning to bloom in Georgia, but in Florida everything was a kaleidoscope of radiant colors.

Even though I wasn't good with identifying flowers, I gaped at the beautiful colors of gold, red, purple, and yellow. All evoked their own special dominance of beauty along the walkway. There were chrysanthemums, daffodils, tulips, azaleas, mums, and daisies of every shape and size and color of the rainbow. There were other flowers I didn't have a clue as to their names. They were simply beautiful. But I can tell you their elegant splendor paraded their colossal beauty against the backdrop of the campus as the sun found its way to the other side of the world.

I was in awe at the sight of the beautiful sunshine of God's creation and I felt very blessed to see, to touch God's wonderment of color. The campus reminded me of an enchanted garden overflowing with God's arrangement of radiance. As I walked closer to the hotel, I didn't want to go inside. I was mesmerized, even astonished by the grandeur of the campus.

"I'm glad I came here, Lord. Even beyond checking my heart. I'm glad I came."

In front of the hotel was a small lake and surrounding it on each corner were bunches of cattail plants. I watched the ducks as they swam out of the pond wagging their tail feathers; shaking off the excess water from their breasts. Then in an instant, the ducks turned around with their big bellies and slowly waddled back into the pool. It was a breathtaking sight to see.

Surrounding the pond was a stream of daisies of all shapes, colors, and sizes. The petals from the daisies gently fell from the flowers and sprinkled into the air, finally settling into the pond. I watched the flowers float around in the lake. It was all very special that afternoon as I watched nature at its finest. I watched bumble bees crowd into nearby mums and butterflies fly from one end of the pond to the other. I watched in amazement as the pond beamed with life and energy.

And then I heard my stomach growling and I knew it was time for me to leave the pond and return to my hotel room. I was very thankful at that moment.

"My stomach is growling," I said with some surprise. I hadn't eaten since that morning. I hadn't had the time.

And before I knew it, 30 more minutes had passed into oblivion as I studied the pond's fanfare. I looked at my watch and it was almost 5:00 p.m. Reluctantly, I walked away from the pond and into the lobby, smiling as I closed the door behind me. It was one of those special afternoons as I watched the habitat around the pond come alive with insects and animals of all kinds.

I knew it was time for me to put the chipped pieces of my life back together and go on. As I watched the bees pollinate the flowers, the butterflies dance over the budding flowers, and the Junebug display its neon armor of purple, green, and gold, I felt blessed to be alive. I was at peace...real peace that afternoon in Jacksonville, Florida. I was ready to go on with my life.

The clouds intruded on the sun's dominance as the afternoon waned to hide the beaming rays of the sun. I looked back one more time and smiled as I waved goodbye in my heart to the duck pond. It had been a humbling moment for me as I listened and became one with nature.

"Thank you, Lord," I said to Him, "for allowing me to witness your awesome power to heal and to comfort me in your care. I will always appreciate you."

Dining Alone Again

Around 6:30 p.m., after a good soaking shower, I decided I had better head down to the restaurant to eat. I knew I had to eat, but I wasn't so thrilled about eating alone.

"Come on girl," I said. "Come on, you can do it. Just put one foot in front of the other and walk down to the lobby. There's not that many people anywhere. It really won't matter. You can do it.

"Yes, I can," I said rather defiantly. "Yes, indeed I can." And I walked out of my hotel room.

Other than two or three families and me, the restaurant was nearly empty. Maybe the other folks knew something I didn't, since most of the visitors were eating off campus.

I could only imagine there were many places to eat in this beautiful oasis, but the food had been pretty good last night, so I was satisfied. The same young lady who had greeted me the previous night greeted me again and escorted me to a table near the window. I felt I could handle being alone and was doing quite well until I spotted two ladies, three tables down from me. One of the ladies was staring at me as I settled into my chair. Her stare became very uncomfortable. She was probably wondering why I was eating alone. Even more so, why I was at the clinic in the first place.

"Ma'am, have you decided what you would like to order tonight?" a voice asked, interrupting my thoughts.

Though startled for a brief moment I responded, "Yes, I am ready; I'll have the stuffed pork chops, baked potatoes, green beans, and lemonade."

"Would you like a salad, Ma'am?" she asked.

"Yes. Thank you. The Caesar salad is fine with a touch of Ranch. Thank you so very much."

"So, do you prefer having Ranch on your Caesar salad instead of Caesar, Ma'am?" she asked to clarify my salad dressing order.

"No, just put the Caesar salad dressing on the salad and give me a small cup of ranch dressing on the side."

"Yes, Ma'am. Certainly."

I looked at the lady again, and it appeared that she was looking over in my direction, possibly saying something about me, I didn't know. *She probably knows why I'm eating alone,* I thought silently. I became extremely uncomfortable as I stared back at the ladies. I decided to eat in my hotel room for the rest of the visit.

In less than an hour, I had eaten my dinner and left the restaurant, leaving a tip for the waitress. Walking briskly to my room, I grabbed some ice from the ice machine and closed my door to the world. I talked to Alex Keith and Mae and told them everything was going well. I went on to tell them that I would be seeing different doctors and undergoing tests of all kinds over the next couple of days. On Friday, I told them, I would be heading home.

I didn't tell Mae about the incident at the restaurant. I knew she would start to worry and I didn't want that to happen. I knew I wouldn't be going down to the restaurant to dine alone again. I wasn't quite ready for that reality, and I decided not to force the issue. It would come in time. For my remaining time at the clinic I ate dinner in my room.

Before going to bed I looked over my schedule, as I had several appointments. One of them I dreaded—the one with the psychologist. I hadn't asked to see a psychologist. As the television was already turned on, I changed it to the news. I guess I was pretty tired from the drive yesterday and the walk to appointments.

I woke up every second during the night, or so it seemed. I missed Clyde. I missed him very much. "If only he could be here with me." I finally fell into a deep sleep.

My Second Day at the Mayo Clinic

My second day at the clinic was filled with brilliant sunshine as I walked to my appointments. Between my doctor appointments, I stopped for lunch. There was really no need for me to go back to the hotel since my appointments were scheduled in increments of two hours. Between appointments, I hung around like most patients did, in the lobby reading, waiting for the next one. There was plenty of coffee to drink and magazines to scan through. I also took advantage of the lull time to tour parts of the facilities and the main lobby. Soon it was time for my appointment with the psychologist. I arrived at the reception desk 15 minutes early.

"Hello. I'm Deborah Slappey," I said to the receptionist. "I'm here for my 2:00 p.m. appointment."

I handed the paperwork over and she verified my appointment in the computer.

"The doctor will be with you shortly, Mrs. Slappey," she said. "You can have a seat and the nurse will call you."

"Thank you so very much."

Within 15 minutes of sitting down, the nurse walked out to the reception area and called my name. "Mrs. Slappey," she said, looking around for me in the crowd.

"Yes, here I am," I replied, waving my hand for her to see me. By this time, I knew the routine.

The nurse escorted me into one of the patients' rooms on the left side of the building. Everyone had been genial since my visit. I felt very special to be financially able to come down and be examined by a world-renowned health care facility. It was a privilege and I was thankful for that.

I walked into the room and sat on the sofa.

"The doctor will be with you shortly," she said and left the room.

"Thank you."

The door swung open within minutes.

"Good afternoon, Mrs. Slappey. My name is Dr. Anthony Beard. And how are you doing today?" the doctor asked as he reached out his right hand to greet me.

"I'm doing okay, Doctor."

The doctor walked directly to the large computer monitor. For each appointment the physician would enter my patient ID and read the summary of my visit so far. Once he finished reviewing my chart, he turned to me and asked again how I was doing.

"I'm doing all right, Doctor," I said. "No, I'm not. I've been having a lot of pain in my chest. It's been going on for sometime now, especially since my husband, Clyde, passed about 11 months ago."

"Yes, and what did he die of, Mrs. Slappey?" he asked, interrupting me.

"Clyde died of a very rare disease of the immune system, called primary amyloidosis. It's rare. The doctors who treated him in Columbus, Georgia didn't know he had it until it was too late. He was 43 years old when he died," I replied, sensing the cracks in my voice.

He seemed very inquisitive about the amyloid disease, just like all the others had been. I told Dr. Beard that the physicians in Rochester were the experts in the field.

"Mrs. Slappey, you talk as if your husband is still here sitting next to you," he said. "You have to let go and come to terms with your husband's death. It's been almost a year and you talk about him as if he's sitting next to you. But he's not."

"You don't seem to understand, Dr. Beard," I responded. "I can't let go, and if I do, I'll let go of me."

"Grief can cause a chemical imbalance in the brain," Dr. Beard began.

Over the next hour, Dr. Beard described the grieving process. He talked about how grief is a normal reaction to a significant loss that causes feelings of sadness and preoccupation with the loss.

Dr. Beard further explained that grieving is a process that typically progresses through stages, from becoming aware of the loss, to feeling and expressing grief, and eventually ending with adjustment to the loss. As there is no specific timeline that one progresses from one stage to the other, he noted, it's important that the progression through the various stages do occur to avoid a person becoming "stuck in one or more of the stages of the grieving process."

"Is that what's wrong with me?…that I'm stuck in my grief, holding on to Clyde?" I asked him.

I hadn't heard that term before, but I knew of a lady who was stuck in her grief. She never got over her son's death. *Had it happened to me?* I wondered. I guess Dr. Beard was describing the process to help me better understand my situation. Later on I would appreciate Dr. Beard talking to me the way he did that afternoon.

He told me there were medications he could prescribe to help me work through my grief. He described the chemical imbalance in the brain in more detail, and after about an hour, Dr. Beard shook my hand kindly and said to me again, "You have to learn to go on with your life, Mrs. Slappey. Your husband would want you to do so. Don't you think?" he asked me.

"Yes. Yes, he would," I replied, holding my head down.

"Take care of yourself," he said, and with a pat on the back of my hand, he said, "Good luck, Mrs. Slappey. Take care of yourself."

I thanked Dr. Beard for seeing me. I knew he'd seen many people in similar situations to mine. It was his job to help me learn to understand that the sting of losing my husband could become crippling, even to the extent of experiencing physical and psychological pain and symptoms, which I was experiencing. Nothing so far explained my chest pains. More and more it was looking like my mental anguish was causing my chest pains. I knew the doctors were coming to this conclusion as well.

As I walked out of the room, his words replayed in my mind like a tape recorder. I didn't want to feel this way. *Is my mourning for Clyde causing my chest pains? Am I simply reliving Clyde's death within my own body?*

"Lord," I said as I pondered his words, "Lord, is it true what the doctor has said? Is my grief causing my body to ache, causing my chest pains? Could it be true?"

I walked out of the room and remained totally preoccupied with the doctor's words.

"Lord," I said, as I walked out of the office, "I can't let him go; I'd let myself go if I did. I can't quite yet!"

With tears rolling down my face, I walked out of the building, wiping them away as they settled in the corners of my lips. Deeply disturbed, I felt the heat of the sun beat against my face as I headed toward the hotel. I didn't want to talk to anyone. I only wanted to keep walking and feel the warm glow of the sun's rays against my face.

"God," I said, as I walked closer to the hotel. "Please take care of me."

It was a good thing I didn't have anymore appointments for the rest of the day. I opened the door to my room and stretched out both arms above my head, collapsing on the bed, bursting into tears.

"Clyde, I really miss you," I said. "I really miss you in my life. Please, Lord, let him come back. Let Clyde come back to me…let him come back."

God took care of me that Tuesday afternoon. He allowed me to go to sleep right then and there and escape my pain and anguish. I felt comforted in my sleep; and I slept peacefully without any dreams. God always knows what is best and what to do in your deepest times of need. I had read about His deep love for us in His holy word, but when I had to experience it firsthand, I knew my Lord was taking care of me solely. I love the Lord for sheltering me during the darkest times of my life.

I awoke and turned my head to the clock. It read 6:41 p.m. I had slept for hours. I felt okay after my usual cry. I knew it was time to get something to eat. I had already told myself I wasn't going back to the restaurant. So room service was the next best thing.

I pulled myself from the bed and walked toward the coffee table, fumbling through the hospitality book to locate the room service number. Flipping to the back of the book, I found it.

I enjoyed the rest of the quiet evening as I ate my steak dinner and crossed my legs in comfort on the soft bedding while listening to the news of the day in beautiful Jacksonville. I was thankful that the week was moving along, but I was ready to go home. It was time for me to get back to Alex Keith and go on with my life.

The fourth day of my visit began early in the morning. The sun's glow epitomized the radiance of a ripe pumpkin ready for the plucking as it lit practically all four corners of the room. It was Thursday and I had one test remaining in cardiology.

I had replayed in my mind the conversation I'd had with Dr. Beard the previous day. He had been very direct with me about Clyde and the physiological changes that had occurred in my body since Clyde's tragic death. The doctor didn't have to tell me I was hanging by a thread. I knew I was. But I kept praying to God to help me one day at a time. I couldn't do much else at the time. My whole world had fallen apart around me, but I was doing better. I knew that. But I didn't want to lose myself and I knew if I didn't think about my conversation with him and heed his advice, I wouldn't make it through my grief. I wasn't ready to give up. I knew Clyde wanted me to take care of myself and so I would.

I really missed hearing the birds singing at home outside my window early in the morning and late at night. I had become accustomed to listening to their happy songs and could only imagine what they were doing at home.

"I really miss them, Lord," I said, "I really miss home."

I was sleeping better since arriving at the Mayo Clinic. It was a good thing I had come down, just to be alone for a short while and to put things in perspective. I knew I would be traveling back the next day and I was very anxious to leave right away, but I knew something had happened to me at the Mayo Clinic. I had found the strength to go on with my life. I felt stronger. I was wrapped and cuddled in hope.

I knew I could be independent. I could do things myself. I was very pleased about that. I had accomplished something I could only appreciate by traveling to Jacksonville.

As I walked to my appointment, the garden was breath-taking beyond words. I wanted to capture the moment and neatly package it into a bottle of priceless perfume to preserve its incandescent splendor for another day. I took deep breaths and as my mind bathed in the fresh scent of the flowers, I felt renewed.

"Lord," I said very quietly beneath the beats of my heart. "It's good to be alive today. It's good to see Your face in every flower, every rosebud, every one of Your magnificent creations. Thank You for letting me hear the birds sing and see the flowers bloom, and to watch the bees dart about their business and pollinate the flowers. Thank you Lord for letting me see what You have given us to admire and to enjoy every day of our lives. Forgive me for not clearly seeing your handiwork explicitly until now. Thank you, Lord, for allowing me to see that everything is in Your glorious hands and You decide when it's time for us to leave this earth and come to You. I have nothing to do with it, nor will I ever. Everything is in Your hand, including Clyde. Please forgive me and thank You for allowing me to see, to really see."

I looked up at the sky as I opened the door to the clinic's entrance. The sky was placid; I didn't see a cloud. All was beautiful; all was well. That morning, that moment, all was well with my soul.

It's Time to Go Back Home

I would soon be sitting down with Dr. Jones to review my test results. Mentally, I had been in tremendous pain while driving down. During the last 11 months, I had suffered much agony, frustration, despair, and disillusionment. I didn't know if I was suffering from heart trouble or if it was all in my head. But I had to make sure. I had to know; I didn't want my children to be without both parents. My cardiologist in Columbus had told me that I was okay, but it simply wasn't enough for me. It wasn't that I didn't believe her; I just needed a second opinion.

I was going to miss the clinic and the city of Jacksonville. It was a very beautiful, picturesque city and was growing by leaps and bounds. I walked out of the lobby over to the beautiful small pond for the last time. I knew I would always remember sitting near the pond on the first day of my arrival. I wouldn't ever forget seeing nature's parade of butterflies and lily pads, and ducks and every other semblance of nature before my eyes. It had been my tranquility.

I didn't have much of a wait for Dr. Jones. The reception area wasn't as full as the previous four days. The few people in the room were waiting to hear their test results, I surmised.

"Mrs. Slappey?" the lady called from the reception desk.

"Yes," I said rising from my chair.

"Dr. Jones will see you now."

I grabbed my things and followed her to the examining room.

"Thank you so very much. I appreciate it," I said as she pointed to the sofa where I would sit and wait for the doctor.

"He will be with you shortly," she said.

I knew what shortly meant. It meant maybe an hour. *I hope he will hurry up and tell me my results,* I thought silently.

"It's time to go, Debbie; you know that," I said.

To my surprise, Dr. Jones walked in within 10 minutes.

"Hello, Mrs. Slappey. I hope you're doing well."

I'm doing okay, Dr. Jones," I said to him anxiously, waiting to hear my test results.

"Mrs. Slappey, we didn't find anything wrong with your heart. Of course, you already knew about your mitro-valve prolapse," he said. "The regimen that your cardiologist in Columbus is administering for you is the same that we would recommend as well. You need to continue your medication and get regular checkups.

"All of your tests are within normal limits. You are anemic as you know, so you'll need to take your iron supplement daily."

He hesitated for a moment. "Mrs. Slappey...I believe that Dr. Beard talked with you about your husband and recommended medication to help you with your depression."

I listened to Dr. Jones and knew he had a genuine concern for me. He felt the cause of my chest pain was a result of the tremendous stress I had endured over the past year. He ended by saying that the stress of grief had affected me physically and psychologically. His last words were, "Mrs. Slappey, you must come to grips with your husband's death. He's not coming back."

The tears flowed as his words throbbed incessantly in my mind. *He's not coming back. Clyde's not coming back to me...*

"Mrs. Slappey," he continued, "grief is hard work. Grief can cause physical and mental anxieties, and if not treated with the proper medication, it can cause major health problems, including heart and other conditions."

He touched the back of my hand kindly and continued.

"Mrs. Slappey, take care of yourself. I don't know what you're feeling. I still have my spouse and I don't really know what I would do if I lost her. But I've listened to the way you describe Mr. Slappey, and I don't feel he would want you to become sick. As you described him, he was a wonderful man. So, I know he would want you to take care of yourself so you can take care of your children. So, I say to you, take care of yourself, Mrs. Slappey.

"I'm going to give you a copy of our report to give to your medical doctor. Your heart is fine. You are just grieving. Let me know if I can do anything else for you. It was a pleasure to know you, Mrs. Slappey. Good luck. I wish you well," he said.

"Thank you Dr. Jones," I replied. "I appreciate your squeezing me in this morning. Thank you for everything and I will take care of myself."

I shook his hand and said goodbye. The nurse came in after a few minutes and gave me a copy of my report along with several prescription medications. I thanked her and the clinic and walked out of the room and into the reception area where there was no one around. Coming down to the clinic had been a turning point for me. I was glad I had come. I felt empowered to go on. I knew it wouldn't be easy. I knew I would cry many more nights, and I really didn't know if the crying would ever end. But I would keep trying, taking it one day at a time.

I opened the door and looked up to capture the stunning blue sky, like the waters surrounding the Caribbean Islands. Except for a few stray clouds, the sky was absolutely gorgeous.

"I'll see you, Mayo Clinic," I said as I walked out of the building.

I caught the shuttle back to the hotel and to my car. After tidying up a bit, I drove away from the hotel onto San Pablo Drive. I took another short right and was back on the interstate headed for Lakeland, Florida. I was going home and it was all that mattered that late Friday morning. I had already called Mae to let her know I would be arriving home sometime late afternoon. As I drove out of the city limits of Jacksonville, I felt hopeful; I felt victorious as I pointed my car toward Georgia.

I felt peaceful and grateful to God for letting me be all right physically. I now had to work on my psychological health. I knew I would have to work through my grief, having learned more about the grieving process than ever after talking to the psychologist. I also knew that God would be there for me every step of the way as I yearned to live again in a brand new world.

CHAPTER SEVENTEEN

Shadow Living...
Paintings of Grief

*Learning to live without Clyde has been the most difficult thing in
my life. I had arrived at the final stage of the grieving process—
acknowledgment. I would always remember my husband, but I had
to learn to live without him and to accept that he was gone. It was my
new reality. It wouldn't be easy, but with God's help I would live on.*

IT DIDN'T TAKE ME LONG to drive home. I was
familiar with the roads and used the same directions I used to
travel to Jacksonville to get back to Georgia. I watched each
small town come into focus as I waved goodbye to the state of
Florida and welcomed Georgia as my car wheels glided through
Valdosta, Tifton, Albany, Dawson, all the way to Columbus. By
the time I arrived home, Alex Keith was standing in the driveway waiting to greet me.

I had done it! I had truly done it! I was happy to be home.
It took me five hours to drive down to Jacksonville, but only
4½ hours to drive back. I made up the 30 minutes by relaxing
and enjoying the ride. It made all the difference in the world.
That night as I prepared for bed, I talked with Mae after Alex
Keith had retired.

"Mae, the doctor feels that I'm grieving too hard," I said. "He says that I talk about Clyde as though he's still here, sitting next to me. I told him I couldn't let go, not yet."

"Debbie, you'll know when it's time, and when it's time you will do what you need to do. Trust yourself," she said, touching my shoulder gently as only a mother could.

"Maybe one day I'll be able to, but not now. Thank you, Mae. Love you," I said. "You know I'm beyond tired. It has been a very long day, a very long week. Since I was up early this morning I should sleep really well tonight. Good night, Mae. I love you."

"Good night, Debbie. I love you, too. Try to get some sleep, okay?" she responded, patting me on my shoulder.

I was very tired, pretty much worn out. I felt a gentle calm within myself, having accomplished a major milestone in my life, driving more than 600 miles roundtrip by myself. I had accomplished what I had set out to do—to become independent again, to learn to do things on my own. I really had no choice at this point. The trip helped me to believe in myself again.

"Clyde, you would be very proud of me," I said to him as I looked over at his picture on the end table in my bedroom. "Yes, you definitely would be proud of your Debbie."

I prepared for bed, said my prayers and crawled into my warm, comfortable bed, pulling my sheet and the blanket close to my face. Before I could even turn over to Clyde's side of the bed and squeeze his pillow gently, I fell asleep. It had been a long trip.

The next day I took Mae back home to Americus. After driving to Jacksonville, I felt I could drive just about anywhere in the world. We stayed at Mae's house for a few hours and then Alex Keith and I headed back home.

Back in Columbus, I decided to treat Alex Keith to dinner. We had dinner and then went to a movie. I wanted to be with my son since I had been away from him an entire week. Alex

Keith and I had a great time enjoying our meal and the movie. We hadn't done much in the way of leisure activities since Clyde's illness. It was time.

Sunday arrived and we went to church. I listened to Brother Clayton very closely that morning. Over the past year, I had been pretty much out of touch. But on this day, I decided to really tune in to what he was saying in his sermon. Brother Clayton was a dynamic, charismatic gospel preacher. He had a wonderful, loving, caring attitude and everyone knew he was genuine to the core.

After church Alex Keith and I sat in the den and watched a television show together. It didn't matter what show we watched as long as we were together. And if and when Alex Keith was ready to talk about his father, I would be there for him.

We kept each other company that afternoon and it would become one of many weekends we would sit in the den and talk and laugh together. I wanted my boys to be well. I wanted the entire Slappey family to be all right and for Clyde Daryl and Alex Keith to grow into mature Christian men. The world had its issues, but I knew as long as they had God in their lives, strong, sealed and walking hand-in-hand in Him, they would be able to conquer any obstacle in their lives.

My heart ached for Clyde day and night. But something had happened to me when I drove to Jacksonville. God gave me the strength to lean on Him and His unchanging hands through the storm of death. I was stripped of myself when I began to rely totally on God. I allowed Him to take over completely and deliver me from my pain and agony. God was carrying me now. He was always carrying me.

I had no idea that the drive to Jacksonville would have such a monumental impact on me. I knew Clyde wanted me to be strong. When I looked at the future, it scared me to death. So much so, that I wanted to run for shelter and crawl into my tiny place of despair and not come out again. But when I kept reading my Bible, listening to God, and asking Him to help me take it one day at a time, I began to put one foot in front of the other.

Again, Alex Keith and I sat on the sofa and watched a show about deadly snakes on *National Geographic*. It felt good to sit down and watch TV together again. I was very careful what I watched on television. I avoided watching dramas that dealt with death such as *Touched by an Angel*. I didn't want to see anyone die, nor did I want Alex Keith to see it either. I was very cautious about what I read as well. I did everything I could to protect my family and myself from unnecessary pain and anguish.

I learned later though that this was a normal occurrence after losing someone to death. I was fragile, delicately splintered. I was no longer seeing Clyde in other people's faces. Even though I yearned to see him again, I never did. The mind can play tricks on you, especially when you want to see someone as desperately as I had wanted to see him. I learned during the first year that I had to take life one day at a time, especially since I didn't have much of a choice.

Monday morning came and I knew I had to go back to work. I still wanted to stay in the sanctity of my home. Alex Keith was off to school, so I really wanted to stay home and rest. I called my boss that morning and told her about my test results at Mayo. I asked her if it would be all right if I stayed home. I was exhausted and worn out from the trip; I wanted to be alone. I was glad she approved my request. She had been very supportive and I was grateful.

I felt I needed to stay at home and reflect over the week's event. With God's strength, I had driven to Jacksonville and back. I lay down on my queen-size bed and meditated over the week. It was a very quiet morning.

"Lord," I began to pray, "Will I ever be right again? Will I ever smile? I mean, really smile again? I really don't feel like it. I'm okay now, but I know the anguish will return. Everything seems temporary, almost suspended in time. I cry and I get tired of crying and the next moment I smile and then I cry again.

"Will it ever be over...the pain, that is? Will I ever be able to laugh out loud again, throw my head into the wind and laugh, even to the point that it hurts my stomach to do so? Will I ever feel that way again, Lord?"

The tears washed down my cheeks and I knew the answer to my own questions.

No! I won't ever be the same again. I won't. I can't. I'll be better. Clyde and I were one, truly one and he has passed on. But I will laugh again.

I touched the tears with my ring finger and wiped my face gently with a tissue. Life had changed for me, the children, and the entire family forever. I knew I wouldn't ever be the same person again. I prayed that I would be better. I wiped the tears dripping down my mouth and walked into the bathroom and washed my face.

"Yesterday, I felt strong, Lord. But today, I'm fragmented again. Just how do I handle this sort of despair? It comes, it goes, and it comes again. Maybe the doctor was right when he said I need to let go, but Lord, how do I let go?"

I finished washing my face, placed my washcloth on top of the bathroom sink and stared in the mirror. My hair was turning grey. The stress of Clyde's death had aged me. I recalled what the doctor had told me in Jacksonville. I guess that's why he was telling me I needed to learn to cope with Clyde's death better with medication. Dr. Beard warned me about becoming stuck between my new reality without Clyde and living in the shadows of the past.

I walked into Alex Keith's bathroom and grabbed the octagonal shaped mirror and positioned it to the back of my head.

I placed the mirror down on the vanity and walked into the kitchen, popped a bagel in the toaster, and put a few pieces of bacon in the microwave. Walking back to my room, I had my bagel and bacon sandwich in hand, and when I bit it, I was more than satisfied. I made a promise to myself that I would do better about taking care of myself so I would be physically and mentally able to take care of my children. When I finished my sandwich I lay down again and opened my Bible. I wanted to read from the Psalms, so I turned to Psalm 27 and read the last few verses:

Wait on the Lord: Be of good courage, and He shall strengthen thine heart: Wait, I say, on the Lord.

I closed my eyes and medicated on His words.

"Please help me find my way back from this. Please, I pray," I pleaded.

I laid my head against my pillow softly. I didn't want to think about anything else but Psalm 27. I didn't want to do anything. I didn't want to go anywhere. I didn't want to think about what I would do the next hour or the next day. I wanted to stay right where I was—not thinking, not crying, not even reacting.

After about an hour or so, my eyes grew weary and God gently closed them for me. As I turned onto my back on the soft feather pillow, I listened to a sound coming from my window. At first I didn't want to open my eyes. I wanted to remain still and listen as the sound penetrated the inner core of my brain. I kept listening and my ears began to grow closer to the sound.

Then something unusual began to happen. I began to hear different sounds practically throughout the house. I heard something similar to a train that appeared to be coming from the refrigerator motor. Then came a whoof, whoof sound, but where was it coming from? I didn't quite know. Next, I heard a buzzing sound coming from the computer in the next room.

And then I heard a familiar sound from outside—sounds of crickets, in fact a bunch of crickets. All the sounds I was experiencing were blending into one rhythmic hum. I kept listening as I was intimately enticed by the sounds culminating outside my window. That's when I heard the birds sing. The sounds cooled my spirit as I became one with them.

I had been listening for a long time. I was obliged to God for giving me this time to be alone with Him and to understand that life was more than working a 9 to 5 job and taking the children to baseball games. It was much more. It was about understanding and appreciating the little things in life that most people, including myself, didn't pay much attention to until forced to do so.

I heard the birds again. They were singing, whispering, humming, and chirping. All was well with my soul as I listened to the birds sing. I walked over to my double window and peeked between the openings of the mini blind and spotted a robin perched on a limb of the pine tree. I watched the bird sway playfully on the tree branches with seemingly no particular care in the world. The robin simply looked around and watched, doing absolutely nothing. He perched himself upon the branch for hours.

I watched for a little while longer and then laid down again and closed my eyes in thankfulness for opening my ears, eyes, and heart that morning to a world of possibilities.

We would continue to go to school, go to church, go to work. We would continue to live in this world that we all called home until our Father in Heaven bowed His head to let us know it was time to travel home. I knew I would continue to cry, wipe my tears, and make it through another day. Alex Keith and I would continue with grief therapy together and we would lean on God's unchanging hand to help us through the bitter days ahead.

Life wouldn't ever be the same again. How could it? I guess that's what Helen Davis was trying to tell me when I asked her how you make it through the maze of grief and survive. I now knew. As I listened to the birds sing, my heart began to rise from despair.

"God," I said, "please give me the strength to be better than I am. Please help me to be better."

Using my wrist, I wiped the tears from my face again and screamed as loud as I could on that placid Monday morning.

"But now I must keep going because I want to in my heart. Please Lord, help me hear the birds sing in my mind again. Help me to hear them sing."

I arose from the bed and took a nice warm bath. Afterward, I walked into the den and pulled out a family video and placed it in the recorder. I fast forwarded it and pressed the play button. And then I saw his face and touched it on the screen as the video played. I stared into his face and pressed the rewind button again and again with tear-filled eyes.

"I'm going to miss you, my friend," I said crying. "I'm going to miss you. But please save a place for me somewhere beyond the sky."

I froze the recorder so I could touch his handsome face. I stared at him for a long time, retracing the painful lines in his face. I pressed the eject button and took the video out of the machine very carefully and walked back into my bedroom and placed the video in my middle dresser, its safe place.

"God," I said, as I walked back into the den to sit down. "Please help me, Lord. I need You now, more than ever."

I walked back into my bedroom hoping to hear the voices of the morning. I yearned for the sounds of peace, tranquility and soothing serenity. As I listened, I mumbled under my breath,

"Lord, thank you very much for helping me to face each day one moment at a time."

With my eyes swelled with tears, I closed them and gently listened. As the clock struck 10:00 a.m., I looked around my room one more time.

I fell on my knees and whispered softly, "Lord, thank you for letting me hear the birds sing and for letting me see the light of day."

It was time for me to rise from the dreary dungeon of grief and to go on with my life. I knew it wouldn't be easy, but I had to keep going. I knew as long as I had the Lord to carry me through the shadows of death, I would make it through the lonely, teary nights and awake once again to experience life renewed once again. As I continued to listen to the birds singing, I walked to my bed, laid down, closed my eyes and fell into a deep sleep on a quiet Monday morning.

CHAPTER EIGHTEEN

A Closer Look at Grief

During my first few years as a grieving spouse, I experienced several phases of grief. Through my own research I've learned that shock, denial, anger, bargaining, fear, depression, and acknowledgment or acceptance are common phases of the grieving process. I've outlined more details about each phase in this chapter.

I WAS VERY NAÏVE WHEN it came to grief and even understanding the stages of grief. As I said in *I Feel Okay*, I had watched Clyde suffer from primary amyloidosis, and when he died, I was grateful to God he wasn't suffering anymore. I knew I would miss Clyde terribly, but I had no idea that grief would grip me in an unending web of despair, sorrow, and remorse after his death.

As Clyde closed his eyes in death, I was overwhelmed with misery of missing him beyond my comprehension. I felt cold inside. I was stripped naked with remorse as I lost myself to grief. When Clyde breathed his last breath, I died too. It took me many years to understand the depth of grief that I carried inside year after year. I didn't understand what was happening to my body as I began to experience psychological, physiological, and even spiritual changes in my life as I wallowed in the depths of grief.

As I did in *I Feel Okay*, I wanted to devote an entire chapter to talk about the stages of the grieving process and educate others. At some point in our lives we will experience the death of a loved one. During my first year after Clyde's death, I earnestly looked for books and anything I could find to read to help me understand the psychological and physiological changes that were happening to me.

I was thankful to receive a book about grief that the late Helen Davis had given me. She had lost her husband a year before Clyde passed away and wanted to share the book with me since someone had given it to her. She gave it to me with one stipulation. She asked that after I read that I pass it to another person who was in the midst of grieving. I read the book and began to understand grief in more detail. Grief was more than a five-letter word. It would take me years, even a lifetime, to cope with Clyde's death. Only time would heal my broken heart.

Based upon Helen's request, I gave the book to another sister whose husband had died recently, and as Helen told me, I told her to pass the book to another griever after she read it. I continued to attend my group therapy and learned more about the grieving process.

As a result, I organized a luncheon for widows and friends from the church. We decided to meet every quarter at local restaurants and would sit and talk for hours. I guess we had organized our own grief support group. We didn't call it a support group at first, but it turned out to be one. It was one of the best things I could have done for myself and other grievers. We cried, laughed, and supported each other as we all braved the road to recovery. The impact of those support luncheons was far reaching and it helped us to cope with the sting of grief.

For the first time, I began to put a face to grief. It's important to work through grief because if you aren't careful it will consume you. The stages of grief are responses to feelings that can last for minutes or hours as one progress from one stage to another. We don't enter and leave each individual stage in a linear fashion. We may feel one, then another, several at once, and possibly back again to the first stage of grief.

People put undue pressure on grievers. I believe if you don't know what to say to a person who is suffering with grief, don't scold them for wanting to hold on to their loved one. The best thing you can do is to hug them. They'll remember that hug more than any words. Grief is physical and mental torture. Grief hurts. It's painful and unnerving. Grief affects every part of a person's being, both physical and mental capacity. Everything aches within with excruciating pain. So, next time when you are with a relative or friend who's grieving, take them by the hand and hug them closely. They'll truly appreciate this gesture of compassion more than you'll ever know.

According to Elisabeth Kübler-Ross and David Kessler, the five stages of grief are denial, anger, bargaining, depression, and acceptance.[2] In addition to the five they discuss, I would add two more—shock and fear. At least, I experienced shock and fear as I worked to come to terms with my loss. I've listed the seven stages as I experienced them in the following table.

My Seven Stages of Grief

Shock
Denial
Anger
Fear
Bargaining
Depression
Acknowledgment

Over the years, I've read several interpretations of the grieving process, but I believe Kübler-Ross and Kessler have captured the universal model that is consistent with the grieving process. However, there is no one formula for grief and this is why I've added two other stages. I experienced them, so I'm sure others have as well. We'll start with shock.

• Shock

I had traveled with Clyde for five months scavenging the countryside in the hope of finding someone to treat primary amyloidosis. Even though I knew that Clyde could pass out at any given moment and never wake up, I was still shocked when it happened. I had hoped I wouldn't have to face it.

I didn't understand what it meant for him to be deceased. My mind knew Clyde was dead, but my subconscious, somehow, blocked this reality from my mind. My reality was often confusing to me. I knew Clyde had left me, but I still wanted him to walk into the den. I guess my mind shut down temporarily, shielding me from the full impact of Clyde's death. It would have paralyzed me.

I was in shock when I let him go while holding his hand on that Wednesday afternoon, April 19, 1995, at 4:20 p.m. I was in shock when I made the arrangements for his funeral, even though Clyde and I had spoken at great length about his funeral and carrying out his wishes if he succumbed to death. And I was also in shock when I walked into the church building for Clyde's funeral. I couldn't believe my husband was lying in a coffin only a few feet away from me and he wouldn't get up again. I couldn't fathom this thought. My eyes saw him lie still in the coffin, but my mind didn't acknowledge what my eyes were seeing.

According to experts, many people feel shock and numbness in the first few days after a loved one passes away. They may also experience shortness of breath, tightness in the throat, difficulty concentrating, hallucinations, and lack of or too much sleeping and eating.

"A lot of it comes from stress and the anxiety that happens to people after the death of a loved one. It all sort of wreaks havoc on our natural defense systems," says Kathy Wood, a spokeswoman for AARP's End of Life Program.[3]

"After the initial shock wave of hurt," Wood adds, "it is not uncommon for grievers to lack energy and have headaches or tension. These physical symptoms often share center stage with the magnified emotions of sadness, confusion, fear, guilt, anger, and a sense of emptiness."[4]

"Besides experiencing the strain of stress, of emotional overload, and of not taking care of oneself properly, it is also possible for grievers to be at higher risk for health problems. Various studies have shown that surviving spouses may have increased odds of suffering heart disease, cancer, depression, alcoholism, and suicide," says Dan Leviton, Ph.D., first president of the Association for Death Education and Counseling.

Dr. Leviton notes, though, that not everyone has a higher risk for disease because they may cope well with loss. The sting of loss can be even more dramatic for those who lose a husband or wife."[5]

Many people would tell me, "Deborah, you're doing so well. You must be strong!" They couldn't believe our tranquil behavior at the funeral. But what they didn't know, what they missed on that sad Monday, April 24, 1995, was that the entire family was in shock. I have learned over time that God helps us through our grief, one step at a time. He's always there to help us and support us. God was with the Slappey family on that day. But when the funeral was over my sons lifted me from the church bench, and with their assistance, I walked behind my husband's coffin. Then and only then did the tears began to flow, because I knew I couldn't go where he was now. I walked slowly behind Clyde for the last time out of the church to his permanent place of rest.

I knew Clyde had left me. He had really left me forever and there was nothing I could do about it. I felt stripped of all consciousness and will. I was lost in a quagmire of despair and sadness. I had no place to go, so I retreated into what I call shadow living. I was petrified knowing that the love of my life had left me to go to his final resting place in Andersonville National Cemetery.

• Denial

I could only peek into my reality for short spurts of time. And if I stayed more than a moment, the reality was too horrifying—Clyde was gone. *How could he be gone? I just spoke to him the night before. Was I on the verge of insanity?* At first I couldn't handle the reality that Clyde was gone, so I retreated to my safe place—my bedroom where I closed the door to the world.

Grief takes hold of you and pulls away your skin one layer at a time. One minute I would be happy, and the next moment, I would be dying inside. I would be screaming inside for my sweetheart to come back to me even though I knew he wasn't coming back.

Denial is a natural response that gives the griever time to handle a new reality. It's another alternative for retreating from a reality that is too painful to experience at the time. And as irrational as it may seem to others, denial is meaningful to the griever at the time. It is a psychological emergency stop gate or a temporary holding pattern until the grief-stricken individual is able to begin to cope with his loss.[6]

I didn't care how God planned to bring Clyde back, I just wanted him back. Many times I felt I was completely out of my mind. The only stabilizing agent in my life at the time was my children. I knew I needed to take care of them, and God gave me the strength to hold on to them. But God made sure I stayed away from the edge of despair. I knew I had to take care of Alex Keith and ensure that Clyde Daryl stayed in school. Since they needed me, I felt I desperately needed to hold on for dear life.

I would see other couples walking and holding hands. I yearned desperately to walk hand in hand again with Clyde as an expression of our love and devotion. I could sense that the other couples were extremely in love with each other. They were holding hands and walking very close together. It was a beautiful sight; a tender expression of their love. I became envious as I watched them stroll down the sidewalk together. I desperately wanted to do the same with Clyde. It saddened me to think that we wouldn't experience growing old together.

The mind can play more tricks than one can ever imagine during the grieving process, oftentimes witnessing manifestations of your loved one. But God saw something in me that passed my understanding. He made sure I had my children to help me to hold on to His hand.

"What a God we serve!" I would recount these words as the years passed by. God is great. No words will ever describe His love for His children because He saved me from myself. He kept me from drowning in my grief.

During the first four months, every evening around 6:00, I would stare at the French doors in the den waiting for Clyde to walk in, but he never did. Many times I thought I distinctly heard the deadbolt turn, and I would come rushing from the kitchen or the bedroom, calling his name. Clyde's normal work schedule was 7:30 a.m. to 4:30 p.m.; if he worked overtime he would come home around 6:30 p.m. I remember one time when Clyde had to work late to restore electricity to customers because of an ice storm. By that time, I had already arrived home and started dinner. I couldn't wait for him to walk through the door after a hard day's work.

From the kitchen window, I would see Clyde drive up, and would wait for him to walk into the den and tell me how his day had gone. We always greeted each other with a warm, affectionate kiss. Several times he would surprise me by sneaking behind me and placing his arms around my waist. I remembered those times and smiled.

Clyde took pride in his work. He made sure that every *T* was crossed and every *I* dotted. He was proud and always went the extra mile to exemplify quality in his work. I was very proud of him and told him so many times. We had a mutual respect for each other.

Months passed and I still stared at the door hoping, even praying, to hear the rattle of Clyde's keychain and for the door to swing open. Grief affected my psyche to such an extent that I imagined hearing the key unlock the door. And without thinking, I would rush to the door calling his name.

I would rehearse our reunion in my mind. The door would open, Clyde would walk in and I would rise up from the sofa and run and jump into his arms. I would experience joyful bliss as I touched his smiling face. We would be overjoyed.

But he never came home to me or his family; he never did and never would. Grief robs one of sensible thinking. Nothing much is rational or coherent anymore. I felt like I was in a daze and living in the shadows. Denying a loved one's death is a saving grace in the beginning because it's the only way to survive as the next stage unfolds—anger.

• Anger

I don't remember exactly when I began to feel anger, but it rushed in like a mighty storm. First, I became angry with other married couples. Then I became angry with Clyde for leaving his family. I felt Clyde should have been able to hang on for another two weeks to receive his life-saving heart transplant. Everything would have been wonderful. He would have a new heart and we would be a happy family again.

I was very angry at him for leaving me to survive alone with our two young boys. "It isn't fair he's gone and left me here. I've done all I can, Lord, for the children. They need their father now, not me! They need their father's voice in their lives as they grow into young men. They need him!" I would repeat often.

I was very angry with Clyde, but it didn't last long. I had to let it go. Everything was a blur—a fog of some kind. I wanted Clyde to be alive. That's all. I would do or say anything to bring him back to me. As I pleaded with God, I knew nothing was going to change. I knew Clyde was gone from the earth and if I was ever going to see him again, it would be at the resurrection, in heaven with our Lord and Savior. Still, I wanted my family back.

This made me very sad and angry at the same time. But there was nothing I could do about it. I was powerless. I felt sick to my stomach as the anguish ripped my insides, leaving me with only shreds of tortured flesh, torn into minute pieces of nothing.

I had no strength in me. I had nothing inside but pain and anguish. The only solace of being left alone was to turn to God in tears, pleading for him to help me through the unbearable nights. I was angry with myself. I felt I should have left earlier in the week before Clyde passed out. Perhaps he wouldn't have died if I had been at his side in the hospital. I would have known what to do to revive him. He wouldn't be dead now.

I hated myself for not listening to my inner voice when I wanted to fly out sooner to the Mayo Clinic. I beat myself numerous times, but in the end I knew what Clyde would have said.

"Debbie, I want you to take care of Alex Keith," he would say.

That's exactly what he would be saying to me. I knew him too well.

I also blamed myself for not finding the information sooner about the Mayo Clinic and the heart transplant. I beat against my chest and blamed myself for Clyde leaving us so soon. My emotions drifted one to the other. They were off the chart.

I felt as though someone put his hand inside my chest and ripped my bleeding, wretched heart from its chamber. I learned that grief is more than pain; it's a prison of everyday sorrow, anger, and disillusionment all packaged into relentless agony and despair.

Anger doesn't have to be logical or valid. I was very angry with the doctors for misdiagnosing Clyde for years, and my anger was further fueled by their inability to save him.

When I came to myself, I prayed to God and asked him to help me. I knew Clyde didn't want to leave his family. I knew I had done all I could have imagined to help Clyde. But many times my heart fought the anguish, so I floated between reality and shadow living, my own self-made fog world of grief. I was living in the shadows of grief and I lived between reality and my faux reality for years.

There was nothing I could do except work my way through the shadowy world of grief with God's help. I didn't like it one bit. It was a very grueling place to be. I hated it and dreaded to wake up and face my dire reality as each new day only confirmed he was dead.

• Bargaining

This stage of grief takes on an even more collaborative existence. I had prayed to God passionately for Clyde to get better. I had asked God to heal Clyde's body and I would end my prayers with, "Thy will be done, Lord."

But when Clyde died I became angry with God. I found myself asking God to bring Clyde back to me and if he did, I would take his place. I didn't know it at the time, but I was attempting to bargain with God to bring Clyde back. I wanted our sons to have their father back. I would gladly take his place.

I begged for him to do so many times. I wanted God to wake me from my half-hearted existence. I wanted the pain to go away so I could feel normal again. I wanted my husband to lie next to me in our bed so I could gently stroke his forehead to ease his pain.

"Is this too much to ask for, my Lord?" I would ask God many times.

"If only I could have found out about NORD (National Organization of Rare Disorders) earlier. I would have called them back in December 1994. I wouldn't have wasted our time at the hospital in Atlanta. We would have gone directly to the Mayo Clinic instead. And Clyde would have received a new heart earlier, possibly in December, maybe even in early January. If only I had known earlier about clinical trials at the Mayo Clinic, Lord knows, he might have been alive now. Clyde would be alive and kicking."

I tried to bargain with God in many other ways. I remember asking God to let Clyde live again and if he did, I wouldn't tell him ever to clean the bathroom mirror again. He would leave specks of toothpaste all over the mirror and wouldn't clean it up. I even went on to negotiate with the Lord that if Clyde came back to me he could take the tube of toothpaste and smear it all over the mirror, sink, and bathtub if he wanted to; I wouldn't mind it a bit. As a matter of fact, I wouldn't say a word. I only wanted him to be alive again. It's amazing how the small things really don't matter when you understand the bigger picture. I wanted my husband back—case closed.

I wanted everything to be put back the way things were before Clyde became sick with the dreadful disease. I wanted the pain to go away and I wanted Clyde to walk back into our house the same way he walked out, standing. I would sit, sometimes hours on end, and stare at Clyde's picture in my bedroom.

"Lord, I want my life back!" I said many times as I walked through the house sobbing endlessly. I peeked out of the kitchen and living room windows looking for Clyde out in the yard. "What do I have to do to get my life back, Lord?"

And the bare fact hit me square in the eyes. I was a widow and Clyde wouldn't be coming back to me in this world ever again, not ever. As I said earlier, I would have done anything to spare my husband—bargaining would have been just fine with me.

The griever plagues himself with "if onlys" and "perhaps if I'd done this," then my loved one would have been spared from death. We may even bargain with awful pain inside of us and we will do anything to alleviate the pain and sorrow. We remain in the past, trying desperately to negotiate our way out of the pain. That's why I termed grieving the loss of a loved one as shadow living.[7]

• Fear

Fear can be very debilitating. The magnitude of fear depends upon the griever, that is, some people can be overwhelmed by fear, while others don't experience fear at all after the death of a loved one. Common fears include the fear that we could die ourselves at any moment and fear that we won't be able to function with the loss of a loved one.[8]

With Clyde gone, I was riddled with despair. My heart throbbed constantly, and at times, my heart ached. It hurt to breathe. I felt I was going to die and it saddened me because I didn't want to leave my children alone, without their father and now their mother. I was weak and emotionally drained most of the time. I couldn't sleep or eat and many times I didn't have the ability to concentrate. Food no longer gave me pleasure. Food was bland, and for the first six months of living without Clyde, my taste buds went on an extended holiday. Over the course of months, I was totally consumed in my grief and lost about 25 pounds.

Once Alex Keith was asleep, I would close my door to the world and cry like a hungry baby into the late evening. And then I would be paralyzed with exhaustion the next day, having slept less than four hours most nights. I repeated this cycle well into the first few years of living in the shadows of grief.

More than anything, I yearned to see Clyde. Darkness was my enemy. I hated saying goodbye to the light of day. The darkness reminded me of pain, agony, and sadness. My heart would beat rapidly and the panic attacks would begin as I kept the lamps on in my bedroom and den. I was surrounded by a multitude of light.

If only I could stop the night from coming, I would say many times. *If only I could change time. I would reverse time and bring Clyde back to life.*

Many times when I drove from work, without warning I was overtaken with an excruciating chest pain. It scared me to death. I pleaded to God, asking him not to let me die and to allow me to stay with Alex Keith and Clyde Daryl so I could help them.

"Lord, please," I said, as I held onto my chest. "Please let me be okay. Please don't let our children lose both their parents. Please, Lord, let me be okay. My heart hurts. My head hurts."

I would pray to God throughout the day, asking Him to give me the strength to keep going, even though there were times when I didn't have the energy. But I knew God was taking care of me. I knew deep inside He wouldn't leave me because His child was in deep despair.

I was fighting for my life. There were times when I thought I was losing my battle with grief. Grief was winning categorically. I kept trying, though. But my greatest fear was dying and leaving my children in this lonely world to grieve alone. Thank God I felt they needed me. I continued to struggle and ask God to help my family and me get through the pain-filled days.

As darkness smothered the evening light, I felt my chest pain worsen. I was in constant misery. I wanted desperately to escape my pain in sleep, but many times sleep held me hostage in my dreams as I found myself descending into Clyde's grave. I couldn't escape the pain and misery of death, even in my dreams. I prayed to God constantly to help me gain strength to survive the definitive blows of grief.

• **Depression**

I don't remember when I wandered into the stage of depression, because most of the time I didn't know if I was coming or going, or even what day it was. All days blurred into one sad compilation of days. I knew I had to get up and go to work, and most days I did. But there were some days I didn't have the strength. I didn't want to work. In fact it was the last thing on my mind. I didn't want to eat or do anything other than wallow in my sorrow. I only wanted to lie in bed and stare at the television in a muted mode. I guess I should have known I was suffering from depression. Once we had discovered that Clyde had an incurable disease, I was sad most of the time, but when I was around Clyde and the boys, I made sure they wouldn't detect my sadness. I was all smiles for their sake. I had to keep their spirits up. I would deal with mine at another time.

But when Clyde died, I became immobile. Everyone's grief experiences will be different, but most grievers will experience loneliness, anger, abandonment, and denial.

Empty feelings present themselves and grief enters our lives on a deeper level, deeper than we ever imagined. This depressive stage feels as though it will last forever. It's important to understand that depression is not a sign of mental illness. Quite the contrary, it's an appropriate response to a great loss. We withdraw from life because of the intense sadness and wondering if there is any reason for trying to live alone. Morning comes, but it doesn't really matter. A voice in your head says it is time to get out of bed, but you have no desire to do so. Life feels useless, even pointless. To get out of bed sometimes is like trying to climb Mount Everett.[9]

During the first six months, as each day passed I found myself asking, "When will it ever end?" My heart throbbed with sadness, anxiety, and sorrow. I hated to hold my head up because it was far too painful. I didn't dare open the mini blinds in my bedroom.

I would hear my inner voice say many times, *Now, Debbie, you know you need to get up and take your bath and comb your hair and put some lipstick on, girl! Get up!* Sometimes I did; sometimes I didn't. I heard my own voice speak to me. But I didn't feel like it. Much of the time I didn't have the strength to even lift my head from the pillow. I didn't have much energy after battling sleepless nights, so whatever energy was left I used at work. I was barely functioning and lived in the shadows of grief for years.

I saw myself floating through life on a lily pad. I had lost the love of my life and was only a shell of a person. There wasn't much else left in me. What was the point anyway? Clyde was gone.

Clyde Daryl and Alex Keith were my saving grace. They kept me going in spite of my pain and agony and the huge void I felt inside. I knew Clyde would have wanted me to keep living for them, to take care of them, so as much as I wanted to lie down and sleep away forever, I didn't because I knew they needed me more. I kept clawing my way back, one claw at a time.

I remember one particular Sunday morning. I'd had one of those hectic sleepless nights. I didn't have the energy to get myself ready for church. I've always prided myself in dress and appearance. I usually wore suits, but on this particular morning I didn't have the strength to "dress up."

I found a skirt in the closet and slipped it on. I didn't have the strength to put on pantyhose, so I went to church barelegged. This wasn't my customary dressing style. This was far from the Debbie I knew inside. At that time we were in the old church building of the Church of Christ on Cusseta Road and I distinctly remember going downstairs to the fellowship hall and seeing one of my brethren. I looked awful and was pretty emaciated and I knew it, but I didn't care at the time. I read the ghastly expression on his face, but he never uttered one word, other than to say hello. I was in a tunnel of despair and no one could help me but the Lord. In spite of my emaciated existence I kept going to church with Alex Keith because I wanted to make sure he still had some form of normalcy in his life.

Eventually, I was able to recognize some of the signs of depression as I began to study my symptoms. I felt drained most of the time, with no energy. I avoided most people and during my first year, I visited Clyde's grave almost every week. Whereas though some people are drawn away from the graveyard, I was drawn to the cemetery because it provided a solace of peace.

The severe shock and devastation can be so overwhelming to the griever that he will want to follow his companion into death as well. Many times the griever manifests similar symptoms of pain and anguish that their loved one experienced prior to death. Some grievers find relief as the burden of a caregiver is lifted when their loved one dies.[10]

I would drive to the cemetery and take fresh flowers for Clyde's grave. I must have spent a nice fortune on the purchase of flower arrangements—roses, carnations, sprays of just about every flower, I bought for Clyde's grave. I took numerous pictures. I wanted to capture every moment I visited Clyde in the hope that one day I would create a scrapbook. As the months folded into years, I still haven't had the strength to create the scrapbook. Maybe one day I will.

In the beginning I was consumed with being close to Clyde. I surrounded myself with every picture I could find to keep his memory alive and for him to be next to me. I allowed tons of mail to pile up in my bed because I didn't want to bother with it. For moments in time, I stepped out of reality to wander in my self-made shadow world of grief. Before Clyde passed, I always balanced the checkbook to the very penny, but when he died, I never balanced it again. Balancing the checkbook was simply no longer a priority in my life. It was now a trivial task I had no interest in pursuing.

I've always been rather tidy and neat—not extreme, but neat. When Clyde died, my tidiness seemed to dissipate into small puddles of water. I didn't care much about things anymore. My bedroom had stuff everywhere—from clothing I hadn't hung up to the mail piled into organized heaps on my bed. I knew I needed to discard some of the stuff but many times, I didn't have the strength to fool with it.

Many times I forgot to pay my bills. This wasn't like me. I had lost myself somewhere in the fog of night and I didn't know how to feel my way back from my confused existence. As I always did, I continued to pray even when I didn't know what to say. God knew what I was trying to say. He knew my deepest feelings. As my depression deepened, I lost all sense of reality. I would take my plethora of teddy bears and squeeze them softly and gently and pretend I was holding Clyde in my arms. And while Alex Keith was in school, I would indulge in my world of self-pity and regret.

I didn't want to talk about Clyde's passing. I didn't want to acknowledge he had left me. I wanted to be left alone with my grief. In my dark room, I knew it was just me and grief. And that was fine with me. When I had to take Alex Keith to some event, I would pretend. I would put on the perfect face and with a big smile I'd tell everyone I was okay. People said, "You look so good. You are doing all right. Just keep on doing well."

But they didn't have a clue I was rotting with gangrene on the inside from sorrow and despair. Only God knew the pain I was bearing in my body—only Him. I confided in Him and cried out many weary nights as the days passed into months.

God alone was able to pull me back from the caverns of despair. And for it, I am forever grateful to Him.

• Acknowledgment

I had to acknowledge or accept that my Innisfree, my partner for life, died at the tender age of 43. I've come to realize that Clyde is gone and he isn't coming back. I don't know exactly when I began to acknowledge this fact, but I know that it didn't happen overnight or even in a year or so. It happened gradually over time.

Acknowledgment is often confused with the notion that you are okay with what has happened with your loved one. This isn't the case. Acknowledgment is accepting the reality that our loved one is physically gone away from the earth and this is the new reality, whether we like it or not. It's real. It is the new norm with which we must learn to live our life as best we know how. We must try to live now in a world where our loved one is no longer a physical part. As we move through the episodes of grief, healing somehow brings us to a peaceful reality about our loved one, and brings us closer to them. A new relationship begins as we begin the work to put our lives back together as much as possible and go on. God gives us the strength to go on. We learn to live without our loved ones, but we never forget them. We acknowledge their physical death.[11]

I finally realized through God's infinite wisdom that He had given me one of His jewels to love and cherish for a little while on this earth. All jewels are precious to Him and must return to our God in Heaven.

I acknowledged that Clyde and I had had a beautiful life together and nothing on this earth would ever change the fact that our love would endure forever, even beyond the grave. It took me some years to understand my grief and what I had lost. Our relationship was priceless (from God) and I would never meet another person like Clyde on this earth. But I have learned to love again and to appreciate Marshall Pitts, my husband, and his loving kindness and uniqueness in my life.

This is what I consider acknowledgment. I learned to cope with the death of Clyde by accepting his brief presence in my life and thanking our Lord and Savior Jesus Christ for giving me the opportunity to know him and for the two of us to have two fine young men through our union together.

I likened the grieving process to being strapped to a raging roller coaster. The roller coaster travels high in the sky and descends quickly. One minute you are filled with exhaustion, with pain and sorrow; the next minute you are smiling and even happy and excited. You feel empowered that everything is going to be all right. And before you can even catch your breath from the storm, along comes the rain to blanket you in smoldering despair.

Clyde was always the "fixer" around the house. If something was broken, Clyde would fix it. Less than two months after Clyde had passed, the air conditioning compressor in the house, the car battery, and even the alternator all quit working within a few days of each other. These situations scared me silly, but God took care of me as He always did. As I said before, I believe God puts things in motion to help us to be stronger. God knew I hadn't handled the mechanical things before, so He helped me to find someone who could handle them for me. One of the brethren in the Church of Christ installed a new air conditioner for me, and Western Auto installed a new battery and alternator in my 1993 Oldsmobile. I was rolling down the highway again.

Acknowledgment means I will do my very best to keep going because I know Clyde would want me to continue with life. Tomorrow isn't promised to any of us. We must live the time we have while it is day. Acknowledgment doesn't mean I have forgotten my soul mate or loved one. It simply means I won't ever forget him; I will keep him close to my heart.

Acknowledgment means that life must go on, even without your loved one being present in a physical sense. It's the path to spiritual healing with a renewed sense of hope to live again. After so many years, I still cry when I think of Clyde and I smile when I remember our precious time together. Now, I tell others to appreciate what they have while they still can.

⁓

The various stages of the grieving process normally lead one to the path of healing. Monitor yourself through the grieving process. It is the path that will take you to the other side, and once you've made it, you can turn around and extend a helping hand to help someone else suffering through the doldrums of grief. You must work through your feelings of grieving and lean on God to direct your path. Sometimes it might require professional help; sometimes not. You must decide.

I know I won't ever be the same person after experiencing the death of my husband. I've traveled through a dark tunnel of despair, loneliness, and confusion. But because of my experience, I've learned to appreciate God's wonderful, kind blessings of love and protection in my trials and tribulations. It's now my turn to help someone else by telling my story of love, sorrow, and faith and with God's help, to help someone else reach the other side of grief to welcomed peace.

One Last Letter

Dear Clyde,

I miss you…I miss you a lot. I thank God for giving us twenty-one years of marriage. I miss you in my life. I know you would have stayed with me if you could have. I know you would. I know you were very tired…the disease had severely drained you. But we got you there, didn't we, sweetheart, we got you to the Mayo Clinic. I'm thankful for that. I know you are resting now in the Lord. You are out of your pain and agony. I'm so glad. It hurt me to see you in pain and I'm glad you are no longer hurting.

As I stand here on your grave I just want to let you know that I'm okay now. I'm learning to live on…to go on. I really don't know where life will take me, but I'm going to keep going…and not because you want me to…no…it's because I want to now. I'm thankful to God that I've known you for a time. It's my blessing and I thank you for our happy times…our family…our lives…we're forever strong. God blessed us with a beautiful family, didn't he?

Clyde, they are doing some great things with amyloidosis. People are being helped and I know you are smiling about that.

But it's still not enough. There is still much work to do. I have to keep going and expose the disease to the world—thousands, now maybe even millions have heard about amyloidosis. That's a good thing—no, that's a blessing.

Thank you for having faith in me. You've been a blessing in my life. I can love again and I'm very grateful. I'm going to keep walking into the sun's radiant glow and I will think of you often. And I won't ever forget you. With all my heart Clyde, take care and rest. I'm okay now. Really, I'm okay.

Loving you always, Deborah

Epilogue

I RECEIVED A PROMOTION one year after Clyde's death, and one thing I missed most was being able to rush home and tell Clyde my good news.

"Clyde, I got a promotion, honey!" I would say. "I got a promotion!" He would be elated to hear the news. He was always my number one cheerleader and would take me out for dinner to celebrate.

In *Shadow Living...Paintings of Grief*, I've shared my story of grief and pain with you. I pray that it helps you on your journey of suffering and despair to want to live again. You've traveled with me and my grief as I peeked through the days of despair to spiritual rejuvenation in God through our Lord and Savior, Jesus Christ.

Grief is not an easy walk, but God will take your hand in His and lead you through the quicksand, if you allow Him. Grief is real and the physical and mental effects of the grieving process can be totally debilitating.

But help is available and all you have to do is reach for it. Grief, as I've indicated in Chapter Eighteen, "A Closer Look at Grief," can be just as injurious to you physically as it is mentally and psychologically.

When you feel you are losing your grip on life, do your best to rise and fight for dear life. Rise from your bed of despair and seek help for your loved ones and for yourself, and God will be your guiding light.

Take care of yourself. Make sure you get plenty of sleep, eat nutritiously, and obtain a good physical examination. It's very important that you take care of yourself as you face your first years of coping with the death of a loved one. Grief can kill, and the medical profession is currently assessing the long-term impact of grief on a person's mental and physical health. It can be devastating. I've included references where you can read and obtain supplemental information about the grieving process. So, don't give up. Seek help when needed.

I've devoted the last few years of my life traveling the country and speaking about the amyloidosis diseases, and I will continue to do so as long as I'm needed. I've channeled my grief into a mission to educate others about amyloidosis.

As I struggled for years to come to terms with Clyde's death, it is my prayer that you'll learn to live again and find your place and purpose to go on with your life. I've stopped dreaming about Clyde in the grave. But when I dream of him now, he's alive. And he'll always be alive in my heart.

I believe the words of "Hold Your Head Up High" succinctly embodies an anchor of comfort in our loving Father to those who mourn from the riveting pressure of grief. He will deliver you into His solace of peace.

Hold Your Head Up High

Hold your head up high and feel the warmth of God's love,
Give Him your sorrows, give Him your pain and He will comfort you,
Give Him your sleepless nights and He will
wrap His loving arms around you.

Hold your head up high and sense His everlasting love for you,
Give Him your agonizing nights of sorrow and He will give you rest,
Give Him your sadness and despair and He
will ease your burden of distress.

Hold your head up high and receive His wonderful blessings of joy,
Give Him your doubting thoughts and He will bless you in His care,
Give Him your fear and guilt and He will
set you free from your despair.

God meant it when He said He would take care of you,
For God's word will always hold true; God will take care of you,
He will. He said it so true. God will hide you in His bosom
of comfort, love, and joy. This He will definitely do!

Hold your head up high and enjoy the splendor
of God's heavenly blessings of care,
Give Him your love and He will sustain you
in your darkest times of despair,
Give Him your torturing days and He will blanket
you in His arsenal of angelic care.

Hold your head up high and He will ease
your anxiety and don't you cry,
For God is going to wipe away every tear from your eye,
He will ease your mourning and allow you
to enjoy life again by and by.

Hold your head up high and feel the warm
sunshine against your sad face,
He is the one who will give you rest from
your labor; from your distress,
Give Him your lonely nights, your lifeless days and
He will ease your stress and will do the rest.

So, hold your head up high, higher than high. And don't despair. For our God in Heaven will wipe away your tears and will lift you into His refuge and keep you forever in His care.

Lean absolutely on God's unchanging hand as you journey through the valley of grief. He will take your hand in His and lead you onto the other side where you can experience the depth of love, the fullness of joy, and the radiance of peace in your life once again. God bless you.

Keep Pressing, Keep Pushing, and Keep Going on!
Deborah Slappey Pitts

An Amyloidosis Update

I COULDN'T WRITE THE SEQUEL to *I Feel Okay* without providing you with the latest information on the research front to find a cure for the amyloidosis diseases. I'm thankful to report that within the last few years several new regimens of treatment have emerged. Though not a cure, inroads to treatment are promising as researchers from around the world are busy at work conducting clinical trials and learning more about the menacing group of amyloidosis diseases.

In addition to the Amyloidosis Network, which is based in Houston, Texas, a number of other organizations have surfaced within the past 10 years with the objective to provide information, offer support, and bring awareness to the medical community, patients and family, and to the general public. The Amyloidosis Support Groups, Inc., based in Wood Dale, Illinois, is dedicated to supporting and educating amyloidosis patients, their families, and caregivers through face-to-face support services. Numerous support groups with patients, families, and caregivers are strategically organized throughout the continental United States, and more are being formed across the country. Ms. Muriel Finkel is the founder and President of the Amyloidosis Support Groups, Inc. The telephone number and website are listed in this update.

The Amyloidosis Support Network, Inc., is dedicated to promoting amyloidosis awareness in the medical community, providing patient and family education, advocacy and support resources, and supporting high-value research projects at research hospitals. Additionally, the support organization's goal is to make a difference in patient's lives and families so the disease can be recognized earlier and appropriately treated.

Even more promising on the amyloidosis frontier is the establishment of the Amyloidosis Research Foundation, Inc., with the determination to raise funds for research to find the cause for the disease and develop more effective means of early diagnosis and treatment. The foundation was founded by Mrs. Mary E. O'Donnell and her late husband, Mr. Don Brockman.

As you can see, several patient advocacy groups have been organized over the last twelve years, and all have made a profound impact to further research and education, and provide support for victims and families.

The significant events that follow are bringing about positive impacts to further amyloid research and education.

- Medicare is now covering the cost of bone marrow transplants for all patients, including those over 65 years old. This is a huge triumph for amyloidosis patients who need medical assistance to support the cost of a bone marrow transplant.
- Mr. Terry R. Peel of Bethesda, Maryland spoke before the Subcommittee on Labor, Health and Human services in 2004 about the need to address the understudied amyloidosis diseases. Based upon his and other statements by world medical experts, including Dr. Martha Skinner of the Amyloid Treatment Program at Boston University Medical Center, before the Committee, Congress urged

the National Institutes of Health to assess the current state of science and to determine the steps to increase understanding, prevention, and treatment of the amyloid diseases. Currently, the National Institutes of Health are involved in a number of clinical trials for amyloidosis.

- Experts at Boston Medical Hospital, the Mayo Clinic, Memorial Sloan-Kettering, and a host of other U.S. and international hospitals and organizations are using high dose chemotherapy treatments and new drug combinations after bone marrow transplantation in order to suppress the replication of the amyloid fibrils in organs and tissues. Physicians are combining Melphalan with Dexamethasone as a regimen of treatment for some patients. Of course, trial studies are on-going at this time. The protocol for chemotherapy treatments is dependent upon the type of amyloidosis diagnosed.

- Within the last few years newer classes of drug regimens, developed initially for patients with multiple myeloma, are being used as alternative treatments for battling amyloidosis. These new drugs include Thalidomide, Revlimid, Dexamethasone, and Velcade. Major clinical trials and research are underway at amyloidosis treatment centers, including Boston University Medical Center, the Mayo Clinic, Memorial Sloan-Kettering, Indiana University, and numerous others to ascertain the long-term effectiveness of the new drugs. This is incredibly gratifying to me as just 12 years ago, only a few drug regimens, such as Melphalan, Prednisone, and Colchicine were available to fight amyloidosis, coupled with bone marrow transplantation, then in its infancy.

- An International Symposium on Amyloidosis was held in late November 2006 to bring together amyloidosis experts from around the world to discuss the latest research on amyloidosis in an effort to achieve greater understanding of the disease and its components.

- The National Amyloidosis Centre, London, England, has developed a whole body scan, known as SAP (scintigraphy or amyloid scan) which is diagnostic in most cases, and shows the location and quantity of amyloid deposits in organs throughout the body. SAP scans provide a whole body overview and can monitor changes in the amount of amyloid in the body. Even though hollow or moving organs such as the heart cannot be assessed reliably by SAP scans, it does provide an overall picturesque of amyloid in the body. Without a doubt, this is a very encouraging development.

- Long-term survival of patients with cardiac involvement has improved because of increased awareness of the disease and medical treatment. Also, teaching and research hospitals are training new physicians about amyloidosis. Previously the amyloidosis diseases had been given a brief mention in medical school lectures, but now educators are devoting additional class time to discuss the understudied disease. This is also very encouraging.

- In *I Feel Okay,* I identified ten symptoms of primary amyloidosis. In recent years, other symptoms have been added as a link to the disease. These include wheezing, weakness, decreased urine output, tongue issues, rashes, clay-colored stools, muscle contractions, joint pain, and hoarseness or changing voice. You can refer to periodicals or my book, *I Feel Okay,* to read more about the symptoms.

- Also encouraging is the airing of an episode on the hit TV series *House* that aired on the *Fox Network* in 2006, this is helping to teach the general public about the rare amyloidosis disease. As indicated on the television series, doctors have difficulty diagnosing it. Like most diseases, early detection is the difference between life and death. It was a rare look at the disease up close and personal, and the episode gave millions of people around the world their first glimpse of this deadly disease. The depiction of the disease was devastatingly accurate.

As you can see, major strides are being made in teaching and research hospitals around the world with the primary goal to learn more about this silent killer. But more is needed to fight the insidious effects of amyloidosis. There is much work yet to do. Your financial support to advance amyloidosis research and to assist support groups is desperately needed to:

- advance amyloidosis research
- educate physicians across the country and their understanding of the amyloid disease, both at teaching and non-teaching hospitals
- educate patients, patient families, caregivers, and the general public about amyloidosis

Unlike 12 years ago, help is now just a telephone call away in most metropolitan areas of the country. Protocols for amyloidosis treatment have become standard at Boston Medical and the Mayo Clinic. The research teams are ready to communicate the treatment protocol and assist other physicians by broadening their understanding of this rare disease.

To learn more about amyloidosis, contact the following organizations.

Patient Advocacy Organizations

Amyloidosis Research Foundation
4174 Meyers Avenue
Waterford, MI 48329
(248) 884-0156
amyloidosisresearchfoundation.org
info@amyloidosisresearchfoundation.org

Amyloidosis Network International
7118 Cole Creek Drive
Houston, TX 77092
(888)-269-5643 or (713) 466-4351

Amyloidosis Support Groups, Inc.
232 Orchard Drive
Wood Dale, IL 60191
(866) 404-7539, (630) 350-7539 (intl'l)
AmyloidosisSupport.com
muriel@finkelsupply.com

Amyloidosis Support Network, Inc.
1490 Herndon Lane
Marietta, GA 30062
(800) 689-1238 or (770) 977-1500
www.amyloidosis.org
info@amyloidosis.org

Major Amyloidosis Treatment Centers

Boston University Medical Center
Boston, MA
Amyloid Treatment and Research Program
www.bu.edu/Amyloid
(617) 638-4317

The Mayo Clinic, Rochester, MN
www.mayoclinic.org/amyloidosis/index.html
(507) 284-2111

Memorial Sloan Kettering, New York City
www.mskcc.org/prg/prg/bios/532.cfm
(212) 639-8086

Other U.S. Physicians with Specific Clinical Expertise

Familial Amyloidosis–Merrill Benson, MD
University of Indiana
Amyloid Research Group
(317) 278-3426
www.iupui.edu/~amyloid

Cardiac Amyloidosis
Rodney H. Falk, MD
Harvard Vanguard Medical Associates
Harvard Medical School, Brigham and Women's Hospital
Boston, MA
rfalk@partners.org
(617) 421-6050

International Amyloid Centers and Patient Advocacy Groups

Center for the Study and Cure of Systemic Amyloidosis
Pavia, Italy
www.amiloidosi.it

National Amyloidosis Centre, London, UK
www.ucl.ac.uk/medicine/amyloidosis/nac/

Association Francaise contre l'Amylose
www.amylose.net/accueil.php

Amyloidosis Australia
www.amyloidosisaustralia.org

Association Amylose_Infos
www.amylose.net/accueil.php

Other Sources
NORD (National Organization for Rare Disorders)
www.rarediseases.org
(800) 999-NORD (6673) or (203) 744-0100

Leukemia & Lymphoma Society
www.leukemia-lymphoma.org/hm_lls
(800) 955-4572

Another Voice in the Fight

Deborah Slappey Pitts, Author
HarobedHouse™
Edifying the World Thru Words
Post Office Box 9105
Columbus, Georgia 31909
www.deborahslappeypitts.com
slappeyterrymax@aol.com

The Lord heals,
The Lord is the healer of my life,
The Lord heals,
The Lord is the healer of my wounds.

The Lord heals,
The Lord is the healer of my pain,
The Lord heals,
The Lord is the healer of my suffering.

The Lord heals!
The Lord heals!
And the Lord heals!

—DEBORAH SLAPPEY PITTS

End Notes

1. Michael Alan Marsh, *Andersonville: The Story Behind the Scenery*, Second Printing, 2004, p. 14.

2. Elisabeth Kübler-Ross, David Kessler, *On Grief and Grieving*, Scribner, New York, 2005, p. 267.

3. Kathy Wood, *End of Life Program*, AARP, End of Life Program, p. 269.

4. Ibid.

5. Dan Leviton, Ph.D., Association for Death Education and Counseling, p. 269.

6. Brook Noel and Pamela D. Blair, Ph.D., *I Wasn't Ready to Say Goodbye* Champion Press, Ltd., Milwaukee, Wisconsin, 2000, p. 270.

7. Elisabeth Kübler-Ross and David Kessler. *On Grief and Grieving*, Scribner, New York, NY, 2005, p. 276.

8. Brook Noel and Pamela D. Blair, Ph.D., *I Wasn't Ready to Say Goodbye* Champion Press, Ltd., Milwaukee, Wisconsin, 2000, p. 276.

9. Elisabeth Kübler-Ross and David Kessler. *On Grief and Grieving,* Scribner, New York, NY, 2005, p. 278.

10. Tom Golden. *Swallowed by a Snake: The Gift of the Masculine Side of Healing,* LCSW, 2000, p. 280.

11. Elisabeth Kübler-Ross and David Kessler. *On Grief and Grieving,* Scribner, New York, NY, 2005, p. 282.

References

Golden, Tom, *Swallowed by a Snake: The Gift of the Masculine Side of Healing*, LCSW, 2000.

Kübler-Ross, Elisabeth, Kessler, David. *On Grief and Grieving*. Scribner, New York, NY, 2005.

Leviton, Dan, Ph.D., Association for Death Education and Counseling.

Noel, Brook, Blair, Pamela D. Ph.D. *I Wasn't Ready to Say Goodbye*. Champion Press, Ltd., Milwaukee, Wisconsin, 2000.

Marsh, Michael Alan, *Andersonville: The Story Behind the Scenery*, Second Printing, 2004.

The Physician's Guide to Amyloidosis, NORD (National Organization for Rare Disorders), 2006.

Wood, Kathy, *End of Life Program*, AARP, End of Life Program.

Recommended Reading

Cohen, Alan S., MD, *Amyloid, The Journal of Protein Folding Disorders*. The Official Journal of the International Society of Amyloidosis. Volume 13, Number 1, Taylor and Francis Group, March 2006.

Golden, Tom, *Swallowed by a Snake: The Gift of the Masculine Side of Healing*, LCSW, 2000.

Kübler-Ross, Elisabeth, Kessler, David. *On Grief and Grieving*. Scribner, New York, NY 10020, 2005.

Lewis, C.S., *A Grief Observed*. San Francisco: HarperCollins, 1961, 1996.

Noel, Brook, Blair, Pamela D. Ph.D. *I Wasn't Ready to Say Goodbye*. Champion Press, Ltd., Milwaukee, Wisconsin, 2000.

Pitts, Deborah Slappey, *I Feel Okay*. AuthorHouse, Bloomington, Indiana, May 2005.

The Physician's Guide to Amyloidosis, NORD (National Organization for Rare Disorders), 2006.

Wood, Kathy, *End of Life Program*, AARP, End of Life Program.

Shadow Living...Paintings of Grief
DISCUSSION GUIDE

1. Does everyone experience grieving the same way, or is it different for every person?

2. What are the stages of grief?

3. Does a person experience every stage of the grieving process?

4. Why do people avoid talking about grief and grieving?

5. How are children affected by the death of a loved one?

6. Do children grieve differently than adults?

7. Does grieving ever cease for the loss of a loved one?

8. Where can a person find additional information about the grieving process?

9. Are local or regional grief support groups or programs available for the griever?

10. Why is grief so painful at times?

11. What are the physical effects of grieving the loss of a loved one?

12. What are the psychological effects of grieving the loss of a loved one?

I Feel Okay

Deborah Slappey Pitts

"*I FEEL OKAY* is a story of love, faith and determination. It's a touching story that truly shows the meaning of for better or worse, in sickness and in health, that is stated in the marriage vows. It shows a woman of strength, courage and faith who wanted to do all she could to find answers for her husband during his time of suffering. Deborah wanted to tell her story with the hopes that it could help someone else. It took her nine years after the death of her husband to tell the story.

"After reading this story, I felt a connection to the Slappey family. My heart went out to them and I felt as though I was there on the journey with them. This book was meant to inspire those to educate themselves about the disease and to never give up. I believe the goal of the book was achieved." (Review by Eraina B. Tinnin, The RAWSISTAZ Reviewers)

ISBN: 978-1420806090 (soft cover)
ISBN: 978-1420806083 (hard cover)
1-888-280-7715
www.deborahslappeypitts.com
www.ifeelokay.com
Bookstores and Online

About the Author

Deborah Slappey Pitts is the author of *I Feel Okay*, a heart-wrenching account of love, loss, and inspiration listed in *Booking Matters* as a national best-seller.

A native of Americus, Georgia, Pitts is a graduate of Georgia Southwestern University in Americus and Albany State University in Albany, Georgia. Pitts travels the country as an inspirational and motivational speaker to talk about the devastating effects of the amyloidosis diseases and the psychological and physiological effects of grief.

Pitts has two sons, Clyde Daryl and Alex Keith, and resides in Columbus, Georgia, with her husband, Marshall Pitts. To learn more, visit her website at *www.deborahslappeypitts.com*.

HarobedHouse™
Post Office Box 9105
Columbus, Georgia 31908
www.deborahslappeypitts.com
Inspirational/Self Help/Spirituality